A PEDAGOGY OF WITNESSING

SUNY series, Transforming Subjects:
Psychoanalysis, Culture, and Studies in Education

Deborah P. Britzman, editor

A PEDAGOGY OF WITNESSING

CURATORIAL PRACTICE AND THE PURSUIT OF SOCIAL JUSTICE

ROGER I. SIMON

SUNY PRESS

Cover image, *Run Up 2002* from the series Searching California's Hanging Trees, photography by Ken Gonzales-Day, is used by permission. The Simon Family thanks the artist.

Figure 2.1, "Schematic diagram of *Without Sanctuary* exhibit at the Chicago Historical Society," is used by permission of the Chicago Historical Museum.

Published by State University of New York Press, Albany

Printed in the United States of America

For information, contact State University of New York Press, Albany, NY
www.sunypress.edu

Production by Jenn Bennett
Marketing by Anne M. Valentine

Library of Congress Cataloging-in-Publication Data

Simon, Roger I.
A pedagogy of witnessing : curatorial practice and the pursuit of social justice / Roger I. Spevack.
pages cm
Includes bibliographical references and index.
ISBN 978-1-4384-5269-2 (hc alk. pb)
ISBN 978-1-4384-5270-8 (pb alk. pb)

2014941805

10 9 8 7 6 5 4 3 2 1

CONTENTS

FOREWORD

Roger Simon was a thinker of the remnants. A consistent concern occupied Roger's late thinking. Emerging—but certainly not exclusively originating—from his *Teaching Against the Grain*, Roger became more and more focused on drawing out a pedagogical responsiveness to past sufferings, to a legacy of injustices, disposable lives and forlorn histories that still wound and implicate our present. In contrast to the commonplace manner of understanding the past simply through the social, emotional, and political needs of the present, Roger sought to underscore the ethical possibilities that open up when we gain counsel from the past. In his thinking there is a certain priority and *alterity* that the past must retain over the present. In his *Touch of the Past,* Roger cites Alain Finkielkraut to remind us that "memory does not consist of subordinating the past to the needs of the present. He who looks to gather the materials of memory places himself in the service of the dead, and not the other way around." Roger insisted on attending to the past not as a way of escaping our time. His was a complex appreciation of our need to think through our contemporary moment, and, for him, working with the past was the way to preserve critical learning and hope in the present.

Giorgio Agamben tells us that a thinker of the contemporary is someone who perceives in the darkness of our times a light that strives to reach us but cannot. Such a thinker is someone who, while acknowledging what will always evade us, nevertheless finds and can point us to a trace of luminosity, which despite coming from elsewhere persists—however vaguely—amid the obscure conditions of the present. To be contemporary is to hold steadfast to an untimely, often unexpected, glimmer that can cast the world anew and so allow us to act on our time. For Roger, the past offers us this threateningly faint illumination. More precisely, as a thinker of the contemporary, Roger draws us to the past in order to draw us to the hope and possibility of our learning from an untimely (radically unexpected) encounter. He understood that it is through our being gathered and summoned to attend to the past—as something new—that we can learn to see and so act on our present: drawing on the past anew to counter, displace, and interrupt what is expected in the here and now. Throughout his later thinking he consistently emphasizes that the past "teaches" only when it "comes to me, comes to the present, from outside," as something other, "for only that which 'I am not' (which I think not, which I am not already capable of speaking of) can teach me."

In this period of his work we find a method of study, an approach—let us say—to the remnants. His approach urges us to stay near, and extend care and attention to the details of unredeemed sufferings, to the scattered material fragments of a past that remains at the edge of legibility, enigmatic, forlorn, and consequently a potential (untimely) opening for our present. Fond of Walter Benjamin's thinking, Roger often invoked Benjamin's words and mood for helping us approach the remnants. Through his work, he asks us to consider Benjamin's musing, in his essay "Paris, Capital of the 19th Century," that "to live means to leave traces." We invariably and uniquely shed the remnants of our daily lives for other times to come. Moreover, remnants themselves, to be sure, possess the chance for an afterlife; they hold an inherent capacity to allow for other possible meanings with the passing of time and under altering cultural conditions. Though Roger acknowledges that remnants possess a certain durability, he also shares a melancholic sensibility with Benjamin, regarding the ways in which remnants—the images, stories, and materials of another time—are always partial, fragile, and susceptible to being lost amid the so-called course of history. And like Benjamin, he, too, becomes concerned with the threatening and inhospitable grounds upon which remnants are received in our time.

Drawing on Benjamin's often-cited phrase, from the "Theses on the Philosophy of History," that, "every image of the past that is not recognized by the present as one of its concerns threatens to disappear irretrievably," Roger stays with the difficult point here. He presses us to admit that recognizing the past as one's concern is far from simple, that it is fraught with problems and is never assured. Any plea or urgency for the present to recognize what remains of the past must necessarily take an account of how memorial practices risk falling into facile assurances, assimilations, defenses, and idealizations.

On one level, there is the risk of falling into what Roger terms spectacle: the contemporary condition structuring our attention to the past—our manner of receiving and transmitting, compressing and refiguring the remnants of history. For Roger, spectacle renders the past into quick encapsulations and units of information that can circulate smoothly through the channels of mass mediation. Acknowledging the limits of this mode of attention, he urges us to critically recognize that this present tendency diminishes, rather than cultivates, a care for the particular differences and knots embedded in a difficult past that does not fit the present form of mediation. Circulating through the primary currency of information, images and stories from another time have the lifespan of the moment and thus run the risk of not merely the compression of their form, but also of running out of time—of being stripped of the very time they require to make their contact point, their transactional claim on the present.

On another level, while appreciating the affective intensity and connection to the past that communal affiliations and identifications afford, Roger calls for a critical vigilance here. Especially when engaging with communal memories of suffering, we are always susceptible of falling into a certain compulsive conservatism, mimetic self-enclosure and a competitive memory politics. Accordingly, commemorative practices primarily mobilized by identity and resemblance tend to draw from the past only to the extent that it confirms what we already know and only so that the past does not trouble who we think we are. Hope and critical learning is often foreclosed here.

The problem becomes how to recognize the past "as one of our concerns" without cannibalizing and compressing its *alterity* within the terms of spectacle or identity. How might we foster a particular responsiveness to the remnants so that the past retains for us that which does not expend itself simply as information or become more of the same? How might we work with the past so that it can *teach us, face us,* and *challenge us* as the past, as something admittedly different than the present and yet as something that deeply concerns us today? How might we draw on the untimely to think the contemporary? How might we foster and sustain the *touch of the past*?

Roger sought to respond to these questions on pedagogical terms. Indeed, the novelty of his approach lay in his insistence on conceptualizing remembrance as inherently pedagogical. Accordingly, he points us to heed the pedagogical possibilities afforded through the careful arrangement of artifacts within spaces of learning, the textual practices and curatorial work that might welcome the untimely and activate the touch of the past. And amid all our work with difficult images and stories from the past, he reminds us of the need to revisit what one is learning—not only about what afflicted others in the past, but also what one is learning of and within the disturbances and disruptions inherent in comprehending unsettling events in the present.

Looking back, Roger's deep regard for thinking more thoroughly about what goes on behind the scenes of archiving objects of history led to his pedagogy. In the late 1990s, I worked with Roger on his Vilna Project. This research project brought a number of doctoral students and researchers across the University of Toronto into a remarkable space of learning. Over a period of months and years, under Roger's direction, we worked together building a space for receiving and attending to the remnants of an unsettling past, a space where we carefully grappled with the challenges of ethical witnessing of historical trauma. Specifically, we negotiated the difficulties of what we learned from the lives and experiences of the Jewish inhabitants of Vilna during its German occupation between the years of 1941–43, when most of the Jewish population was ghettoized and systematically murdered.

Our work began with assembling a makeshift archive composed of diaries, memoirs, fiction, poems, plays, photographs, videos, paintings, drawings, and songs—the variegated remnants of that time and that place. We each tended to this archive not only by adding new materials that we came across but also by regularly working through and struggling to tap into the interpretative possibilities and associations that lay congealed amid the details of this past. In other words, we tended to the archive not just by our collecting and adding materials but also by our collecting and activating a living memory in relation to this material. Our learning how to tend to this archive, as Roger explained it, involved us in "wandering the semiotic ruins"—in listening, reading, looking at what is before us, opening ourselves to the surprise, astonishment, unsettlement, and ordeal that the juxtaposition of details can elicit not only to well-known historical emplotments but also to our own transferential attachments.

The Study Group, as we came to refer to it, would meet every two weeks, when one of us would present an aspect of our labors of "remembrance-learning" to the rest of the group. Since what we offered to each other was composed of various citations and fragments of testimonial material, we termed our presentations "juxtapositions." Rather than simply presenting factual accounts, the juxtaposition conveyed the signs of one's study. The actual choices of the testimonial citations and their positions in relation to each other held the traces of how one learned: the questions, anxieties, and affective investments with the archival material encountered.

One of our colleagues in the study group, I recall, presented a juxtaposition composed of multiple images and texts that documented the decision by the Nazis to have a brigade of Jewish slave laborers dig up and cremate the bodies of more than sixty thousand Jews murdered since the German invasion of Vilna. The juxtaposition included photographs of brigade workers digging up bodies, drawings of the scene of cremation by a survivor of the brigade, and testimony given at Nuremberg. With the juxtaposition, our colleague offered a commentary; she noted: "What I'm trying to think through in juxtaposing texts and images in this manner is how to find ways of activating testimonial images so that they become more than either merely information, or disengaged voyeurism." This was a symptomatic concern that often arose in our discussions around the particularities of each of the juxtapositions presented. What preoccupied us was the question of how we might redraw and arrange the remnants of the Vilna Ghetto so that this new constellation could reframe and expand what of this past can be sensed in our present, and so that the remnants of this past might summon us and touch us rather than fall into spectacle.

Also, and importantly, accompanying these concerns was the significance that Roger placed on collective study. In contrast to believing that my remembrance and study begins and ends with my own, lone interpretation of archival texts, the collaborative study that we embarked upon necessitated a reckoning with how one's learning from past remnants is at once stimulated by, and addressed and accountable to the dynamics of being-with-others in a common space of learning and caretaking. This collaborative form of study was thus not simply meant to inform others of historical facts, or to confess autobiographical details about one's readings, but became the very opening up of that reading to an other, for an other, making something audible and visible in that space in between.

In taking up Deborah Britzman's question, "What could it mean to learn *from* (as opposed to about) a difficult past," as found in her *Lost Subjects, Contested Objects: Toward a Psychoanalytic Inquiry of Learning,* Roger turned us to one another, back to ourselves, back to the Vilna ghetto, back to the archive, and in turn to one another once again. With all these turns he got us to care and sense that the past is not simply there in memory, but that it can only become memory when it is enunciated to an other through one another. His approach acknowledged that for remnants to survive they must continue to address and provoke us enough that we grant them articulation through our time and affiliations. Our work truly began when we understood and took on Roger's point that to pass on stories and images from the past involves not merely passing on the content and information that they contain, but also telling an other of the difficult experience of one's receiving, attending and caring for this past in our present time.

Looking back on all this work, I am struck by Roger's immense insight and ability as a pedagogue. He brought us to the realization of how the cultivation of a particular attentiveness toward the past could kindle the compressed interpretative forces that the remnants hold for the present. He taught us to trust the thoughts and feelings that could be ignited when carefully selected details of a past in ruins are pushed together. Oftentimes the juxtapositions that we offered each other allowed the details of the past to flare up like a struck match. But that spark, before dimming down, not only lit up the past but also ourselves in the present act of studying, learning, and attempting to make sense and attend to the stream of associations unleashed by our collective work with the archive—with the difficult work of receiving what is absent and what now requires us to speak.

Roger took seriously how our very possibility for thinking the contemporary involves us in ethically grappling with what is absent and requires our care, time, and solicitude. He would often note that what preserves and cultivates our hope in the present, and what shatters and turns us away from our self-enclosure in the Same, is that the life and death of others truly matters. *Contra* Martin Heidegger's claim that only my own death can genuinely concern me, that the dying of

Others is not something that we can experience in any genuine sense, Roger's approach to memory reminds us that my death can never truly be my own nor primarily my own concern. His teaching and emphasis on extending our solicitude to the precarity of remnants is motivated by the sincere wisdom that a life can only come to a *human* completion through the care and attention offered by others. Roger's work insists, through a not so ordinary way of thinking, that the dead cannot bury the dead; they need those in the present, those whose turn it is to do the work, to offer human significance and a human completion to what remains a remnant. We are thus more than just "there alongside" the dying or the dead, we are responsible. Indeed, because his thinking of solicitude is motivated by a social-pedagogical preoccupation, rather than any ontological preoccupation, he helps us appreciate how enacting our responsibility for the other's passing not only confers meaning, but is simultaneously the depositing of hope in the present: an opening to the time of the other—to a way of being for that which is before and after my time. Profoundly influenced by Emmanuel Levinas's thinking, Roger would ask us to take seriously what is pedagogically at stake for our work with memory when, in "Meaning and Sense," Levinas writes, "To be *for* a time that would be without me, *for* a time after my time, over and beyond the famous 'being for death,' is not an ordinary thought which is extrapolating from my own duration; it is the passage to the time of the other."

Mario Di Paolantonio

PREFACE

"Forgetfulness leads to exile while remembrance is the secret of redemption." Attributed to eighteenth-century rabbi Yisroel ben Eliezer, the *Baal Shem Tov,* these words are placed at the exit of the *Yad Vashem* Holocaust Memorial Museum in Jerusalem. Living in era that has seen the proliferation of the ways in which memories of past aggression and cruelty are used to rationalize contemporary violence, I continue to have my doubts about the rabbi's wisdom. The enigmatic character of his words remains for me a provocation to thought. Is not some degree of forgetting important in regard to the challenges of living after events of suffering and loss? Given that remembrance can be accomplished in many ways with differing consequences for what one makes of the past, what forms of remembering might be considered redemptive? And given that redemption is an anticipation of a future still to come, what sort of future may this be and how can remembrance contribute to it?

For more than two decades, I have studied the various ways remembrance has employed the past not only to contest injustice but also justify various forms of brutality and aggression. This study has led to a continuing interest in how differing practices of remembrance are manifest in various forms of public history, particularly those that take shape as exhibitions held in museums and galleries. Not just content to study existing exhibitions, a little over ten years ago I began to work through concrete problems of exhibition design in order to foster my ideas as to what would constitute a critical pedagogy of public history.

This led to a series of collaborations that resulted in an exhibition proposal entitled "The Terrible Gift: Difficult Memories for the 21st Century." This proposal was accepted for development at the *Musée* de *la civilisation de Québec*. While the funding necessary for this exhibition was unfortunately never realized, the opportunity to put together a proposal generated several research studies whose intent was to provide insight into the challenges of what has become known as "curating difficult knowledge." These took the form of comparative case studies of exhibitions designed to present text, images, and artifacts that referenced systemic forms of violence and oppression resulting in degradation, suffering, and death. The basic idea was that a consideration of comparative differences and similarities among various exhibition frameworks and designs would be fertile ground for eliciting a conceptual language through which issues in the practical work of curating difficult knowledge may become newly thought or thought anew.

In this context, I became aware that there had been multiple, but differing, exhibitions in the United States that drew upon the same archive of historical images, photographs that had been taken at lynchings held between 1880 and 1960. Thus, an unusual opportunity presented itself. Here was a chance do to a comparative study of how different museums decided to present images from the same archive. Rather than doing a comprehensive survey of every exhibition that had presented these images, I wanted this comparative work to be in-depth, including not only very detailed descriptions of specific exhibition designs, but interviews with museum staff and an extensive analysis of differences among visitor comments. For this reason, it was decided to limit the comparison to exhibitions held at two museums with quite different frameworks for displaying the images. The six chapters of this book present the comparison between the exhibitions, a discussion of what might be learned from this, and how such learning is applicable beyond the specifics of the lynching photograph exhibitions. Chapter 1 introduces the conceptual project of the book and the problems associated with curating difficult knowledge. Here I also discuss the relation between curatorial practice and pedagogy, in particular a pedagogy of bearing witness. Chapter 2 provides a detailed description of the two exhibitions studied and begins a discussion of their differences. Drawing from interviews with museum staff, Chapter 3 documents and discusses the thinking behind the different curatorial frameworks that defined each of the exhibitions studied. Chapter 4 offers an extensive presentation of differences in written visitor comments collected at each of the two exhibitions. This discussion not only traces differences in comments related to aspects of exhibition design but also considers the way the collection of comments as a whole performs a particular conversation about race in America. Chapter 5 furthers the discussion of the differences between the exhibitions elaborating on the relation of affect and thought as central to the work of curating difficult knowledge. I also extend the relevance of this conceptualization in a consideration of contrasting exhibitions of photographs of atrocities committed by the German army on the Eastern Front during World War II as well as photographs taken at the Khmer Rouge S-21 torture and killing center. Chapter 6 revisits the importance of comparative study of exhibitions. It also elaborates the fundamental relation of remembrance and hope and considers a series of contrasting curatorial frameworks for establishing a temporal bond between the past, present, and future.

There have been many people who have made important contributions to the study reported on in this book. My colleague Lynne Teather was an essential partner in the conceptualization of the project who visited the museums and collected the information on which much of the study is based. In this regard Lynne and I were also supported by Claire Estelle Daitch, who at the time was a student in the Museum Studies Program at the University of Toronto. Furthermore, I am grateful to the staff each of the museums visited. Their time and forthrightness were greatly appreciated. Samantha Cutrara and Esther Simmonds-MacAdam provided essential help in the analysis of visitor comments, as did Laura Thrasher. Laura also provided extensive and also insightful suggestions in regard to the writing of the manuscript, as did Mario DiPaolantonio, Aparna Mishra Tarc, and Kim Simon. Also providing research support were Brian Beaton, Mark Clamen, Ana Laura Pachulo, and Ricky Varghese. This book has greatly benefited from the dedication and thoughtfulness of all those above. Nevertheless, the completion of the manuscript would not have been possible without the unending love and support of my wife Wendy Simon.

Roger I. Simon
Rosseau, Ontario
July 3, 2012

Used with permission to reprint, portions of this manuscript were originally published as: "The Public Rendition of *Images Médusée:* Exhibiting Souvenir Photographs Taken at Lynchings in America," *Storio della Historiografia* [*History of Historiography*] 55, no. 1 (2009); "A Shock to Thought: Curatorial Judgment and the Public Exhibition of 'Difficult Knowledge,'" *Memory Studies* 4, no. 4 (2011): 432–49; "The Public Rendition of *Images Médusée*: Exhibiting Souvenir Photographs Taken at Lynchings in America," in *Presence: Philosophy, History and Cultural Theory for the 21st Century,* edited by Ranjan Gosh and Ethan Kleinberg (Ithaca: Cornell University Press, 2013). Used by permission of the publisher.

Editor's note: Deborah Britzman, editor of this book series, *Transforming subjects,* has provided editorial assistance and has overseen the manuscript through acceptance and production to press. Thanks go to Laura Thrasher for her keen editorial support in this process and to the Roger Simon family—Wendy Simon, Kim Simon, and Bart Simon.

ONE

Exhibiting Archival Photographs of Racial Violence as a Pedagogy of Witness

> If you are a generous person, grant to the photographers the possibility of undeserved grace that their images and craft may be used for nobler causes today.
>
> —Benediction offered by Theophus (Thee) Smith at the opening of the exhibition *Without Sanctuary: Lynching Photography in America*, Martin Luther King Jr. National Historic Site, Atlanta, Georgia, May 1, 2002

In a speech at Fisk University, James Allen offered the following reflections on his decision to make available for presentation the collection of lynching photographs and picture postcards he and John Littlefield accumulated over a twenty-year period:

> For every victim that lies pasted in some racist family's photo album . . . or stored in a trunk with grandma and grandpa's Klan robe, or still pinned to the wall of a service station in some holdout sorry-ass little town—if we can acquire and place their photos in an accurate, respectful context, identify and record them for the first time, I feel some slight awareness of what is meant by resurrection.[1]

With these extraordinary remarks, Allen puts forth the idea that a rendition of images previously occluded from public view might serve as a quite specific form of remedy and restitution. Through a prudent, considered presentation of selected photographs in his collection, Allen intimates that the dead might yet be revived, returned, and brought forth into presence. The conditional possibility inherent in this "resurrection" has been widely embraced and understood as not only the rescue of those murdered from the oblivion of forgetting, but also the animation of specters that has the potential to deeply haunt the formation of contemporary consciousness and conscience.[2] There is no simplistic presumption here that the re-presentation of these photographs can compel an altered future. The public rendition of these images gives no guarantee as to their progressive endowment. Nevertheless, in the struggle to redeem a violent malevolent past, the claim is that the images do possess a potential force that might yet unstick the present from its seemingly necessary future, impelling us to see the work that still needs to be done today.[3] In this respect, the assumption is that the lynching photographs in the Allen and Littlefield collection carry what Walter Benjamin called "a weak messianic power to which the past has a claim."[4] The premise that grounds the contextual articulation of this claim is that properly recontextualized and circulated within curated practices of public presentation, the recovery and subsequent formal display of historical photographs of the perpetration of racist brutality and murder has something fundamentally transformative to offer to contemporary America and its future possibilities.

The provocative, viscerally confrontational force of the public rendition of lynching photographs was expressed clearly by Roberta Smith in her review of the very first exhibition in which a selection of images from the Allen and Littlefield collection were put on view. Smith wrote:

> These images make the past present. They refute the notion that photographs of charged historical subjects lose their power. . . . These images are not going softly into any artistic realm. Instead they send shock waves through the brain . . . in many ways reaching up to the present. They give one a deeper and far sadder understanding of what it has meant to be white and to be black in America. And what it still means.[5]

Yet Smith still expresses the prospect that "horrific as they are [the] photographs are a kind of gift, the gift of knowledge, the chance for greater consciousness and caring" (para. 15). In rendering the photographs as a horrific gift, Smith puts forward an all-too-familiar, particular sense of hope. This familiar notion of hope is grounded in the often-expressed anticipation that an awareness and remembrance of past evil will help prevent its reoccurrence. That such a prospect has increasingly been called into question and regarded as naive is really no surprise. Despite the recent willingness of cultural institutions across the globe to substantially take on the challenge of presenting histories related to injustice, violence, loss, and death, hence offering a more complex public history that is both inspiring and despairing, there is little evidence that human-instigated affliction and misery are disappearing from the world. As a way of explaining the seeming inefficacy of public histories of violence and injustice, critics have argued that such a use of memory has done little more than encourage a form of abjection enacted through identification with either victims or those who have sought to prevent or contest victimization. Such identifications result in placing the self at a comfortable, distinguishing distance from those rendered as malefic, malicious perpetrators of injustice, eviscerating the force of memory for rethinking how one might alter the way one lives in the present. No doubt the claim of past generations made through the call to remembrance requires something more than an egoism that predefines remembrance as that which confirms who one is and what one knows. Indeed, skepticism in regard to the progressive prospect of historical memory is both warranted and welcome as long as it is not used to justify an injudicious dismissal of the social and political importance of the public practice of remembrance. If we are to get beyond both the hortatory injunctions to remember that take for granted memory's critical potential and the shallow dismissal of memory as simply self-referential and self-serving, we must begin with the realization that practices of remembrance can be accomplished in different ways with different consequences.

Public practices of remembrance are most commonly employed to address the problem of maintaining social coherence and cohesion. State-oriented commemorations and ethno-cultural memorialization enact the reiteration of iconic images and narratives that serve to reinforce established frameworks of social cohesiveness and strengthen corporate commitments via the dynamics of recognition, identification, and affirmation. When loss is referenced, as in remembrance of those who died in military service, this loss is typically rendered as a necessary sacrifice for the collective good (e.g., "to preserve our way of life"). The rites of addressing this loss are designed to structure remembrance as a practice necessary for securing national or group identities and fortifying existing social bonds. The staging of commemorative events has been said to mark the end of a collectively perceived traumatic experience signaling that "we" have moved on beyond the violence of past times.[6] It would be a mistake, however, to reduce every practice of public remembrance of unjust violence and its consequent loss to these terms. Such remembrance practices are far more complex, often being justified on three counts: as medium for the development of historical understanding; as a way of retaining and rearticulating memory over and against the desire and necessity of forgetting; and as a means for instigating contemporary practices of justice, compassion, and tolerance. These three justifications are assumed to complement each other in a synergistic, productive alignment of education, memorialization, and ethics. While in my view, such a framework is a more useful starting point for a consideration of the importance of practices of remembrance, it is only the barest of beginnings. Once we take seriously the study of public memory as a form of cultural praxis, it is immediately evident that the focus of such study must be on the different possibilities for enacting practices of remembrance. If practices of public remembrance are understood to instantiate a serviceable alignment of education, memorialization, and ethics, then the potentiality in any such alignment can be traced in part to how such practices are accomplished. This is why those of us interested in a praxis of public history need to turn our attention to the interlinked problems of formulating a conceptual language within which to explore various differences among practices of remembrance and concretely studying ways specific remembrance practices differently foster their inherent pedagogical and political potential.

This move to a comparative study of pedagogy of remembrance is one way in which we can return and reopen the problem of the relation between remembrance and hope. While a full conceptual discussion of the possibilities of an imaginable, productive coupling of remembrance and hope will have to wait until the last chapter, some preliminary comments are appropriate here. As is evident in Smith's remarks above, hope understood as both telos and emotion is routinely associated with an anticipation of a future that bears a fresh beginning. Paradoxically, this notion of hope that so often accompanies the justification of the memory of past violence and injustice is always constituted in a deferral to a desired time yet to come. Of course, such hope is not to be dismissed. Clearly, various practices of remembrance have instantiated the anticipation of a future better time that serves as a motivating force sustaining human efforts to mobilize acts of compassion and justice intended to transform ways of living together. It has long been acknowledged that remembrance of a broken past may carry with it not only a hope for a better tomorrow but also serve as a basis for critical judgment as to the inadequacies of the present and manifest the light emanating from a desired future. Yet there is a need for pause here. Is there another way of conceptualizing what is at stake in the notion of hope that practices of remembrance may sustain? Without mitigating the desire for a better world, can there be an additional way in which practices of remembrance of violence may bear on contemporary life beyond instantiating summary judgments that constitute the present as a form of lack? It is a fundamental premise of this book that the notion of hope embedded in acts of remembrance be rethought as both a desire for a future time different from the past/present *and* as an affectively driven by a force to thought with the potential to generate critical insight into the complex, often contradictory terms and conditions of everyday life.

I will take up this consideration of the potential for hope inherent in the remembrance of violence and loss through an investigation grounded in the concrete, situated realities of particular pedagogical practices of public history. In this respect, my interest is in the various ways one may conceive of and enact a curatorial project. Such a project is comprised of manifold judgments as to what and how aspects of lives lived and events that happened in the past can be brought to public attention so as to inform thought and action. What frames these judgments is a desire to find a way for the past to matter, to structure and inscribe a form of historical consciousness that may yet transform the present and its possible futures. My focus in this book will be on various practices of remembrance enacted through institutionally situated attempts to realize specific curatorial projects. Thus, my concern with the design, development, and presentation of exhibitions held in museums, galleries, and/or other spaces wherein it is possible to encounter a complex interrelated set of objects, images, and texts.[7] As will be evident in the unfolding of my discussion of different exhibitions of lynching photographs from the Allen and Littlefield collection, I view an exhibition as a discursively contextualized event that gathers people together over a specific duration, giving form to their encounter with not only what has been put on display but also with each other. In this context, I will be attending to how differing curatorial projects create various exhibition mise-en-scènes, an idiom I will use throughout this book. While commonplace in discussions of theatre or cinema, I have adapted this term so as to deepen the significance of what is meant by rendering an exhibition as an *event.* Its content or its forms of representation do not solely define the mise-en-scène of an exhibition. Rather than referring to the complex totality of the visual spectacle of a particular theatrical scene or film shot, an exhibition mise-en-scène is here to be understood as a material social practice that enables (but also can obstruct) various forms of thought and social relationships. In other words, an exhibition mise-en-scène is potentially constitutive of subjectivity and sociality. My interest then is in what exhibitions (as events) might do. In particular, I will be concerned with how an exhibition mise-en-scène informs the possibility of an advent—an event defined by the arrival of traces of past events with potential to impact on one's present.

Since the year 2000, there have been seven distinct exhibitions that have presented images from the Allen and Littlefield collection of 140 photographs taken at lynchings that occurred in the United States between 1870 and 1960, an overwhelming number of which targeted African Americans.[8] Not just clandestine acts witnessed in secret by a few, many lynchings were events attended by scores of men, women, and children. Often at these events, commercial photographers would appear and take photographs not only of the person(s) subjected to torture and death, but also the crowd who witnessed the spectacle. The photographs would then be sold as souvenirs, often in the form of picture postcards. Rather than creating a traveling exhibition more or less uniformly presented at different venues, various museums, galleries, and historic sites in the United States have differently drawn from the Allen and Littlefield collection, staging and supplementing the presentation of selected photographs in, at times, quite dissimilar ways. This unusual (though not unique) situation, wherein multiple exhibitions have drawn differently from the same archival source, provides the opportunity to explore how different museums have variously pursued the practice of reframing the presentation of the photographs.[9]

While I will be discussing in detail the extensive differences evident in the contrasting exhibitions of photographs from the Allen and Littlefield collection held at the Andy Warhol Museum and the Chicago Historical Society, my ambitions are considerably broader. Through this comparative study of the different ways of re-presenting images of the criminal, systemic perpetration of deadly violence, my intent is additionally to offer a conceptual language for considering how and why differences among curatorial projects matter, particularly as these differences shape varying pedagogies of public history. While different pedagogies may be grounded in a conviction that a collective encounter with such images is both necessary and desirable, it is how such encounters are conceived that is a core curatorial concern.

In invoking the notion of a curatorial project, I am writing against the grain of institutional arrangements in museums and galleries that hive off curatorial work from education and marketing departments. Rather, my notion of the range of practices that make up a curatorial project is considerably more expansive. Materialized as the design and development of a mise-en-scène into which a person would enter, a curatorial project is enacted through judgments as to: what is to be shown, the placement of such in space, the discursive environment that will inscribe that space and the materials in it (including such texts as object or image labels, brochures, and press releases), and the "programming" initiated to dialectically foster thought and understanding in a manner that might make evident shared concerns and various perspectives held by people visiting a given exhibit. It is axiomatic that such practices are inherently pedagogical and by implication integrally political. Yet as an educational praxis, the terms on which curating operates are very much dependent on the particular decisions that determine a specific exhibition mise-en-scène. As I will endeavor to make clear in the rest of this chapter, how one understands what constitutes the very possibilities of education inherent in curatorial practice is integral to how one might enact a cultural pedagogy of remembrance of violence and loss that might yet become truly hopeful.

THE CURATION OF DIFFICULT KNOWLEDGE

When the photographs taken at lynchings were first circulated by those who purchased them as souvenirs, their viewing was not intended to provoke either guilt, shame, or pity. Neither was their viewing intended to initiate the ameliorative action that would put an end to such violence. Rather, the production and circulation of these photographs was meant to manifest a dominant racial solidarity, terrorize African Americans, and produce income for the photographers who took the photographs. With this history of the production and circulation of the photographs in mind, contemporary exhibitions of the images from the Allen and Littlefield collection have attempted (though in different ways) to render what were once viewed as tokens of racial dominance and superiority into dreadful yet instructive scenes documenting instances of historical injustice and shameful barbarity. In this respect, these exhibitions have echoed the efforts of the extensive anti-lynching campaigns during the first three decades of the twentieth century. These campaigns also made use of photographs taken at lynchings, publishing them in the context of newspaper articles and pamphlets. These publications endeavored to rewrite the perpetrators' narrative so that the act of a lynching came to represent the savagery and shameless immorality of white mobs rather than a confirmation of white domination and suppression of black depravity.[10] As the history of the journalistic rendition of American racial violence well illustrates, more than one hundred years ago narratives and images of the lynching of African Americans were common content in news and opinion media in the United States. Jacqueline Goldsby has pointed out that "in the periodical press alone there were at least three hundred articles on the topic published between 1882 and 1922."[11] In this context, the problem that anti-lynching activists often confronted was not that lynching was a secret history known only to a few, but rather how they might convey information about the widely known recurrence of lynchings in a manner that would arouse a demand for action that would prevent the repetition of such acts. This is well illustrated by the following remarks of anti-lynching activist Winthrop Sheldon commenting on the problem of the widespread indifference to images of suffering of African Americans offered by the media. In 1906, Sheldon wrote:

> The American citizen, as he partakes of his morning roll and coffee and reads in his newspaper the sickening account of the latest lynching tragedy, is moved for the time being with a thrill of horror. He lays his paper aside, goes to his daily work, becomes absorbed in the business of money-making and—that is the end of it. The incident is closed. It is only a few days' sensation and soon forgotten.[12]

While many commentators have traced the phenomena of indifference to representations of suffering to a contemporary media environment saturated with images of violence, Sheldon's comments clearly exemplify the historical persistence of the pedagogical question of how to present the suffering of others so as to provoke sustained attention, concern, and corrective action. A century later, the present-day exhibitions of lynching photographs share related objectives, though differently in a different context. All recent exhibitions of lynching photographs have put been put forward with the explicit assumption that a collective remembrance of the brutality and outrage of lynching is an integral aspect of American historical memory, a public memory that deeply matters to present and future societal relationships. That such a memory matters, that it can make a difference in how we live our lives, obviously cedes an important pedagogical function to practices of remembrance, and it is precisely the complexity and manifold character of this function that the comparative study of exhibitions of lynching photographs seeks to illuminate.

Even though the contemporary exhibitions of lynching photographs share similar broad objectives with past forms of anti-lynching activism, it is important to recognize that the exhibitions held during the first decade of the twenty-first century were situated in a markedly dissimilar time than the period during which Sheldon wrote his remarks. This is evident in the many comments written by exhibition attendees who expressed a deep sense of surprise, shock, and dismay in learning that Americans had perpetrated with impunity such bestial and horrendous acts of racist violence.[13] One might suspect that the extent of this shock experience would be related to one's position in the long and deeply stratified racial formation of the United States. Certainly, studies such as William Carrigan's investigation of community memories of the 1916 lynching of Jesse Washington in Waco, Texas, have shown that in certain sites where lynchings have taken place there are vast differences in the overt remembrance and acknowledgment of lynching by members of black and white communities.[14] Yet in regard to the lynching photograph exhibitions, it is not just those marked racially as white that expressed considerable surprise on seeing the images. Many younger African Americans reported being intensely stunned by what they saw, experiencing the images as shocking and unimaginable. The wealth of similar responses across a wide range of visitor groups indicated that even though lynching continues to be evoked both as a symbol of a racialized threat and injustice, there is little contemporary awareness and discussion of particular circumstances that spawned so many incidents of lynching in the United States. Even more so, there is little knowledge and understanding as to what specifically happened at these events, with what consequences. The reasons for this social amnesia are multiple, a full discussion of which cannot be my concern here. No doubt the attenuation of a well-articulated, contemporary American public memory of lynching attests to the lessening legitimacy of lynching spectacles after World War II and a corresponding tendency to suppress open discussion of terrible events enacted in the past.[15] Likely this lessened legitimacy could be traced, in part, to the success of anti-lynching campaigns that solidified lynching as shameful practice and thus one to be publically disavowed, particularly by a New South trying to integrate fully into American economic and political life. As well, it is likely that the rise of an affirmative ethnic culture in which images of black victimization were seen as dysfunctional for the education of the youth of a new generation also diminished the force of the cultural memory of violence perpetrated during the Jim Crow era.

While such statements can only be an inadequate gesture toward a social history of the public memory of lynching in America, they are intended to underscore the character of the contemporary context in which relatively recent exhibitions of lynching photographs have taken place. In this respect, each of the various exhibitions of photographs from the Allen and Littlefield collection had to address the question of how to return to a public sphere images of lynching that, for many, would be experienced as an unthinkable and deeply disturbing revelation. For this reason, the staff of each of the institutions presenting the photographs felt it necessary to come to grips not only with the question of why they were justified in displaying images of extreme cruelty, degradation, and death, but also how their exhibition plans would take into account that the photographs would appear in a landscape of memory in which the commonplace character of such extreme racist violence was greatly attenuated. In this respect, each exhibition of lynching photographs called for curatorial judgments as to the design of a mise-en-scène that would stage a display within which exhibition attendees might encounter and work through the difficult knowledge engendered in this setting. The difficulty inherent in such knowledge is not only constituted in the substance of images and narratives of violent death and wounding loss, but also in the consequent personal and social aftermath of such that are embodied in and sustained by particular practices of remembrance. In this respect, each of the exhibitions of the lynching photographs was characterized as offering an encounter that would require viewers to bear the burden of negative emotions, that is, the vexing and troublesome feelings of revulsion, grief, anger, and/or shame that histories can produce, particularly if they raise the possibility of the complicity of one's country, culture, or family in systemic racist violence. Compounding this expectation was a further anticipation that exhibitions of the lynching photographs might also evoke a heightened anxiety (and the potential for secondary traumatization) as a result of alternatively dissimilar, yet still troubling, identifications with the victims of violence, the perpetrators of such violence, or those identified as bystanders passively acquiescent in regard to scenes of brutalization to which they were a witness.

As is evident in these anticipations of difficulty, what is experienced as "difficult knowledge"[16] does not lie inherently within particular artifacts, images, and discourses, or within the histories of those events to which these indexically refer. Rather, the experience of difficulty resides in the problematic but poetic relation between the affects provoked by engaging aspects of the mise-en-scène of an exhibition and the sense articulated within one's experience of this exhibit. In other words, at the heart of the matter regarding questions of difficult knowledge is the provocation of affect, and most importantly, affect's relation to the instigation and possibilities of thought. Affect here is not to be taken as simply an equivalent term for emotion. Rather the denotation "affect" is a reference to a nonspecific, immediate sensation not pre-coded by a representational system that settles its substance within specific linguistic markers that offer an understanding of just what it is that one is feeling (e.g., the emotions of sadness, anger, etc.). This notion of affect is not dichotomously opposed to or forestalling thought, but felt as a force that incites and compels thought as to the range of emotions is one is feeling, as well as to what in the encounter has provoked these feelings and, consequently, in what ways this encounter might become significant to one's framework for acting in the world.[17] In other words, the emotions we feel are, in part, conditioned by the way in which our conscious and unconscious interpretations of the world encode affect within interpretable sensations. Given this distinction between affect and emotion, at the heart of the matter regarding questions of the difficult knowledge associated with attending an exhibition of lynching photographs is the way the scene of an exhibition operates as a provocation of affect as well as a way of structuring affect's relation to the possibilities of thought and judgment.[18]

This means that what is particularly difficult about difficult knowledge is what comes to the fore when the affective force of an encounter provokes substantial problems in settling (at least provisionally) on the meaning and significance of the images, objects, and texts encountered within an exhibition. In their explorations of what constitutes difficult knowledge, Alice Pitt and Deborah Britzman make it clear that what is difficult in narratives of the experience of others is not only a matter of what histories are presented but also the prospect of "encountering the self through the otherness of knowledge."[19] What Pitt and Britzman are referring to here are those moments when knowledge appears disturbingly foreign or inconceivable to the self, bringing oneself up against the limits of what one is willing and capable of understanding. On such terms, what is difficult about historical knowledge associated with violence and conflict is not just that the materials exhibited elicit anger, horror, and disgust, and judgments that past actions were shameful and unjust. More to the point, what defines the difficult in the encounters offered by exhibitions addressing violence and conflict is what happens in that moment when one receives "the terrible gift"[20] that an exhibition enacts, when one comes face to face with the task of inheriting the troubling consequences of what Britzman and Pitt term "the otherness of knowledge" (755). Understood on these terms, difficulty happens when one's conceptual frameworks, emotional attachments, and conscious and unconscious desires delimit one's ability to come to terms with the meaning of past events. In such moments one's sense of mastery is undone and correspondingly one may undergo an experience that mixes partial understanding with confusion and disorientation, the certainty of another's fear and suffering with one's own diffuse anxiety and disquiet.

While chapter 4 will provide a detailed, comparative analysis of visitor comments written in regard to the exhibitions at the Chicago Historical Society and the Andy Warhol Museum, to provide a better sense of what is at stake in the notion of the difficult knowledge encountered in these exhibitions consider the following remarks drawn from a sample of comments written by visitors in response to the exhibition "Without Sanctuary: Lynching Photographs in America" presented at the Warhol Museum in the Fall of 2001:

> I'm not really sure what I'm supposed to do when I leave here today. Things just can't go back to normal. I feel very sad when I look at the black faces hanging from those trees they look like my family, friends, people I see on the street every day. What makes [me] more upset is to see those white faces, looking at the bodies with pride and accomplishment. Those white faces also look like the people I see on the street. (I'm very confused as what I should feel right now) peace. (Visitor Comment, Andy Warhol Museum)

The notion of "difficulty" introduced above is evident in these remarks. Expressed here is a heightened affective intensity provoked by an encounter with images of violence and death. Read symptomatically, one can sense the spectral presence of the past commingling with the everyday surroundings and conscious (and likely unconscious) psychic life of the comment writer. This seems to result in a loss of previously secured meanings and, concomitantly, a deeply felt set of uncertainties as to how to respond. In her consideration of such moments, Britzman has explored how the affects spawned by aspects of transference lead to a resistance to thought and a narrowing of what might be learned from such encounters.[21] No doubt a disruptive affective force may be provoked by the sight of deadly violence, intensified not only by identifications bolstered by existing sets of social relationships but also as unresolved psychic conflicts in one's own past. While these considerations are clearly apparent in the comment, there is something else at work, something that points in a rather different direction.

The concluding word of the comment is the orthographically marked, strongly underlined word *peace,* a word written under subjection to the force of the exhibition. In this respect, it cannot be read as simply a conventional gesture of closing for a communication. It is offered simultaneously as a relational posture, a plea, a moral injunction, a question, and a hope for oneself. It reads as an overdetermined response that suggests an inability to remain indifferent to what one has just seen. Something must be done, though what it is, is not apparent. Most importantly, the ambivalence of this sign is a semiotic trace of an embodied situation in which, as a consequence of visiting an exhibition, a person has become charged with an affect that is itself a force to thought, particularly to the extent to which this thought is that which seeks some alteration as a result of the encounter that provoked it. I do not mean that this affect is only an epistemophilic desire to understand or make intelligible (i.e., to master) the violence and brutality one has just seen (although this desire may indeed be operative here as it is in many other similar responses). Differently, I want to suggest that this affect as a force to thought (and possibly action) is the first moment of what Stanley Cavell calls "acknowledgment"[22] of another's pain and what Emmanuel Levinas has understood as the responsibility inherent in the suffering for the suffering of others.[23] In suggesting this, my intent is to open a conversation regarding curatorial practices that would recognize and work with the potential of a mise-en-scène of images, texts, and objects to elicit a force to thought, not simply tied to issues of identification, but to an a priori ethical responsibility rooted in the physical response to the suffering of another. It is in this respect that this book will be most concerned with the question of curatorial judgment and how the potency of a specific mise-en-scène constitutes an exhibition as an *event,* framing and channeling the movement of affect and impacting on the new possibilities for thought that any given exhibition potentially enacts.

To grasp the significance of thinking of an exhibition as an event, one has to consider what the notion of an event may entail beyond its reference to an occurrence. A discussion of the philosophical consideration of an event is not my purpose here. However, as my concern is how an exhibition might be conceived as an event, I have found it helpful to consider the implications of current writings that rethink the question of what is at stake in the notion of an image. Clearly, the most commonplace mode of apprehending an image is to consider it as a representation that draws its significance from its always-imperfect relation to that which it purports to represent. This is most evident in the way most people attend to photographs. If one trusts that a photograph has not been intentionally altered, it is usually taken for granted that such images are representations that underwrite the "realness" of a past presence that was there in front of the lens at the time a picture was taken. At the same time, as "only" a representation (and not the thing or person represented), a photograph is always defined by its partiality. In this sense, it "gives itself to thought in terms of that which it is not, that is, in relation to a more basic kind of entity—an object, a person, a state of affairs—whose presence it re-presents."[24]

In contrast to apprehending an image as a representation are the various positions that emphasize an image's agency. While there are substantial differences among these positions, what they share is that rather than focusing on images that can be said to be about the world, they are addressed to the manner in which images are encountered as in the world.[25] This address is in part based on the recognition that images are not self-sufficient objects. How they operate in the world is a contextual matter. Indeed, images are subject to the always already situated character of all representations, which Edward Said referred to as "texts-in-the-world."[26] While it is certainly important to argue that the meanings of images are never produced in isolation but always as situated within a broader discursive economy of other images and written discourses, limiting one's understanding of an image to questions regarding its status as a representation (i.e., how it is given to meaning) fails to address how an image might be said to hold a certain force that bears on those who engage it.

While a full discussion of the various ways the force of the image is to be theorized is beyond my purpose here, there a few basic premises that need explicit mention. First of all, given that an image is fundamentally visual, it may be said not only to be perceptible or visible, but specifically as that which offers itself to sight. As Hagi Kenaan puts it, "The image is never just present but always already self-presenting, addressing itself to the eye. The image is a turning toward the eye, a facing of the viewer."[27] In this respect, images are never just there, present as inert objects, but always "show themselves in a manner that is . . . intricately tied to the condition [and circumstance] of being viewed" (157). This "in-built relational structure" means that an image "is never simply what it is" (157). As Kenaan argues, "Its being-there is a being beyond itself toward the viewer: a facing. As such, an image can never be reduced to a representation, understood as a specific determination of visual content" (157). Rather, "what we face when we look at pictures is never given, but alternatively, a giving" (157). This notion of an image registers not as a *thing* but something predicative, as transitive, and hence a movement that is potentially "an entry, a trespassing into our sphere of the ego" (154). It is in this potential for images to operate as a force that a situated appearance of and encounter with an exhibition may be understood as an event.

Part of the pedagogical intent of the early-twentieth-century anti-lynching activists in publishing lynching photographs was to employ the force of a photographic image to disrupt prevailing discourses. This was to be done by denaturalizing and contesting codes secured by the dominant racialized class alliance that secured the oppressive and often violent forms of discrimination of a Jim Crow society. Yet given that the force of a visual image is inherently indeterminate, it remains self-evident that one cannot specify in advance if and how any given image will be understood and integrated (or not) with one's existing thoughts, commitments, and desires.[28] Certainly, in the context of photography, it is commonly agreed that there is something in photographic images that resists or eludes efforts to fix their meaning. No doubt this indeterminacy accounts for a degree of the anxiousness associated with curatorial projects that present photographs as traces of past events, particularly those incorporating highly charged aspects of human existence. It is why one can read calls to resist "the pornography of the 'direct' representation of misery" by placing language between the viewer and "visual experience."[29] Indeed, no museum or gallery would present an exhibition of lynching photographs totally unsupervised by words, even if supervisory authority of these words is rendered all but mute at the moment of encounter between a viewer and an image.[30] In attending to the mise-en-scène of an exhibition of lynching photographs, rather than simply its discursive contextualization, I am framing my concern at the organization and framing of such encounters, recognizing in the process that any given set of curatorial judgments will inevitably inform the pedagogical limits and possibilities inherent in the "difficult" engagements such encounters afford.

I will have much more to say about the substance of these encounters in subsequent chapters. For the moment it must suffice to state that the "difficulty" referenced here resides in the problematic relation between the material content that defines the subject matter of an exhibition, the affective force provoked in an encounter with this exhibition, and the struggle to make sense of one's experience of this force through the enactment of thought and conversation. Certainly, the contemporary display of the Allen and Littlefield lynching photographs were intended not only to inform museum visitors about particular violent events in U.S. history and to memorialize those victimized, but as well to publicly indict particular acts of murder and the systemic racism that legitimated them. However, the significance of these photographs does not just rest on what history they signify but also on the consequences of what their contemporary presentation does to those who view them. That the photographs were often colloquially described as "shocking" is an inadequate but still telling indication that the public re-presentation of these difficult images rendered a presence that cast forward a force whose very tactility embodied an indeterminate provocation of affect. It is also an indication that shifting the temporal frame in which the photographs were encountered reconstituted the possibility and trajectory of this affect.[31] While, clearly, curatorial practice can never attempt to fix responses to images present, how different exhibitions were variously designed and developed so as to exert influence upon the movement between affect and thought will become the central concern of much of the chapters that follow.

What is at stake here for any museum or gallery offering visitors encounters with images of suffering and death is suitably illustrated by Mieke Bal in her discussion of the photography exhibition *Beautiful Suffering: Photography and the Traffic in Pain,* presented at the Williams College Museum of Art in 2006.[32] This exhibition presented a wide range of contemporary photography of various instances of human suffering attempting to explore photography's "traffic in pain." At the beginning of her commentary on this exhibition, Bal ruminates on her visceral response to Nicholas Nixon's "Tom Moran, October 1987," a photograph of a man looking at his mirror image, showing his body devastated by disease. Reading the young man's face as "beautiful but skeletal" and his chest as "emaciated," and noting the date of the photograph, Bal associates the image with the ravages of AIDS (93). This visual encounter provokes a sense of anxiety. Standing before the photograph she feels something that she interprets as "grief, compassion, and anger" (93). But she is also aware that simply rendering her feelings on these terms leaves her with "nowhere to go" (93). As she put it, "Alone, I am not witnessing anyone's suffering. In all likelihood, the man is long dead, and he will never know that, in 2006, someone unknown to him felt an emotion for him that might approximate grief" (93). It is this diffuse quality of sensation, reflexively coded as grief but without direction, that Bal labels the core problem that the exhibition *Beautiful Suffering* "analyzes and questions and to an extent, inevitably and boldly performs" (93–94). Bal understands quite clearly that this difficulty in the relation of affect and thought is not simply a consequence of particular photographs being viscerally difficult to look at. Rather, the problem of undirected emotions (and possibly an indifference that might act as a shield to bear their weight) is apprehended as an underlying curatorial problem of the exhibition itself. That is, Bal directs us to the question of the possible ways an exhibition's mise-en-scène might help frame, forge, and support a mode of public vision within which the affective force of images could be directed toward thought regarding one's responsibilities in the face of the felt injunction to bear witness to the scenes of suffering just encountered. As we shall see below, what constitutes such a practice of bearing witness is very much an open question. However, as Bal's comments suggest the question of what constitutes bearing witness to an encounter with the scenes of suffering and death presented in an exhibition at the very least opens a curatorial consideration of the possible relation between affect and thought, a relation (it bears repeating) whose precise content can never be specified in advance.

THE PROBLEMATIC PEDAGOGY OF "BEARING WITNESS"

In a parallel but somewhat different idiom from James Allen's remarks cited at the beginning of this chapter, Joseph Jordan, curator of the exhibition of lynching photographs held at the Martin Luther King Jr. National Historic Site in Atlanta, noted that "[i]f we put these photographs back into the trunks, or slide them back into the crumbling envelopes and conceal them in a corner of the drawer, we deny to the victims, once again, the witness they deserve. We deny them the opportunity to demand recognition of their humanity, and for us to bear witness to that humanity."[33] For Jordan, the public exhibition of recontextualized, recovered images taken at lynchings was a way of allowing the dead "to speak" and in doing so make claims on those living in the present. In this regard, Jordan put forward the notion that an exhibition of photographs can be a specific mode of enacting visual testimony.[34] However, such assertions only beg the question: In what sense can it be said that an exhibition of photographs "testifies"? If we presume that as an event an exhibition does something, if it can be said to in some specific way "attest," an exhibition of historical photographs can be taken as a practice that affirms something about the past and functions as a call to witness that affirmation. In principle, then, an exhibition as a practice of visual testimony may be understood as an event that constitutes an encounter with the potential to provoke a consideration of the substance and significance of prior events and experiences (however partial such considerations must be). On these terms, testimony enacted by an exhibition has an inherent pedagogical character that I will refer to here as its pedagogy of witness.

At root, the testamentary character of a photograph exhibition, addressed to those who attend, commands them to see and remember. Jordan most certainly understood this command as a moral injunction, that those murdered (and the loss engendered by these murders) should not be forgotten. For such to be the case, he insisted that we must enact the recognition that the all too untimely death of those murdered remains deeply grievable. This is a demand for recognition that requires more than the visible apprehension of the dead and the public acknowledgment of the crimes perpetrated against them. Something much more is at stake in Jordan's proposition that an exhibition of lynching photographs is a way of initiating a claim on us to "bear witness" to the humanity of the victims of such crimes. The visual testimony of an exhibition of lynching photographs is comprised not only of an attempt to transmit information about the past and to keep specific events before one's eyes; it constitutes as well a force intended to open questions as to the significance of a specific practice of re-presenting the photographs for public viewing. Yet how such viewing is to be accomplished, and what remembrance might mean when mediated through any given exhibition, entails pedagogical, ethical, and epistemological considerations.

Always directed toward another, testimony places the one who receives it under the obligation of response to an embodied singular experience not recognizable as one's own. Amid testimony's tensile mix of gift and demand, there is an underlying entreaty to see, read, and/or hear that which is given over to those of us ready and able to accept the requirements of its encounter. On such terms, testimony (visual or otherwise) has the potential to transform the way in which we understand ourselves in and through our relations with others. If we embrace the premise that subjectivities are fundamentally intersubjective and dialogic, then there is a transformative potency in an act of testimony that depends on one's capacity to inherit it as a bequest. This is a capacity that depends on one's address-ability and response-ability in the face of how it is that testimony gives over its witness. In this respect, witnessing testimony is not something accomplished by merely enduring the apprehension of demanding images and/or stories; rather, one must work through ways of transporting and translating these beyond their moment of appearance and enunciation. Thus, central to witnessing is the enactment of one's relationship with others in ways that make evident that one's thought and practice has been informed by the living memory of prior testimony. By invoking these obligations as central to witnessing, witnessing is constituted as first and foremost an ethical concept. In other words, witnessing is to be defined through a normative structure of expectations and obligations that sets the conditions of possibility for testimony's participation in a "just remembrance."[35] As Kelly Oliver has indicated, the fundamental question regarding an encounter with testimony is, "How can we witness and bear witness to oppression, domination, subordination, enslavement, and torture in ways that open up the possibility of a more humane and ethical future beyond violence?"[36]

Oliver's question is not simply rhetorical. There is a warranted, acute equivocation regarding the practice of publicly displaying photographs of death and suffering, even when it is done as a call to a witness that would recognize loss, initiate a demand for justice, and warn against as the destructive consequences of racism (or other forms of discrimination and oppression). Clearly, there is long history of the public display of visual imagery depicting violence and violations not only as a demand for justice for past crimes but as well to mobilize transformations in existing and future social relations. A classic instance is Francisco Goya's famous aquatint plates, which subsequent to his death were published and became known as the series *The Disasters of War*.[37] It is generally assumed that Goya intended these graphics as a transformative visual report of the horror, brutality, torture, and the savagery witnessed during the 1808 Spanish nationalist insurrection against Joseph Bonaparte and the subsequent Peninsular War. While graphic artists over the centuries have rendered images of the inhumanity of violence that bear witness to atrocity and injustice, after the invention of photography in 1839 and the rapid advances made in technologies of image reproduction and distribution, the photographic image became the privileged mode of documentation through which barbarism could be made evident to a previously uninformed citizenry. Early important instances of such exhibition practices that continue to draw critical consideration are the Congo Reform Movement's exhibition of atrocity photographs in the context of their human rights campaign against Belgian King Leopold, colonial ruler of the Congo Free State (c.1904–13)[38] and Ernst Friedrich's Berlin Anti-War Museum (1925–1933) founded with the intent of publicly displaying the mass death and mutilation inflicted during the trench warfare of World War I.[39] Both instances exemplify exhibitions of photographs documenting the consequences of immoral and unwarranted actions that should be stopped or prevented from recurring. Despite these instances, and many more recent examples of the use of photography as central to a pedagogy of witness, the privileged position of this reproductive technology has not obscured the fact that photography's relation to death and suffering remains one of deep ambivalence.

On the one hand, such "socially concerned" photographic exhibitions are still commonly accepted as indexical depictions of reality. Such depictions are not only offered as information (as "news"), but often are intended as an indictment, a moral charge directed at the people, ideologies, and structural conditions responsible for the actions and/or circumstances depicted. Through a pedagogy of display, it is assumed that photographic images can direct attention and inform public opinion so as to mobilize action to promote justice via prosecution, restitution, or reparations, as well as instantiating a normative order that would constrain such violence in the future. This privileging of photography is grounded by an epistemological trust in the representational truth of an image as well as the hope that in informing a public, it will awaken compassion, understanding, and the desire for and action toward the amelioration of suffering. This is a trust constituted in a gaze that turns a photograph into "a sign to be drawn on in speaking out" against injustice.[40]

On the other hand, there remains considerable anxiety in regard to the appropriateness of this assignation of photographic technology with the attempts to visually render the factual realities and experience of pain, anguish, and death. This anxiety specifically takes the form of a significant unease regarding photography's complicity in the impropriety inherent in the act of taking such images and subsequently staging their viewing, an impropriety that verges on the production of an exploitative sensationalism. In commenting on the moment of exploitation in the public display of images of impending death, Bal reminds us that it is the imminent expectation of death that is the reason such images have been put on display.[41] Bal argues that death on public display indicates that death has been turned into (perhaps stolen as) symbolic merchandise, and thus on these terms such presentations are an inherently disrespectful, exploitative practice. Such concerns were evident as early as the controversy that ensued over the 1862 New York City public exhibition of Matthew Brady's Civil War battlefield images. While making evident the horror of war, many of these images offered what Susan Sontag called an "intolerable realism" that for some was considered quite indecent, particularly as Brady hoped to profit from their exhibition.[42] Such issues continue to be raised in more contemporary contexts. For example, in 2002 photographer Thomas Condon was convicted of "corpse abuse" subsequent to a call to the police made by a technician who was developing his prints.[43] With the permission of a local Cincinnati coroner (but without permission of the relatives of those deceased), Condon had opened a number of body bags in order to take photographs of material remains for a series intended to portray the cycle of life and death. In sentencing Condon, County Court Judge Norbert Nadel judged that his photographs were "disrespectful," "the worst invasion of privacy," and contained no redeeming value (para. 5). As well, lawyers representing families of the photographed dead filed a class action suit seeking damages from Condon as well as from the coroner and the county. The suit charged that the defendants violated the privacy of the dead and that the county failed to exercise proper custodial care of the corpses. However, not everyone thought Condon's sentence was justified. The U.S.-based National Coalition against Censorship quickly circulated a petition urging his release and the case was extensively discussed in digital forums across the Internet, with many people expressing views that supported Condon's project.

Such controversies obviously raise the question as to when the display of a dead human body might be judged a desecration, an issue clearly relevant to the staffs of the museums that decided to exhibit images from the Allen and Littlefield collection. Homer, in books 22–24 of the *Iliad*, described how Achilles avenges the death of his friend Patroclus by killing his slayer Hector.[44] Still enraged after killing Hector, Achilles fastened Hector's feet to a chariot and then dragged the body round the city ["[Hector's] head . . . tumbled in the dust . . . defiled in the land of his fathers" (446)]. Priam, Hector's father, groaned in anguish at this sight and entreated Achilles to "have respect for my age." But Achilles, still beside himself, again dragged Hector's body three times around Patroclus's tomb. At the sight of this desecration Apollo, in a speech to the gods, announced that Achilles "has destroyed pity, and there is not in him any shame [*aidos*]" (476). In treating the remains of Hector's body in this way Achilles demeaned himself through an act of desecration, and as Apollo says, "nothing is gained thereby for his good, or his honour" (476). Indeed, we might extend Apollo's charge and say that those who desecrate a body and those who publicly display such desecration might on this account be judged has having "no shame," and without shame one is disgraced and dishonored. This is one framework within which one might mount a critique of the public exhibition of the photographic images of lynchings. Even if these exhibitions were intended as a mode of dissemination broadly useful as a means of informing and mobilizing relevant publics, nonetheless such views express an opinion that such utilitarian display of human remains is evidence of institutional hubris and violates the necessity of respect for the body of the dead.

The exhibitions of lynching photographs that I will be discussing throughout this book, specifically those at the Chicago Historical Society and the Andy Warhol Museum, were efforts not only to inform various publics about a shameful past in American history and in this respect initiate a pedagogy of witness, but, as well, were intended to honor those victimized. On such terms, it would be a scandalous exaggeration to suggest that either of these exhibitions had any affinity to Achilles's act of dragging Hector's body in the dust. Clearly, what was intended in exhibiting the photographs was not a prolongation of the desecration of the bodies of those murdered in acts of lynching, but a redemptive reclaiming of these images of desecration, noting that it was those who engaged in these acts that had "no shame." This is a reclamation that was intended to pose questions about how and why the condition of having "no shame" came to pass, how and why the conditions for its continuance operate today, and what would have to be done for this to change. Thus, one might argue that whether or not the public display of the lynching photographs enacted a desecration is a matter of curatorial intent. But intent is not the final word here. It certainly seems legitimate to ask how it is that public exhibitions might avoid complicity in the violation of dead bodies. Good intentions aside, still at issue is the question of what particular concerns a thoughtful curatorial project must try to take into account when attempting to realize progressive pedagogical objectives. In this regard, there are a series of concerns that are commonly acknowledged and discussed that offer significant challenges for anyone initiating an exhibition within the framework of a pedagogy of witness.

The first of these concerns is the fear that the exhibitions were complicit with the perpetuation of an entrenched social hierarchy often enmeshed in the justification of violence. This concern is rooted in the thought that if one "type" of dead/wounded body is more easily made available for public display than others, the differences in the distribution and display of these bodies will continue to enforce intensely violent distinctions regarding the differential value of life and its grievability.[45] Such an argument has recently been made regarding policies that have differentially determined which bodies of those killed in the wars in Iraq and Afghanistan could be publicly shown and which could not. Largely out of a sense of moral decency and respect for families of those killed, contemporary media rarely provided images of the bodies of American and European dead (instead publishing earlier photographed portraits of these individuals in uniform). However, as Susan Sontag noted, this was "a dignity not thought necessary to accord to others" (70). This view is amply illustrated by Luc Delahaye's full frontal photographs of dead Taliban soldiers, published in *Newsweek* magazine 2001 as part of the article, "The Fall of the Taliban."[46] While few questioned the ethics behind the widespread circulation of these images, it would be hard to imagine that this would have been the case if the dead had been U.S. soldiers. A similar concern has been expressed in regard to the exhibition of lynching photographs. Here, the argument is that for too long racist hierarchies have differentially determined the respect accorded to human life. While defending the necessity of public exhibition of the photographs, Dora Apel acknowledged that in displaying the vulnerable black body, such exhibition risked "reproducing the prurient interest and humiliating effect of racist violence."[47] Nevertheless, Apel's position is that this was a risk worth running. She argued that as a nation, the United States could not afford to be innocent of these photos and by refusing to see these images there would be a loss to historical understanding that would only serve to whitewash the crimes of white supremacy. In these comments, Apel recognized the difficulty in reading lynching photographs against the grain: against the photographer's gaze refracted within the composition of the image. Indeed, she makes clear that it is important to register that onlookers may be affected not only by what they see but as well by how they are made to see it via the composition of an image and the conditions of the image's subsequent presentation. Despite this acknowledgment, Apel emphatically defended the decision to exhibit the photographs by evoking the necessity and efficacy of a pedagogy of witness. As she states, "Through the act of bearing witness to these photographs, the traumatic history they represent is re-framed through the shifted context of contemporary exhibitions, providing new insights into this deeply troubling part of American history and countering a demonstrated will to historical amnesia" (3).

Yet such arguments as Apel's do not dispel another concern regarding such a pedagogy of witness, a concern that stems from a serious trepidation regarding the implications as to what is involved in the very act of viewing images, particularly when such images are those of anguish and suffering. This concern is concretely expressed in the worry that any given exhibition of lynching photographs would function to extend the moment of violation of the humanity of those shown, those who are dead or dying. What is being argued is that the ritual of racial degradation is prolonged through contemporary practices of public exhibition in a way that spectatorially parallels one or more of the original mise-en-scènes of these images. Examples of such moments include instances when friends and family viewed postcards of lynching images sent to them in the mail or when such images were sent to anti-lynching activists as a form of threat of further violence still to come. In an interview discussing the placement of photographs in his novels, W.G. Sebald noted two functions of photographs: verification and the arrest of time.[48] Sebald was arguing that looking at a photograph released one from the passage of time, slowing down the comprehension of narrative. Applying this to the viewing of lynching photographs, this arrest of time situates one as entrapped in the spectacle of death, complicit in the subjection of those violated to an enduring public abasement constituted by the fascinated gaze of those who cannot help but stand before the scene as onlookers. On such terms we must acknowledge the possibility that an image of suffering might compound or add to suffering. Such an argument recognizes the violence that the act of photography itself enacts in such situations.

While the majority of lynchings likely took place without the presence of photographers, the taking of pictures at lynchings can also be said to be integral to the event, not incidental. More specifically, the camera was an additional instrument of abuse not exhausted in the moment of murder. In this sense, when a perpetrator photograph can be understood as depicting the scene of perpetration and participating in the perpetration itself, both the photographer and the photograph must be considered perpetrators. A similar argument has been made in regard to the infamous photographs of torture taken at the Abu Ghraib prison in Iraq. As Mark Reinhardt noted,

> The torture in the prison could have been carried out without the aid of photography . . . but the cameras that were, in this instance, ubiquitous did not merely record what happened: they were instruments used to abuse and humiliate prisoners. Nor was their use exhausted in the initial encounter. In many pictures, the faces of the tortured stare out at us in a moment not only of fear and pain but also of shame, as we, by looking, prolong the suffering. Viewing and disseminating these pictures thus complete the rituals of degradation first enacted in prison.[49]

Despite recognizing the importance of making the Abu Ghraib photographs public, Reinhardt admits that "insofar as photographs of this kind are performative artifacts that help to create or prolong the very suffering they document, we have good reasons—rather different from those, say, of *Fox News* or the *New York Post*—for hesitating over their re-presentation" (17). Reinhardt's comments clearly have resonance for the design of public exhibitions of lynching photographs.

As if the above concerns weren't enough, there is even a further disquiet expressed in regard to the public exhibition of images of lynchings. This is the concern that despite the commendable curatorial intentions behind any given exhibition of suffering and death, these intentions harbor a naive trust in the power of the photographic image to provoke a significant acknowledgment of previously unknown unjust suffering, specifically an acknowledgment that might make a difference in the realities of the present. This concern is cogently stated by Alan Sekula in his classic work *Photography Against the Grain*. In Sekula's words, "Documentary photography has amassed mountains of evidence. And yet, the genre has simultaneously contributed much to spectacle, to retinal excitation, to voyeurism, to terror, envy and nostalgia, and only a little to the critical understanding of the social world."[50] Such remarks are reminiscent of Roland Barthes's statement that a "shock photograph" is one that arrests interpretation and about which there is nothing useful that can be said.[51] However, Sekula's worry goes farther. As discussed by Mark Simpson, what Sekula suggests is that there is an enticement to the seeing of the previously unseen horrors of the past—a solicitation that holds the possibility that one might slip from critical remembering into a fetishistic, self-gratifying gaze that narcissistically appropriates the pain of others.[52] Furthermore, this gaze might be considered exploitative since it can leave one feeling good about oneself, enjoying the fact that one is able "to feel oneself feeling."[53] In such circumstances, there is a concern that the act of viewing photographic images of suffering and death will be taken in itself as a sufficient act of witness, sufficient as an act of reparation and repair requiring no further thought and action. The worry here is that the opportunity to view images of suffering will initiate a condescending, self-satisfied complacence that is complicit with the very conditions that have produced suffering in the first place. Thus, the concern that, after attending an exhibition of lynching photographs, museum and gallery visitors may feel that they need to look no farther to understand the events rendered by these photographs. Such might be the case if one assumes that the violence depicted is adequately addressed within a compassionate, empathic response to past victimization and an affirmation "that times have changed."[54] As Martha Rosler has argued, such responses invite unwarranted projection and hence lean "toward the self-congratulatory and the cathartic," putting the viewer into a voyeuristic position and objective relation to those depicted.[55]

PEDAGOGY AND CURATION

Given this combination of faith and doubt regarding the promise of photography to ameliorate the violence that it documents, it is no surprise that there is an extensive commentary on practices that attempt to mobilize this promise. This is a commentary that continues to struggle with the question of what might reasonably be the hope of or for the photographic display of suffering and death. The stakes in the photographic representation of suffering are high, not only because the issues in the world beyond the image are as large as life and death, but also because of the consequential and difficult choices involved in the determination of the mise-en-scène in which such images make their appearance. Clearly, the particular contexts for viewing any given photograph (or sets of photographs) may offer very different purposes for its (their) contemporary presentation, hence altering the significance of the photograph(s) as a social sign. However, in instances where the intent is to reframe images such as those of the Allen and Littlefield collection, there are obviously complexities that arise that cannot be ignored. These curatorial practices of reframing were clearly intended to offer more than social rituals wherein those possessing a consciousness of the history of racial injustice would gain some satisfaction by experiencing the grief and indignation provoked by viewing irrefutable evidence of the horror of lynching. Furthermore, the call to witness intended by these reframed presentations was not one to be satisfied by the provocation of an emotional shock that left visitors numb or depressed, but without thought regarding what one had just seen. So how might we understand the pedagogy of witness intended by these museum practices? In all cases where exhibitions of lynching photographs have been presented, the institutional staff fully recognized the virtual impossibility of looking at these images without their becoming imbricated with one's psychic network of knowledge, identifications, and desires. They knew full well that the witness provoked by lynching photograph exhibitions inevitably would raise questions as to pedagogical implications of museum visitors' affective responses, questions rooted in the realization that those who saw their exhibitions would likely be personally moved by the force of these images toward various but indeterminate states of feeling and related frames of thought. Given this indeterminacy of visitor response—one often emphasized in discussions of museum education—one might conclude that what constitutes a witness to the exhibition of lynching photographs must inevitably depend on the idiosyncrasies that individual visitors bring to a gallery or museum. Such a presumptive conclusion evinces a deep skepticism about any notion of a curatorial pedagogy given that a visitor's knowledge, interests, and obsessions will overdetermine any intentions associated with the mounting of an exhibition. Such skepticism is, unfortunately, the root of the failure to imagine a practice of public history as anything other than a restrictive disciplinary regime whose legitimacy is underwritten by institutional authorities. However, the indeterminacy of visitor feeling and thought does not at all cancel the interest in a pedagogy of witness. Rather, it demands a further clarification of the possibilities for enacting an ethically defensible pedagogical project that would mitigate the considerable risks run by placing another's suffering on display.

To begin this clarification, consider what is at stake in attempting to mitigate the possibility that a display of lynching photographs might enact an ethically compromised spectacle. Stating that a spectacle is something *enacted* underscores the importance of considering a spectacle as something different than a commonplace way of characterizing an event.[56] Understood as a predicate, the formation of a spectacle is something that happens in the enactment of a particular mode of attentiveness. This mode of attentiveness is a consequence of a particular way of apprehending a visual event. It is an apprehension organized within certain forms of thought and feeling that have definite implications for defining one's relationship to the social relations expressed in and constituted by the event itself. One example of this notion of spectacle particularly significant to my discussion in this book is the enactment of the apprehension of any given single image so that all the photographs displayed are grasped as interchangeable signs of inflicted suffering. An exhibition might be said to be complicit with the production of this form of spectacle when a perceived interchangeability of images has been reinforced by the material and discursive terms within which the photographs have been presented. This results in the sense that each image is essentially conveying the same meaning and in this regard is of equivalent significance. Mieke Bal is again helpful here. In the context of her commentary on the aforementioned exhibition *Beautiful Suffering,* she put the issue forward in a characteristically straightforward manner: "Let me phrase it bluntly . . . put about one hundred such photographs together [in an exhibition], and the hardship vanishes" (97). The "hardship" Bal is referring to is the difficulty of making and sustaining a relation with the force of an image. As she put it, "One cannot sustain the difficulty offered by any given photograph through the confrontation with so many photographs" (97). Commenting on the proliferation of various images of the subjection to pain and death presented in *Beautiful Suffering,* she noted that when one encounters an exhibition wherein there is "an image of consequences of famine here, a corpse lying about there, and a wounded figure and lots of blood just over there, soon the turbulent emotions vanish" (97). In the place of this emotional turbulence, a customary ease develops as one grasps the thematic frame that has allowed one to settle the meaning that resides in the presentation of each and all these images. Given this, Bal adds one qualification. Perhaps remaining is an uneasiness that results from the recognition that one's gaze serves no purpose other than a self-affirming reading of the particulars of images on the terms of the moral certainties that we hold dear.

Somewhat in contrast with Bal's position emphasizing the potential problem with exhibitions of multiple images is a recent statement by photographer Edward Burtynsky. In his commentary incorporated in one of the special features made available on the DVD version of the film *Manufactured Landscapes,* Burtynsky offered the view that the singular image means nothing, since alone it is unable to "create a language."[57] For Burtynsky, an exhibition of multiple images is essential to the possibility that photography can articulate a view of the world that opens up different ways of seeing and different forms of thought. Yet, in the context of exhibitions of human suffering, Bal is concerned with precisely the opposite possibility, that the multiplication of images (and the danger of their thematic overdetermination by always-present contextualizing discourses) actually reduces the possibility of any such photographic language adequate to its subject.

What is at issue in the tension between the differing positions of Burtynsky and Bal is the question of how an exhibition might offer traces of a singular life, subject to violence and pain, while also making apparent something of the particularity of any given image. Bal suggests that what distinguishes singularity from particularity in this context "is the possibility, indeed the almost irresistible compulsion, to translate" the singular (105). Drawing on theories of translation that emphasize the importance of safeguarding the visibility of the foreign (that which cannot be incorporated into the target language), Bal argues that translation "opens up an experience to others without encouraging vicarious identification; that is, translation maintains difference, it withstands assimilation" (105). It is this possibility of apprehending the singularity of a photograph (i.e., that which maintains its difference) that resists and undoes the enactment of spectacle. As such, the apprehension of singularity sets out one part of the basic curatorial problem inherent in presenting exhibitions of images of suffering and death. Indeed, the curatorial judgments responsible for the exhibitions of lynching photographs under discussion here, one way or another have had to negotiate the question of how the singularity of an image of a lynching might be preserved and maintained. In other words, all exhibitions of lynching photographs have had to address in practical terms how to mark and maintain some of the noncomparable loneliness of a person undergoing infliction of suffering and death that differentiated each victim of lynching as a unique and grievable person. This is not to be understood as an existential loneliness, but one enforced by the extreme precariousness of life rendered by the social and political networks of power in which this body at one time lived.

Yet there is still a further problem to contend with. The rendering of a photograph of a dead body in an exhibition risks its becoming a curiosity, a symbolic token, or a referential symbol of one's own identity. These are all risks that carry an increased probability that one's encounter with a lynching photograph will turn into a spectacle. Encountering such an image, one is in danger of losing the sense of the victim as unique and grievable since there is nothing in the visage of a dead body that suggests what it was like to be alive, and without that, there is nothing to mourn.[58] This is perhaps the reason that many commentators reading the imagery of lynching photographs focus their gaze intently on the white crowd gathered at lynchings, a gaze that at times has agitated African Americans who see this a tendency to erase the life that had been so violently cut short. This is most starkly illustrated by the photo manipulations of Ken Gonzalez-Day.[59] Using the images appropriated from lynching postcards and archival materials, Gonzalez-Day removed the lynched victim and the ropes from photographs taken at lynchings. For him, this was "a conceptual gesture intended to direct the viewer's attention, not upon the lifeless body of the lynch victim, but upon the mechanisms of lynching themselves: the crowd, the spectacle, the photographer, and even [upon] the impact of flash photography upon this dismal past" (para. 2). Yet it is also a gesture that, by erasing the victim of lynching, radically shifts our attentiveness away from the singularity of this particular death and makes it difficult to apprehend it as grievable.[60] As Judith Butler emphasized, for a death to be grievable what must become apparent is that there was a life there and that this life mattered.[61] When the apprehension of death becomes a spectacle, one may be horrified, but the possibility of thinking through one's relation to this image as the death of another is sharply attenuated. Ariella Azoulay is particularly helpful in clarifying what is at stake here.[62] She emphasizes that a photograph bears the seal of the "photographic event," that moment in which photographed persons and photographer met (14). Azoulay recognizes that to avoid falling into spectacle a photographic encounter requires more than just identifying what is shown and placing it as part of the evidentiary record. Rather, she argues for the importance of not just looking at a photograph but "watching" it as one would a film (14). Azoulay is here asserting that a photograph itself entails a dimension of time and movement that needs to be reanimated in the context of one's response to an image. The implication here is that when and where the subject of the photograph is a person who has suffered some form of injury, it is of decisive importance to constitute a viewing of this photograph that reconstructs the particularity of the photographic situation, making possible a reading of the situation and circumstance implicated in the infliction of injury. This, then, is another part of the basic problem for a curatorial project; preserving and maintaining the particularity of a photograph wherein the death displayed is contingent on the precise circumstance in which, and through which, a given lynching took place. This dual problem of structuring an exhibition so that an encounter with the singularity and particularity of a set of photographs is possible is an issue that I will discuss more fully in the chapters to come. These considerations will, of course, have to be placed in relation to another important aspect of curatorial judgment, one that acknowledges the lack of narrative coherence in any given photograph and the necessity of such coherence for understanding a photograph's historical significance. This, then, is the question of how to re-present lynching photographs so that the experience of lynching is grasped as a comprehendible component of a narrative that conveys how and why this form of violence is integral to the record of racism endemic to American history.

As I will soon demonstrate, the various ways in which this complex curatorial problem was differently confronted at the Chicago Historical Society and the Warhol Museum had a great deal to do with the ways these museums staged different relationships between images and text. There is no question that these differences were in part influenced by the fact that these two museums are quite different institutions, with very different mandates articulated through the divergent discourses of art and visual culture on the one hand, and public history on the other. Each institution conventionally operates within a particular range of disciplinary practices, which no doubt help shape the meaning of the "documentary" images presented. However, what is important to grasp here is that the differences that will become apparent in the succeeding chapters cannot be explained simply as reflections of the genre distinctions between different types of museums. Rather, what we will see at work in the details of this comparative study is how the institutional mandates and operational discourses shaped the way each museum confronted the problem of exhibiting singularity and the subsequent consequences they risked in the process.

CURATORIAL PRACTICE AND THE PURSUIT OF SOCIAL JUSTICE

Given the omnipresent problem of exhibiting singularity and particularity, especially in regard to the desire to mitigate the apprehension of the Allen and Littlefield collection photographs as a form of exploitative spectacle, I need to return to the notion of a pedagogy of witness and begin to rethink the terms on which it might adequately be constituted. Restating the basic aim of the Chicago Historical Society and Andy Warhol Museum exhibitions, the underlying expectation of these events was to provoke a form of witness that might substantially alter the continued existence of what it witnessed. It is quite clear that the contemporary display of the photographs from the Allen and Littlefield collection were done not just to inform visitors about particular events in U.S. history and indict[63] heinous individual acts and the systemic racism that legitimated them. Just as important was the attempt to call forth a consideration of what it would mean to act justly with the weight/force of these images as a part of one's consciousness in the present. Mark Simpson put the matter succinctly: "Riven with fissures and contradictions, lynching's historical crisis exceeds any response that aims to mourn or condemn past crimes without confronting their uncanny powers of return—that settles for static remembrance and not dialectical reckoning."[64] These are pregnant comments whose implications are worth unpacking. In a more general vein, Simpson's comments suggest the need to think through how the historical repair initiated by the rendition and reframing of images of the past will guard the particularity *and* singularity of past and present, facilitating a dialectical connection among temporal events that avoids the collapse of diverse forms of victimization into each other.

But as important as these considerations are for thinking through what is at stake in contemporary exhibitions that have set out to reframe lynching photography, Simpson's comments offer a more specific and direct thought proposal. Drawing on Walter Benjamin's notion of dialectics at a standstill,[65] Simpson argues that an exhibition intended to justly serve both past and present must "arrest the memory of lynching in order to face and know its present spectres" (35). I want to take this suggestion quite literally and explore for the moment the consequences of breaking specific practices of the memory of lynching out of its place in the linear temporal movement of a historiographic narrative, placing them in a constellation with more contemporary concerns, and provoking a dialectical relation between the what-has-been and the now. In other words, an exhibition that would be a call to witness would have to mobilize something that includes, but also goes beyond the historical meaning of a photograph.

What is a stake in this idea is tellingly conveyed by John Willis in a discussion of his own practice teaching the history of slavery in the United States to his ninth grade class.[66] Wills noticed the inability of his students to draw on the history of racial oppression to help think through the implications of contemporary events. While his students had been immersed in the study of African American suffering during slavery, they understood these events as having occurred in a transcended past and hence that they had no obvious connection to events in the present. What the study of these events provided students was a moral discourse for understanding slavery by focusing on the brutal or inhumane treatment of slaves. Missing, however, was a pedagogical and political discourse that could serve as a resource for thinking contemporary events. In other words, the awareness and moral assessment of past events do not automatically constitute a bridge for linking the past and present. Given the underlying aim of exhibitions of lynching photographs, if witnessing simply devolves to the act of refusing to turn away, of looking straight-on at events that are difficult to face, what constitutes an act of witness might remain relatively impoverished. This certainly would be the case if an exhibition of lynching images was to be grasped as a "sad past," but one that has no currency in the present. Most significantly, Willis argues that a moral discourse for apprehending the past must be accompanied by an ethical political discourse capable of bridging past and present without reducing one to the other. To clarify his view of how this might begin to take place, Willis discussed the pedagogical possibilities inherent in presenting two contrasting documents to his class for their consideration. The first was an excerpt from the autobiography of the great African American abolitionist Frederick Douglass, a passage making explicit his personal experience of subjection to the violence of slavery. The second was an excerpt from "What to the Slave is the Fourth of July?" a speech Douglass gave on July 5, 1852. Willis argued that the later text provided his students with a discourse within which to connect the experience of slavery to contemporary events, contending that while provoking a compassionate response, the passage from his autobiography did not.

Thinking through the implications of this example we can further see why the judgments that enact a curatorial project matter so deeply. It is these judgments that make evident divergent answers to questions such as how a photograph of lynching is to be viewed and understood as a historical document, what it could mean to display it publicly, and what such a display would require. Such judgments not only articulate precise modes of displaying juxtapositions of selected texts, images, objects, and sounds that structure divergent ways of viewing and comprehending what is shown, but as well, engage in the practice of consigning, bestowing, and bequeathing a difficult memory in ways that set the terms on which it is to be inherited. Such judgments do not and cannot prescribe what viewers see and comprehend, but they can be understood as implicated in the possibility of modes of apprehension and thought that might be occluded through a too-quick settling of what is felt and understood in regard to one's encounter with an exhibition.

In this sense, the ethical political discourse that Willis suggests is necessary for bridging the past and present rubs against the grain of a common assumption regarding the power of photographs. A reductive version of a pedagogy of witness takes for granted that photographs themselves are invaluable, particularly photographs of violence and suffering. This is because it is assumed that the testimony initiated in their exhibition bears witness by revealing what happened at a particular time and place. Consequently, such revelations are taken as important information essential to rethinking our present and opening new possibilities for a future beyond the repetition of the forms of violence depicted. Understood on these terms, the main requirement is to simply look at such images, or more charitably to work through and overcome our resistance to looking at such images and thus no longer look away. However, as I have argued above, neither the provision of information about past events nor simply registering this information through one's acquisitive gaze, can satisfy what is required by a pedagogy of witness.

If we assume that the mise-en-scène within which one encounters lynching photographs is of some consequence as to how bearing witness might be enacted as a response to an encounter with the images, then in the final analysis curatorial practice would have to be concerned with possibility of mobilizing images so that they are apprehended as expressive, transitive acts that have an impact on feelings, thoughts, and judgments and not just as evidentiary documentation. In other words, we must be concerned with the question of how exhibitions of lynching photographs might be presented so as to serve a *testamentary* function that could open up a reconsideration of the force of history in social life. How then might this testamentary function be understood as something different from the provision of information? While exhibitions of lynching photographs always include what John Austin called a "constative" dimension in that they offer accounts of what has happened in the world in a particular time and place, they also must be understood as "performative."[67] In this respect, it deserves repeating that exhibitions do not just *state* things, but also that they *do* things. What it is that exhibitions *do* is defined through the transitivity that the very act of exhibition implies. More explicitly stated in terms of my interests here, an exhibition of lynching photographs is constitutive of transitive acts providing an account of the past events that arrive in the present making an unanticipated, likely unwanted, claim that may wound or haunt those who have engaged this exhibition. This claim might be said to "wound" or "haunt" through its power to interrupt one's self-sufficiency, demanding an attentiveness that resists reduction to the terms one holds for comprehending and determining the significance of what one sees in the images presented. Inherent in the form of attentiveness demanded is an injunction placed on our practices of viewing and reading that, if acknowledged, evokes and enables the (at times, socio- and psychodynamically difficult) reassessment and revision of the stories about ourselves and our communities. In evoking the notion of transitivity of an exhibition, I am concerned here with how exhibitions that offer images and narratives that trace the lives of those who have lived and died in times and places other than our own, may have some force that enjoins something of our capacities and felt responsibilities. For a pedagogy of witness to unfold through an exhibition, the images of past events must retain what Emmanuel

Levinas referred to as their "face," their summons, their uncompromising time of otherness.[68] The past in this sense must retain that which does not expend itself as information, in order to teach us and face us as the past, in order to be something different than and in the present. And yet, the transmission and condensation of the past through the mediated structures of our grasp of contemporary concerns, is what gives its representation the possibility of a continuous readability and effective circulation.

The viewpoint here is that the exhibitions discussed in this book presented images not simply as documents or artefacts to be interrogated as to their truth value or status as evidence, but as perlocutionary signs of entreaty, embodying an affective force compelling one to respond. While it is no surprise that different people responded to this force in different ways, something discussed in detail in chapter 4, in regard to the possibilities of curatorial judgment and their relation to the notion of a pedagogy of witness it is worth contemplating what sort of response holds the most promise in regard to a witness with the potential to alter what it is that it is witnessing. As Stanley Cavell has so importantly argued, when one is faced by another who states to you that they are in pain, one is "forced to respond, either to acknowledge it in return or avoid it."[69] In either case, no matter what the response, Cavell is insistent that in our response to the pain of others, "the future between us is at stake" (94). If we extrapolate this argument to how one responds to the lynching photographs presented in an exhibition, it is the future of the relationship between these images and us that is at stake. Since these photographs make an ethical and civil claim on viewers, this is a highly politically charged future. Encountering the photographs creates a political space and it remains an open question as to the terms on which the politics of this space will be enacted.

The import of these remarks can be made increasingly evident through a consideration of Mark Reinhardt's comments on the importance of Cavell's thought for developing a basis for the critical assessments of imagery that purports to inform viewers as to the existence of suffering and injustice.[70] Reinhardt notes that in her classic book *On Photography,* Susan Sontag remarked, "photographs do not explain, they acknowledge."[71] While Sontag meant this as a form of familiar complaint against the photograph, Reinhardt, citing Cavell, turns this remark on its head. For Cavell, acknowledgment is precisely what it is that we must offer when confronted with human suffering. It is the difficult, often painful, and thus often avoided act of responding appropriately to the pain of others.[72] "The acknowledgment of another" Cavell wrote, "calls for recognition of the other's specific relation to oneself," a recognition that "entails the revelation of oneself as having denied or distorted that relation."[73] Reinhardt's key insight is the inverse of Sontag's. He recognizes that to avoid acknowledgment is to fundamentally refuse to grapple with one's relation to another. Reinhardt understands Cavell as suggesting that recognition of such relations can come only through acknowledgment and that this work can never be undertaken by knowledge alone. In terms quite similar to some of the previously mentioned concerns about the limits of photography to ameliorate the suffering it portrays, Cavell noted that Charles Dickens worried that the images conjured by his fiction might fail in just this way. Dickens realized that "he could get the Pecksniffs and Murdles of the world to cry over the pictures he presented of poverty and death of children, but this did not get them to see their connection with these pictures."[74] The solicitations of an exhibition certainly may be ignored, nevertheless they may be said to fall short ethically, politically, and pedagogically when what they invite from a responsive viewer is something less than acknowledgment. This falling short, of course, may in part be traced to the particular constructions of any given image, but it also lies within the frame of the curatorial judgments that have determined how the image should be publicly presented.

The implication of Reinhardt's position that to avoid acknowledgement is to refuse to grapple with one's relation to another is made fully evident in his critique of James Nachtwey's deeply troubling photograph "Sudan, 1993." In this photograph, Nachtwey depicts a famine victim receiving rehydration salts from a volunteer aid worker. While the entirety of Reinhardt's critique is worth reading, I quote just a fragment:

> This is a picture in which nothing, it seems, is held back. The photographer shows no inclination to avert his eyes. We are asked to join him: the imperative proposed seems to be, "You must look at this, you must not turn away." For all that, it is hard to fathom what the looking achieves or effects. We, the spectators, may (most likely, will) cringe before it; we may even weep. Our feeling of disturbance will in all likelihood confirm,

> in a gratifying way, our sensitivity and our compassion. But it is not at all clear how the photograph asks us to assess our relationship to—our complicity in—the situation. The image issues no proposal or invitation on this matter. It is a failure of acknowledgment. (32)

Can we say the same about the exhibitions of lynching photographs held at the Chicago Historical Society and Warhol Museum? And if not, in what ways did the curatorial practices that produced these exhibitions solicit acknowledgment such that visitors were able to assess their relationships to the images themselves, or perhaps more importantly, to the scene of their presentation in this contemporary moment? In order to address these questions, I now turn to a detailed account of both exhibitions.

TWO

Without Sanctuary Exhibitions at the Andy Warhol Museum and Chicago Historical Society

As Mieke Bal has emphasized, visual images are not autonomous objects that travel through space and time in selfsame identity.[1] Clearly the particular circumstances for viewing any given set of photographs may offer very different purposes for their presentation, hence altering their significance. As this significance is defined through contingent, socially situated processes of meaning making, an image must be understood as integral to the event of its appearance, an event that is always a conjunctural occurrence in the world. While the conjunctural terms of an exhibition always surpass curatorial determination, there is little question that within an exhibition, the questions asked of an image (for example, what and how it "means") and the force that it is felt to enact (sensed as specific demands and questions posed to those who engage it) are dependent on (though not totally determined by) the mise-en-scène of its presentation. Certainly, in regard to the contemporary rendition of archival images, it is the manifest mise-en-scène that sets the terms on which they become intelligible. The public viewing of such images is of little consequence as long as they are not materially and discursively situated in relation to what is known from elsewhere (however speculative this might be). In notes recorded for his Arcades Project, Walter Benjamin wrote that "the historical index of images not only says that they belong to a particular time; it says, above all, that they attain to legibility only at a particular time. . . . The image that is read—which is to say, the image in the now of its recognizability—bears to the highest degree the imprint of the perilous critical moment on which all reading is founded."[2] Taking Benjamin's thought as a methodological guidepost, a critical comparative study of public history exhibitions must endeavor to make apparent the various ways differing exhibitions attempt to articulate this critical moment of readability and the pedagogical and ethical risks taken as a result. What follows are detailed accounts of the different curatorial projects and subsequent exhibition designs integral to the varying mise-en-scènes within which visitors to the Andy Warhol Museum and the Chicago Historical Society engaged presentations of archival photographs taken at lynchings across the United States. I have no interest here in settling the question of which of the two exhibition designs was preferable. Rather, the primary intent of these accounts is to sketch out the concrete grounds for a discussion of the more general museological problem of displaying difficult, violent images of historical importance as well as the social significance of the divergent curatorial practices for working through this problem.

As will be evident from the descriptive contrasts developed in this chapter, the exhibitions presented at these distinctly dissimilar institutions assumed very different ideas regarding the status of the visual as the primary sensibility through which the history of lynching was to be presented. These differences are apparent in the divergent ways each exhibition constituted the visual weight borne by specific photographs as well as in the contradictory ways these photographs were intended to work within each respective exhibit space. As a consequence of disparate approaches to exhibit design, these exhibitions ceded to the images they displayed quite divergent notions of authority and instrumentality. To make apparent the contrasting modalities of each exhibition and the sensibilities through which they were structured, I will provide considerable detail regarding the differing spatial organization of displayed materials and their intended narrative sequence; the substance of the various photographs, artifacts, and texts exhibited in each space; and the specific labeling practices each museum employed.

Of major interest will be a consideration of the different ways the same or similar images were presented within the tensive grammar of what W. T. J. Mitchell refers to as "image/texts."[3] Mitchell deploys the slash here to create a composite term that references representational practices wherein there is a problematic cleavage or rupture between text and image despite the ensemble of relations that attempt to integrate them into coherent museological presentations. At both institutions, the curatorial teams responsible for the production of each exhibition were astutely aware that the photographs they were making public were difficult. As I will document extensively in chapter 3, they certainly knew that these were images most people would prefer not to see or at least not to spend much time looking at. However, beyond this limited sense of what is meant by a difficult image, there was the acute curatorial recognition that the photographs put forward an excess not fully containable within an exhibition's narrative. This meant working with the unsayable and unimaginable contained by each image yet also against both, making the images sayable and imaginable "in spite of all."[4] As a consequence, the mise-en-scène at each institution was designed with the awareness that the exhibit would have to be engaged as a complex, challenging, disjunctive network of "image/texts." In this regard, I will be paying particular attention to how the exhibitions acknowledged the tensions inherent in such practices of display as well as the ways in which different curatorial projects presumed such tensions might become productive.

Each exhibition enacted different terms on which images and text were integrated into a disciplinary structure—a mix of percepts, affective instigations, and ordering concepts framing institutionally preferred ways of seeing, feeling, and thinking.[5] As a consequence, the mise-en-scènes fashioned at the Andy Warhol Museum and the Chicago Historical Society constituted divergent modes of displaying a selection of texts, images, and artifacts that framed the engagement of what was to be shown. More than this, the varying mise-en-scènes constituted differing practices of consigning, bestowing, and bequeathing the legacy of a terrible history of racist violence and its consequent suffering and death. Given the status of lynching photographs as abject images always in excess of the discourses that attempt to pin down their significance, the legacy on offer in each exhibition cannot be considered transparent or univocal. The two exhibitions of these images, each in its own way, situated the inheritance of the visual history they put on view as if from a secret that insistently whispered, "Read me, will you ever be able to do so?"[6] In this sense, a given mise-en-scène enacted a specific form of an injunction to (re)affirm the significance of what was being passed on. This was an injunction that attempted to force a choice as to whether and how one would make the images participate in one's knowledge and action. This condition of choice meant that one had to consider whether to accept or reject the task of rendering each image as intelligible and working with the felt movement of its force. I now turn to the different ways this was done.

THE *WITHOUT SANCTUARY* EXHIBIT AT THE ANDY WARHOL MUSEUM

Pittsburgh's Andy Warhol Museum opened its exhibition of lynching photographs on September 22, 2001, just eleven days after the attack on the World Trade Center in New York City. The significance of this happenstance will be made evident in chapters 3 and 4 in the context of the discussion of staff perspectives on the exhibition as well as in an analysis of responses to the exhibition written by those who attended its presentation. The exhibit continued at the Andy Warhol Museum until January 21, 2002.[7] As a converted mattress factory, the Warhol Museum has the look of a loft-like contemporary art space. Paying an admission fee and making their way to the sixth floor, visitors approached the exhibit space of *Without Sanctuary: Lynching Photographs in America* by passing along an entry hall until they reached two extensive text panels placed on the right. Positioned on a dark maroon-red wall, these texts offered an introduction of the exhibition. It is important to register that other than quite minimal labels for each of the photographs and documents selected for the exhibition, these introductory panels were the only exhibition text that directly addressed the presentation of the visual images of lynching. It is also important to note that both the Andy Warhol Museum and the Chicago Historical Society had chosen to place extensive text panels at the entrance to their exhibitions. This is testament to the fact that each institution was impelled to justify the public exhibition of rather gruesome, dismaying, difficult images. However, as will become apparent throughout this chapter, the varying mise-en-scènes employed by the two institutions ultimately presented justifications for such display on very different terms. As this is the only text that offered a specific explanatory contextualization of the images displayed, it is necessary to attend to the particulars of how the Andy Warhol Museum introduced the material from the Allen and Littlefield collection.

Written in a third person institutional voice, the first of the Andy Warhol Museum introductory text panels began by explaining what the exhibition consists of, its provenance as part of the compilation of photographs assembled by Allen and Littlefield, with an excerpt from James Allen's previously published statement about his collection,[8] and finally the museum's justification for publicly presenting the material. This text panel is worth citing in its entirety. Note in particular how the text characterizes the exhibit as a moment of public disclosure in remarking that "*Without Sanctuary* holds a unique place as a museum exhibition" given that these images "have rarely been shown publicly." Thus, the exhibition "reveals previously untold history, once hidden among ephemera, and points to the power of photographs, whether documentation or art."

> *Without Sanctuary: Lynching Photography in America*
> The exhibition *Without Sanctuary: Lynching Photography in America* comprises close to 100 photographic prints and postcards, ranging in date from 1870 to 1960, that document the history of lynching in the United States. These photographs are part of the collection of James Allen and John Littlefield, begun in the mid-1980s.
>
> In the publication accompanying the exhibition, James Allen says of the collection: *Until I came upon a postcard of a lynching, postcards seemed trivial to me. . . . Studying these photographs has engendered in me a caution of whites, of the majority, of the young, of religion, of the accepted. Perhaps a certain circumspection concerning these things was already in me, but surely not as actively as after the first sight of a brittle postcard of Leo Frank dead in an oak tree. It wasn't the corpse that bewildered me as much as the canine-thin faces of the pack, lingering in the woods, circling after the kill . . . the photographic art played as significant role in the ritual of torture or souvenir grabbing—creating a sort of two-dimensional biblical swine, a receptacle for a collective sinful self. Lust propelled the commercial reproduction and distribution of the images, facilitating the endless replay of anguish. Even dead, the victims are without sanctuary.*
>
> *Without Sanctuary* holds a unique place as a museum exhibition. Images of this type have rarely been shown publicly. Their exhibition reveals previously untold history, once hidden

> among ephemera, and points to the power of photographs, whether documentation or art. The *Without Sanctuary* photographs are both focal points for extremely strong emotions and potential catalysts to inspire exploration, dialogue, and action.[9]

Subsequent to this justification, the Andy Warhol Museum also acknowledged the local organizations that "joined with us in inviting the community to the *Without Sanctuary* Project." This included the local chapter of the American Civil Liberties Union, the African American Chamber of Commerce, the Anti-Defamation League, the Pittsburgh Branch of the National Association for the Advancement of Colored People (NAACP), the National Conference for Community and Justice (NCCJ), the Urban League of Pittsburgh, and the YWCA Pittsburgh Center for Race Relations. Also acknowledged was a community advisory committee and unspecified "organizations and individuals who have given their time and energy in assisting us." This was followed by a list of a number of organizations that provided financial support for the "project." This subsequent text functioned not only as an acknowledgment of cooperating and supporting organizations but situated the legitimacy of the exhibition, not with the museum itself, but within a network of progressive community institutions that included the Andy Warhol Museum. As will be discussed later, it is important to note that the exhibition of *Without Sanctuary* at the Chicago Historical Society did not include any formal public consultation nor did it attempt to situate the manifestation of the exhibit in Chicago as a collaborative effort of local organizations other than the museum itself. It is also important to note the prominence of the "voice" of James Allen cited in the Warhol Museum text. In extensively citing Allen, the Andy Warhol Museum reiterated and hence reaffirmed his understanding of the significance of his collection and in so doing further justified its exhibition on terms Allen had previously offered when he first made his artifacts publicly available.

The second introductory panel displayed adjacent to the first one offered a narrative that endeavored to historically situate the photographs visitors were about to see. Presented as a historical overview of lynching in the United States, this text provided visitors with a definition of lynching, the time and place coordinates for the majority of lynching activity, an explanation for why African Americans were the primary victims, and which Americans have been at the forefront of anti-lynching struggles. The precise text is as follows.

> Lynching in the United States: An Overview
> What is lynching?
> Lynching is the ritual torture and summary execution of an alleged criminal by a mob. The victim is not convicted of, and usually not even charged with, a crime. Although the most visible method is hanging, lynching could be any form of murder.
>
> Where and when did lynching take place?
> Although most prevalent in southern states, lynching occurred throughout the country in states such as Illinois, Ohio, Minnesota, California, and Pennsylvania. Between Reconstruction (1865–1877) and 1930, and up to the 1950s and 1960s, approximately 5000 people were victimized by lynch mobs. The vast majority of victims were southern black men. Other minorities, women, and children also represent a small percentage of recorded victims.
>
> Why lynching of African Americans?
> Lynching became the most violent manifestation of racism during and after Reconstruction. As African Americans pursued economic and social advancement, a new phase of race relations began. Humiliated by Reconstruction and no longer able to rely on a legally sanctioned slave system to subjugate African Americans, white Southerners moved to reinstate "order" on their own terms. Lynching was rationalized by the idea that black men were seeking supremacy by sexually assaulting white women—the rape myth. The mob took the law into its own hands and meted out punishment for alleged crimes. Lynching had devastating effects on entire communities and acted as a warning against black advancement.
>
> Who fought against lynching?
> Despite an atmosphere of intimidation and terror, leaders and members of the African American community staged effective and sophisticated campaigns to put an end to lynching. One of

> the most significant leaders was African American journalist and activist Ida B. Wells (1862–1931). Her research proved that the vast majority of victims had not been accused of a sexual crime or, frequently, any crime at all (except, perhaps, "talking back" or "testifying against whites"). Anti-lynching legislation was not passed, but, over time, a network of activists emerged. Reformers, educators, church leaders and members, artists, writers, Northerners and Southerners, blacks and whites dedicated themselves to eliminating lynching.

Beyond the placement of the introductory text panels in the sixth floor entrance hall, the Andy Warhol Museum exhibition was laid out in two quite distinct segments. The first of these segments was a gallery containing the lynching photographs and a small number of historical ephemera. The second segment was comprised of two rooms containing material whose purpose was to help heighten the contemporary significance of the historical photographs and facilitate visitor dialogue regarding such significance. The gallery room containing the photographs was a large space (with a half wall divider) in which were displayed ninety-two postcards containing images of lynchings, all of which were drawn from the Allen and Littlefield collection. The postcards/photos were placed in black frames with a large black mat, hung at eye level on muted cream walls with subdued lighting. The collection was presented chronologically and hence sequenced by the date of the lynching pictured in each photograph. If visitors were to start with the earliest image displayed they would be moving left to right.[10] However where one started one's viewing of the images was indeterminate and therefore, there was no specific path that structured a visitor's movement through the exhibition. This gallery also contained several flat table cases for pamphlets and other ephemera as well as additional wall mounted material relevant to the history of lynching being presented through the photographs.[11] In a manner typical of art galleries, the labels for each photograph were in black lettering on white background placed below the frames. These labels included a title and very limited descriptive text for each photograph including the year the photograph was taken, the location, the text of any inscriptions or markings on the image, the medium (e.g., gelatin silver print, real photo postcard), the dimensions (in inches and cm), and finally the notation: In the Allen Littlefield Collection at Special Collections at the Woodruff Library,

Emory University.[12] There was no additional interpretive label text provided.

In addition to the gallery displaying the lynching photographs, the sizable interpretive segment of the exhibition was comprised of four distinct spaces. Presented in these spaces were materials that offered a supplement to the presentation of the photographs in the Allen and Littlefield collection. While clearly separate from the display of lynching photographs, this supplementation was intrinsic to it. Not only was this supplement an amelioration of something sensed as lacking in the gallery display of photographs but, importantly it provided material intended to resonate with and extend and enrich (and hence transform) the significance of the photographic display. In this sense, the supplement presented at the Andy Warhol Museum should not to be understood as contextualization, ornamentation, or simply an "add-on" that is secondary in importance to a primary material display. Rather, the supplementation in this exhibition design put into place an exhibition structure through which the meaning and significance of any one component of the exhibition was transformed through its relation with the others, comprising its entire mise-en-scène. On these terms, the introductory hallway and text panels described in detail above may also be understood as supplementary to the lynching photographs displayed. They provided visitors with what otherwise would have been perceived as a missing justification for presenting such photographs at the Warhol Museum as well as offering a narrative context that might be helpful in rendering the historical significance of this material. Likewise, the extensive interpretive spaces beyond the photography gallery developed at the Andy Warhol Museum were also forms of supplementation. The first of these was reached by exiting the photo gallery into a hallway where one encountered a deep maroon-red wall on which was mounted a forty-foot-long timeline of African American achievements. Designed by the museum, this graphic representation was entitled "African-American Experience, Struggle and Achievement: 1885–1995." As elaborated in chapter 3, several Andy Warhol Museum staff indicated that this timeline became a touchstone for many people and that museum personnel observed groups of visitors pointing to specific dates and/or engaging in conversation about its content with family members and friends.

The next supplement in the visitor path was another gallery space containing three displays of material intended to further deepen the significance of the encounter with the lynching photographs. These included a modest exhibit focused on Billie Holiday and her signature anti-lynching song "Strange Fruit," a display providing information on anti-lynching advocacy during the 1930s on the part of a local newspaper, *The Pittsburgh Courier*, and the presentation of an art work entitled *A Contemporary View: Media, 1996–2001.* Commissioned by the museum, this work by Pittsburgh artist Lonnie Graham was a collage of clippings and other references to news stories related to racism and discrimination. This gallery also included ample space devoted to collecting extensive visitor responses. Several thick portfolios intended for writing visitor comments sat on large tables. Comfortable chairs and writing implements encouraged the reading and writing of visitor comments. As well, placed in this gallery space was a recording booth for collecting video comments. Displayed on two screens beside this booth were several pretaped examples of visitor commentary intended to prompt thought and encourage visitors to enter the booth and leave a record of their thoughts and feelings regarding the exhibition. A third supplementary space extended off of this gallery and was intended as a quiet space for reflection. Hushed and dim, this space contained a few benches and a box of tissues. Outside this gallery and off the main sixth floor hall was a fourth supplementary space intended to encourage visitor dialogue and social action. Part of this gallery was designated for facilitated public dialogues and contained concentric rings of chairs intended to create a degree of conversational intimacy. The dialogues were scheduled at 1:00 p.m. each day and twice on Fridays (this meant the chairs were often left unoccupied yet their presence still signaled the museum's emphasis on public conversation concerning the significance of their exhibition). Next to the spatial forum created by the rings of chairs was a space devoted to a project entitled "Postcards for Tolerance." This area consisted of a large table with blank postcards and writing implements. Here visitors could write a postcard addressed to themselves reflecting on their experience in the exhibition and offering any commitments they were prepared to make regarding future action for either personal or social change. Throughout the exhibition, a changing selection of written cards was on view, posted to a bulletin board attached to a gallery wall. After the exhibition closed, these postcards were mailed to their authors, effectively reminding visitors of their museum experience and the feelings, thoughts, and commitments it provoked. As well, this gallery contained one other seating area with a large table displaying reference material intended to support local and national social justice activism.

Given the layout of the entire exhibition, visitors could quite easily revisit any of the exhibition spaces or at any point during their visit exit the sixth floor via the elevator or stairs.

THE *WITHOUT SANCTUARY* EXHIBIT AT THE CHICAGO HISTORICAL SOCIETY

When the Chicago Historical Society opened their version of a lynching photograph exhibition in June 2005, the gallery space allotted for the photographs was more than double that made available at the Warhol Museum. Nevertheless, in displaying only fifty-five lynching postcards and photographs compared to the ninety-two images displayed in Pittsburgh, the Chicago Historical Society presented just over half the number of images that had been presented at the Warhol. However, it was not just the sheer difference in the number of images shown that marked the divergence in display between the two exhibitions. As the following description will illustrate, the exhibitions markedly differed in the logic through which their mise-en-scènes were constituted. What will be the primary focus in the discussion below is how the Chicago exhibition worked to offer a different potency and cognizance to the visual history offered through the presentation of archival photographs of lynchings in America. While I will comment on differences between the exhibitions in regard to the selection of photographs displayed and their spatial organization, I also will need to discuss in depth how the supplement employed at the Chicago Historical Society was of a different order than that incorporated into the exhibition at the Warhol Museum.

Visitors accessed the Chicago Historical Society exhibition by entering the front doors of the museum,[13] paying the entrance fee, and walking up the main stairs where they saw a large sign on the left marking the entrance to the exhibition that read "*Without Sanctuary: Lynching Photography in America* is organized by the Chicago Historical Society from the collections of James Allen and John Littlefield with the generous support of the Lannan Foundation." Rather than the dramatic, emblematic red and black entrance space that was designed for the Warhol Museum exhibit, the text panel that located and introduced the Chicago Historical Society exhibition was graphically rendered in various fading gray tones. Thus, to be noted are the quite different visual palettes of the two exhibitions; the Andy Warhol Museum set the introduction their exhibition in a visually chromatic register often used to resonate with representations of violent death, while the exhibit design at the Chicago Historical Society offered a more elegantly elegiac setting. Close to this initial signage was mounted a large picture of a thirteen-year-old Emmett Till seated next to his mother. Next to this image was the following quote from a *New York Times* article of May 10, 2004: "The Murder of Emmett Till stands at the crossroads of American civil rights movement. Although too late to save Emmett, the slaying helped galvanize opposition to the brutality of segregation and Jim Crow."[14] A related text read: "In commemoration of the 50th anniversary of the death, the Chicago Historical Society supplements *Without Sanctuary* with material related to Emmett Till." The supplementation of lynching photographs with material related to Till's murder in part was justified by the coincidence[15] of the anniversary of this event and the dates during which the Chicago Historical Society scheduled the exhibition. However, understood as part of the supplement that ordered the exhibition's logic at the Chicago Historical Society, and given Till's enduring identity as being from Chicago, devoting a portion of the exhibition to Till's murder worked to align the significance of the archival photographs with very contemporary local concerns. Indeed, this material was part of the work of justification for the presentation of disturbing images of racial violence that seemed necessary in both Pittsburgh and Chicago. This justification was made quite explicit in the introductory text panels detailed below.

A little farther on, visitors encountered a sign that warned that "The exhibition includes graphic images and may not be appropriate for young children" as well as text printed high on the sand/tan wall offering the words of African American civil rights activist W. E. B. Du Bois: "We must remember, because if the world forgets evil, evil is reborn." Also placed at the exhibition entrance were two large explanatory text panels. The first of these, entitled "Why this Exhibit," was a signed statement by Lonnie Bunch, President of the Chicago Historical Society at the time the exhibition opened. It read as follows:

> *Without Sanctuary* draws from the collections of James Allen and John Littlefield to document the brutal and horrific

> history of racial violence in America. The shocking, unimaginable images reveal much about the terror and lawlessness that shaped race relations in America in the 19th and 20th centuries. They force us to confront a shameful part of our history, a part many of us would rather forget.
>
> We present this exhibition to remember and honor the victims of racial hatred; to help us understand the impact and commemorate the legacy of the murder of Chicagoan Emmett Till; and to challenge us all to accept the notion that, to paraphrase Thomas Jefferson, the price of racial equality is eternal vigilance.
>
> Chicago Historical Society strives to make America's past accessible, useful, and meaningful. We interpret difficult, unpleasant, or controversial issues not to embarrass, cause pain, or be unpatriotic but out of a responsibility to convey a fuller, more inclusive history. By examining these issues, Chicago Historical Society hopes to stimulate greater understanding of the forces and choices that shaped America.[16]

Next to Bunch's institutional justification for displaying the lynching photographs was a panel labeled "A Time of Terror" providing the following initial historical contextualization for the images visitors were about to see.

> From the 1860s to the 1960s, lynch mobs killed thousands of African Americans. Most lynchings occurred in the Deep South—Georgia, Louisiana, Mississippi, and Texas—but no part of the nation was immune to this brand of racial terror. Extralegal violence is deeply entrenched in the nation's heritage, dating from the Revolutionary War to Westward Expansion. After the Civil War, race became the determining factor for lynching violence and African Americans the most likely target. Lynching was the most violent tactic whites used to intimidate blacks and suppress their progress. Although lynching peaked in the 1890s, the practice continued well into the 20th century.
>
> It is conservative to estimate the victims at 5,000.
>
> Documentation is often incomplete and does not include unreported murders, "secret" lynchings, or persons who simply

> disappeared. Records also fail to account for displaced families, terrorized communities, and generations of people inflicted with deep, psychological scars. In the absence of legal protection, African Americans turned within to develop survival strategies—leaving the South, strengthening and building community, and promoting anti-lynching activism.

As mentioned previously, the visual palette of the exhibit space was subdued. Throughout the gallery, the exhibit walls maintained the tan, sand color that marked the exhibit entranceway (although occasional contrast was produced though the use of a deep saturated blue on several half walls). Printed wall texts, similar in format to the Du Bois quote mentioned above, were placed high along the exhibition path. The photographic images were displayed in uniform off-white mats and dark wood frames and as explained below juxtaposed with specific and quite extensive labeling. Passing through the introductory space and into the exhibition proper, the exhibition was organized to guide visitors on a journey through an extensively contextualized juxtaposition of text and image that presented lynching as a historically situated form of systemic violence against African Americans. The entire layout of the Chicago Historical Society exhibition can be seen in the schematic diagram below.

Standing just inside the entranceway to the exhibit, to one's left was a panel listing the exhibition credits. Straight on and quite prominent when entering the exhibit space was a blue wall on which was mounted the first of the photographs on display, a series of images devoted to the lynching of William James in Cairo, Illinois, in 1909. Not only did this placement locate the practice of lynching in relatively close geographic proximity to the city of Chicago, but it also indicated one of the main structuring relations between word and image within which the image/texts in the exhibition were to be presented. Displaying five framed postcard images taken at various stages of the James lynching (of which one was an original composite image of multiple photographs), these were juxtaposed with an extensive text panel addressed to the content of the images. Thus, the associated text explained that:

> On November 9, 1909, William James was lynched for the alleged rape and murder of 24-year-old Anna Pelly. A white mob abducted him from law enforcement authorities and

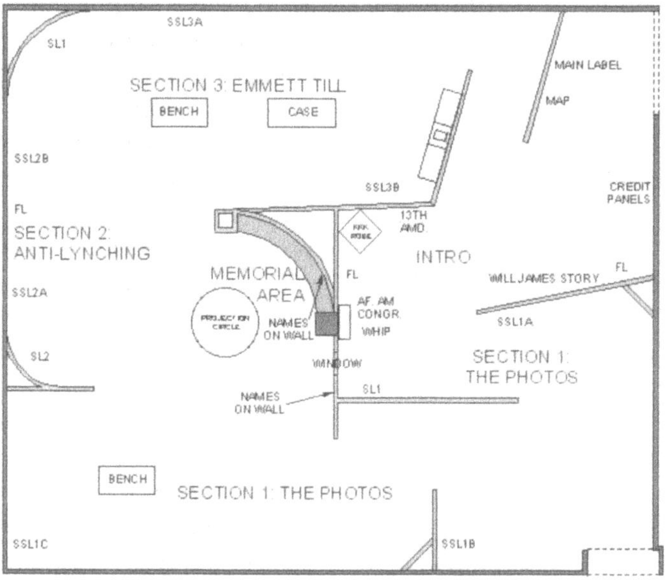

FIGURE 2.1. Schematic diagram of *Without Sanctuary* exhibit at the Chicago Historical Society

> hung him from the steel arch lining Eighth and Commercial Avenues in Cairo, Illinois. The electric lights illuminating the arch dramatized the hanging, which took place in front of thousands.
>
> After James was killed, mob leaders dragged his corpse to the site of Pelly's murder, where they severed his head and placed it on a wooden pole. His organs were then removed for souvenirs, and his body was set on fire. These postcards, addressed to Mrs. Jake Petter of Paducah, Kentucky, visually document Will James's murder and mutilation.

While not all the subsequent images of lynchings had as extensive labeling as that given the James sequence, as will be seen later in this chapter this attempt to provide a basic narrative within which to situate the images presented another significant contrast between the Andy Warhol Museum and the Chicago Historical Society exhibitions.

As one stood facing the wall containing the photographs of the James lynching, to one's right, in immediate spatial proximity, were additional items that further instantiated the strong historical contextualization given in the photographic display. In this set of materials was a map that indicated the patterned distribution of lynchings of African Americans in various states and counties in the United States in the period 1900–1931. The label accompanying this document emphasized that "although lynchings of African Americans peaked in 1890's, a year did not pass without a reported lynching until 1952." Set in display cases in close proximity to this map were a Ku Klux Klan robe, a braided leather whip with a black face carved into the wood along with photographic illustrations of a formerly enslaved man's scars, as well as reproductions of the Thirteenth and Fifteenth Amendments to the United States Constitution.[17]

Thus, when standing just inside the entrance one had visual access to a variety of images, texts, and artifacts. As well, through a window set in the wall to one's right, one could see other visitors moving through the gallery space or sitting near a large light-pond memorial positioned just following the last of the series of lynching photographs presented (more information regarding this memorial is presented below). It should be noted that while visitors could enter the exhibition and immediately read the introductory text, examine the map, and view the cases containing the constitutional amendments, the robe, and the whip, they could also move directly to the blue wall and view the James lynching images and read the associated text and turn to engage the map and display cases (prior to continuing on to the rest of the exhibition). It is not insignificant that on the opposite side of the wall containing the images of the James lynching was another extensive narrative detailing the lynching of Anthony Crawford, a presentation discussed further below.

Moving beyond this initial exhibition space, visitors had to turn left around the blue wall in order to enter a series of open spaces containing the remaining fifty lynching photographs. In contrast with the chronologically ordered, minimally interpreted presentation of postcards at the Andy Warhol Museum, the rest of the lynching postcards displayed at the Chicago Historical Society were ordered by a narrative arrangement in which specific groups of photographs appeared within six thematically organized sections of the exhibition. These six sections included: (1) an explanation of the existence of lynching photography, (2) the way lynching operated as a form of terror, (3) definitions of what constitutes a lynching, (4) who were the people in the mobs that perpetrated lynching, (5) specific information on the existence of lynching photographs and how they were used, concluding with (6) a segment showing and hence acknowledging that, besides African Americans, others who were considered "racial outsiders" in the United States were also lynched (although these were clearly a small minority of the total victims of lynching). The thematic substance of each of these six sections was rendered through particular juxtapositions of wall text, images, and image labels.

As an example that indicates how the image/text in each section was presented, consider the first section, labeled "Lynching Photography in America." This section of the exhibition contained three photographs each specifically labeled as follows:

> Lynching of Bob Addison, Jim Redmond, and Gus Robertson, in Hagersham County, Georgia. May 17, 1892. The Chicago Tribune reported that 241 persons were lynched in 1892; of those 190 were African Americans.
>
> Lynching of John Richards. John Richards was accused of the murder of a local farmer, named Anderson Gurley. On the morning of January 12, 1916 a mob of 200 men dragged him from his jail cell and executed him. Richards probably died from gunshots wounds as he's suspended by a rope under his arms. His lowered pants also suggested he was castrated.
>
> Lynching of David Jackson, McDuffie County, Georgia. December 14, 1961. On the morning of December 14, 1961, two young boys found the corpse of David Jackson a county prison farm trustee hanging from a tree in the woods and reported it to the local authorities. After a brief visit to the scene, the Chief of the Georgia Bureau of Investigation declared the death a suicide. As proof, he stated that Jackson was not handcuffed when found. This photograph was taken and the investigation closed. Thirty years later one of the boys who discovered the body told an Augusta [Georgia] news station that the Chief's statement of was incorrect. Jackson had been handcuffed.

While the photograph of Jackson did appear in the exhibition at the Warhol Museum it was simply labeled "Lynching of African American Male, 1960 [*sic*], McDuffie County, Georgia." The photograph also appears in the James Allen's book *Without Sanctuary* where Jackson is identified and the date and place of his murder is given.[18] Allen also provides the above narrative thus offering some explanatory details regarding Jackson's death. However, the explanation published in the book concludes with the words "This photograph was snapped, and the investigation closed." The curator at the Chicago Historical Society added the information regarding the disclosure of the incorrect report by the Chief of the Georgia Bureau of Investigation. This textual emendation is testimony to the fact that the staff at the Chicago Historical Society did extensive research on the documents in the Allen and Littlefield collection and at times added or rewrote image labels, something we will discuss further below.

The wall panel text at the Chicago Historical Society that accompanied the three photographs mentioned above did not address the specific deaths depicted in these three photographs, nor did it address the specific conditions under which the photographs were taken and subsequently distributed. Rather, it offered a more general framework for understanding how photographs such as these were produced. After first emphasizing the long history of violence against African Americans and the expansion of such violence after emancipation to outright murder, the text noted that in the absence of slavery such violence maintained a form of racial control.[19] Having said this, the exhibition text turned to an explanation for the very existence of the photographs visitors were now seeing.

> Photographers captured racial violence on film.
>
> In a twisted mix of murder and mass production, photographers printed lynching postcards, which whites mailed to friends or saved as souvenirs. Rather than expressing horror over the murder of another human being, lynching spectators often rushed to have their presence recorded. Such morbid visual documentation served to elevate the white perpetrators and devalue the black victims.
>
> The images from the collection of James Allen and John Littlefield are shocking. They reveal the depravity of lynch mobs and show how everyday people participated in maintaining a system of racial violence. These images starkly capture the brutal murder of someone's parent, child, sibling, or friend, and in doing so, document the shame of racial violence in America.

The above mode of juxtaposing text and image illustrates how photographs and expository text were displayed throughout the exhibition of the lynching photographs. Exceptions to this logic of display occurred only when there was both multiple images of a specific lynching and/or enough information pertaining to a particular lynching that made it possible to write a more extensive narrative that conveyed details regarding a specific event. This was illustrated earlier in regard to the description of the wall text devoted to the story of the murder of William James (and will be illustrated again in the account of the Anthony Crawford lynching discussed below). Dispersed throughout the exhibit were additional texts printed high on the walls that provided various poignant statements reinforcing exhibition themes. These ranged from the testamentary ("Back in those days to kill a Negro wasn't nothing. It was like killing a chicken or killing a snake"—Unidentified Black Mississippian) to the exhortative ("We cannot stand still. We cannot permit ourselves to simply be victims"—W. E. B. Du Bois).

Further to this thematically articulated presentation of lynching photographs, the Chicago Historical Society exhibition offered supplementation in the way of a specially designated commemorative space, a display of material pertaining to anti-lynching activism, and a substantial display of materials related to the murder of Emmett Till. In spatial proximity to the last of the lynching photographs was a memorial space designed as a moment of sanctuary offering a respite from the intensity of viewing the photographs. This space was markedly different from the previously mentioned timeline of African American progress presented to Andy Warhol Museum visitors after they completed their viewing of the exhibited photographs. In contrast, moving from their viewing of the lynching photographs, Chicago Historical Society visitors found a space containing a circular light pool at the base of a blue teal semicircular wall on which were written the names of five hundred lynching victims. At the base of the wall and half-surrounding the pool was bench seating. The space was labeled "To Honor and Remember" and the associated panel text explicitly encouraged visitors to reflect on the loss perpetrated in acts of lynching. The precise text is as follows:

> Lynching claimed an unknown number of lives. This space is dedicated to honoring the victims of racial violence and reflecting on the loss all humanity sustains when injustice is accepted

> and perpetrated. The names on these walls represent only a fraction of the documented victims of lynching. Many others remain nameless. We ask you to look at the names, remember the lives, and honor the sacrifices made by the victims and their loved ones in the ongoing struggle for racial equality.

Also projected on the light pool was the following quote by Lois McMaster Bujold: "The dead cannot cry out for justice; it is a duty of the living to do so for them."[20]

Turning away from the memorial space and extending farther into the exhibit was a display of artifacts and memorabilia referencing anti-lynching activism. This section, entitled "Courage in the Face of Terror," focused on the work of Ida B. Wells and the NAACP in the early decades of the twentieth century. Presenting photographs of Wells and her family as well as copies of her various publications, the section also included an extensive biographical wall text. In this text, Wells was introduced as an African American woman, prominent Chicago journalist, and outspoken anti-lynching activist. The text noted that Wells was forced to leave the South due to her outspoken criticism of lynching. Upon settling in Chicago, she continued her investigations into racial violence and the organizing of anti-lynching campaigns. Next to the display of material about Wells were additional text and images that referenced various similar efforts to organize a legal response to the continued practice of lynching. Information was provided and ephemera displayed instantiating the cultural memory of the work of the National Association for the Advancement of Colored People (NAACP) as well as that of the Commission on Interracial Cooperation (CIC), and the Association of Southern Women for the Prevention of Lynching (ASWPL). Included was the widely published photograph of an NAACP flag hanging outside their New York headquarters on which was written in large letters "A man was lynched yesterday."

The final segment of the exhibition marked the fiftieth anniversary of Emmett Till's lynching. This space included several much-enlarged photographs mounted on the final exhibition wall (the only images in the exhibition altered in scale). These included a 1955 portrait of fourteen-year-old Till before his death as well as at his brutally beaten and disfigured face photographed in his open casket at his Chicago funeral.[21] Accompanying the images were a series of text panels giving an extensive account of Till's life and his trip to visit family in Mississippi in the summer of 1955. A few days after he left Chicago for this visit, Emmett Till was dead, murdered subsequent to his being accused of allegedly whistling at a white woman. After his mutilated body was found in the Tallahatchie River by a fisherman, Till's mother, Mamie Till-Mobley, insisted on having her only child's body returned to Chicago for an open casket, public funeral. Till's body was on view from September 3 to September 6. His funeral was attended by more than one hundred thousand Chicagoans. The exhibit text states that Mamie Till's decision "dramatized the injustices of the South's racial codes and helped galvanize the Civil Rights Movement."[22]

Near the images of Till and the information about his murder and funeral was a segment on the 1955 trial of Roy Bryant and J. W. Milam, both charged with Till's murder. The label text explained that despite brave testimony from Mamie Till Bradley and Till's great-uncle Moses Wright, an all-white Mississippian jury acquitted the men after less than an hour of deliberations. Displayed in a longer rectangular glass case were the courtroom sketches and ink-and-wash drawings that Chicago-based artist Frank McMahon furnished for publication in *Life* magazine (these drawings were acquired by the Chicago Historical Society in 2004). The final exhibit label of this sequence was as follows:

> Emmett Till's Enduring Legacy
> Fifty years later, the story of Emmett Till still resonates. Historians cite his murder as a critical turning point in the Civil Rights Movement. Unanswered questions about his death have provoked numerous documentaries and prompted the Justice Department to reopen his case in 2004. Till was not the first or the last to die at hate-filled hands, but his death has become symbolic of the loss communities sustain in the wake of racial violence.
>
> His mother, Mamie Till-Mobley, dedicated her life to helping us remember her son. In doing so, she refused to let us forget where we have been as a nation or how far we have come. Yet, the story of Emmett Till reminds us all that there is still much work to be done.

Just before leaving the exhibition, to the right of the exit, there was a small space containing two visitor comment books and takeaway memorial cards inscribed with the names of each of the victims referenced in the exhibition. These cards were frequently taken by visitors, and as a consequence the museum had to reprint them several times during the duration of the exhibit. On the wall, near the exit, was a wall quote by Martin Luther King Jr., "The arc of the moral universe is long, but it bends towards justice."

THE SELECTION AND LABELING OF THE LYNCHING PHOTOGRAPHS DISPLAYED

Clearly, there were major differences between the exhibitions held at the Chicago Historical Society and the Andy Warhol Museum in regard to the number of lynching photographs displayed (Andy Warhol Museum displayed ninety-two, while the Chicago Historical Society displayed fifty-five), the logic employed to sequence them (Andy Warhol Museum—chronologically; Chicago Historical Society—thematically), and the degree to which they were situated within a narrative context (Andy Warhol Museum—entrance way signage and mininal object labels; Chicago Historical Society—extensive image labels as well as expository and hortatory wall text). However, there were several additional important contrasts between the selection and organization of lynching photographs in the exhibitions that also are important to consider. These bear specifically on the mode through which the Chicago Historical Society exhibition attempted to negotiate the breach between image and text, the incommensurability of what might be offered within a given logic of display. The first of these constrasts is the significant difference in the number of photographs that were used wherein victims were identified. At the Warhol there were twenty-one out of ninety-two photographs in which victims were unidentified (close to one in five) while at the Chicago Historical Society there were only four out of fifty-five (less than one in ten). As we shall see in the next chapter, this was a quite deliberate decision made by the Chicago Historical Society curator Joy Bivins. It will be important to consider her rationale in depth in chapter 3. This facilitated another specific aspect of the Chicago Historical Society exhibit, the possibility of the use of images and text to offer brief "stories" of the circumstances surrounding particular lynchings. As indicated above, the very first images of lynching photographs seen by visitors to the Chicago Historical

Society was the sequence of five images taken at the lynching of Williams James in Cairo, Illinois. Recall that accompanying these images was a narrative account explaining who Will James was and how and why he was so brutally murdered. As mentioned previously, on the other side of the same wall on which the James photographs were displayed was another example of this approach. Here was presented, not an archival lynching photograph, but a newspaper clipping (attributed to the Allen and Littlefield Collection) containing the posed, dignified studio photograph of Anthony Crawford. Accompanying this document was the following label:

> The Lynching of Anthony Crawford. The *Independent*[23] reported the details of the lynching of farmer Anthony Crawford in Abbeville, South Carolina. The article concluded that Crawford's success was the real motivation for his murder.

Offering further context and significance for this document was an adjacent text panel reading as follows:

> A Time of Loss
> In October 1916, Anthony Crawford was tortured and executed in Abbeville, South Carolina. Not one to conform to the era's racial codes, he had asserted himself by arguing with a clerk while negotiating the best price for his cotton. Crawford was one of the region's wealthiest farmers, a patriarch of a large family, and a cornerstone of the black community. His murder caused his family to scatter and delivered a clear message of intimidation to local blacks.
>
> Lynch mobs terrorized entire communities
> Along with other forms of racial violence, lynching served to remind African Americans of their "inferior" status. While whites often justified lynching as "punishment" for black men's sexual assault of white women, these accusations hardly accounted for one-quarter of lynching executions. The stories of Anthony Crawford and countless others reveal that African Americans were primarily murdered for the "crime" of being black or for challenging the racial status quo.

What is particularly interesting about the inclusion of the newspaper document, label, and text panel in the Chicago Historical Society exhibit was the absence any documentation of the Crawford lynching at the Warhol Museum. This further illustrates the emphasis that the staff at the Chicago Historical Society placed on the provision of curator researched *petite histoire* whose consequence was the negation of the anonymity of lynching victims through providing an identity for as many of those pictured in the exhibition as possible. Such a mode of selection and display may be understood as an attempt to bring the lives of lynching victims into presence so that they could be suitably, in the words of Lonnie Bunch, "remembered and honored."[24] But more than this, the Crawford document and narrative, placed as it was early on in the sequence of lynching photographs, also illustrates a mode of supplementation that attempts to articulate the significance of the visual images displayed to a strong narrative of racial injustice. It was perhaps not inconsequential that just prior to the Chicago Historical Society exhibition, in the context of the campaign to have the United States Senate apologize for the historical injustice of the lynching of African Americans, Crawford's murder was publicly cited by then Senator Barack Obama and interviews were given by some of Crawford's surviving relatives. Thus, it is likely that visitors familiar with some of contemporary media reportage on this campaign would recognize the intertextual connection between the exhibition and what many considered an important moment of social justice activism.

An additional feature of the Chicago Historical Society exhibition that marked its difference from that at the Warhol Museum was the display, not just of documents not presented in Pittsburgh (such as the clipping from *The Independent* mentioned above), but as well of lynching photographs not in the Allen and Littlefield collection. An example of this was the series of four postcards in three frames and accompanying text that told the story of the lynching of George Hughes in Sherman, Texas, on May 9, 1930. This was a widely reported news story at the time since it involved a large crowd that attacked a detail of Texas Rangers sent to protect the courthouse during Hughes's trial. As the prosecution attempted to proceed with a trial, the crowd suceeded in burning the courthouse, killing Hughes, and subsequently brutalizing and burning his corpse. Photographs taken at this murder where published across the United States. Dora Apel notes that it is likely the grotesque photograph of Hughes's burned body that appeared in the

June 1930 issue of the International Labour Defense's *Labor Defender* that served as a basis for Isamu Noguchi's difficult, yet still iconic sculpture made for an anti-lynching exhibition held in New York in 1935.[25] Another example of an image/text presented in Chicago but neither present in Pittsburgh nor in the *Without Sancutary* print publication is the widely cited lynching postcard entitled "Dogwood Tree circa 1908" (this image has been reproduced in curriculum material on racial injustice and was mentioned in several newspaper accounts of the 2005 United States Senate apology). Its appearance at the Chicago Historical Society exhibition is consistent with the strategy of offering supplementary images that would underwrite the main narrative frame through which the Allen and Littlefield images were shown. On the front of this card is a photograph of five African Americans hanging from a single tree. Also on the front of the card, below the image the following text is printed.

> Scene in Stain County Texas, June 15, 1908
> "The Dogwood Tree"
>
> This is only the branch of the Dogwood tree;
> An emblem of WHITE SUPREMACY.A lesson once taught in the Pioneer's school,
> That this is a land of WHITE MAN'S RULE.
> The Red Man once in an early day,
> Was told by the Whites to mend his way.
>
> The negro, now, by eternal grace,
> Must learn to stay in the negro's place.
> In the Sunny South, the Land of the Free,
> Let the WHITE SUPREME forever be.
> Let this a warning to all negroes be,
> Or they'll suffer the fate of the DOGWOOD TREE.
>
> Copyrighted—Pub. by HarkriderDrug Company, Center, Tex.

In a quite different vein, it is worth noting one instance where the Chicago Historical Society considered, but chose not to show, an image that was presented at the Warhol Museum. Of the eight images of the lynching of William James displayed at the Andy Warhol Museum, the

Chicago Historical Society only showed six (two were in one frame). Purposely excluded was the "Half Burned Head of James on Pole" in Candee Park, Cairo, Illinois. As will be discussed more fully in chapter 3, the curatorial staff at the Chicago Historical Society decided not to present this image. First of all, it was decided that it was not needed to tell Willam James's story and hence the presentation of the gruesome photograph would be exploitative. Secondly, it was thought appropriate to temper the emotional assault inherent in the viewing of photographs by excluding this particular instance of body mutilation. Thus, while the exhibition at the Chicago Historical Society did not defer the presentation of quite disturbing images, each presented was justified in regard to its function in the narrative coherence of either accounts of individual lynchings or the overall thematic historical narrative that organized the entire presentation.

Another mode of contrast that amply illustrates the different frameworks employed by the Andy Warhol Museum and the Chicago Historical Society is the comparison between the image lablels that each institution wrote for the exact same photographs. For example, consider the labels placed under the photograph entitled "The lynching of Rubin Stacy, July 19, 1935, Fort Lauderdale, Florida." The Warhol Museum used this title under which appeared the following text: "Onlookers, including four young girls. Gelatin silver print, 8 x 10 in. (20.3 x 25.4 cm.). In the Allen Littlefield Collection at Special Collections at Woodruff Library, Emory University." In contrast, at the Chicago Historical Society, after the same title the following text appeared:

> After he allegedly assaulted a white woman, the police arrested Ruben Stacy and slated him for transfer to the Dade County Jail in Miami. According to Deputy Virgil Wright, more than 100 masked men overpowered his deputies during the transfer. The mob seized Stacy, shot him and hung him from a roadside tree, and continued to riddle his body with bullets. According to the *New York Times*, subsequent investigation revealed that Stacy, a homeless tenant farmer, had gone to a house to ask for food. The woman became frightened and screamed when she saw Stacy's face. The number of young witness participants at Stacy's lynching is almost as troubling as this unjust murder. Capturing the disconcerting tone of this photograph, James Weldon Johnson describes the epidemic of the lynching of

African Americans as "problem saving Black America's body and white America's soul." The NAACP later used this photo in their anti-lynching propaganda.

Another example of constrasting practices of labeling is illustrated by a comparsion of the labels given photographs of the lynching of Leo Frank. The exhibition at the Warhol Museum provided two images from the Allen and Littlefield collection and labeled them as follows:

> (1) The lynching of Leo Frank, August 17, 1915
> Marietta, Georgia.
> gelatin silver print, real photo postcard
> 5 1/2 x 3 1/2 in. (14 x 8.9 cm.)
> In the Allen Littlefield Collection at Special Collections at Woodruff Library, Emory University
>
> (2) The lynching of Leo Frank, August 17, 1915
> Marietta, Georgia.
> Printed over the image: "THE END OF LEO FRANK HUNG BY A MOB AT MARIETTA. GA. AUG. 17. 1915."
> gelatin silver print, lithographed postcard
> 3 1/2 x 5 1/2 in. (8.9 x 14 cm.)
> In the Allen Littlefield Collection at Special Collections at Woodruff Library, Emory University

At the Chicago Historical Society one postcard photograph of the lynching of Frank was displayed along with the following story as part of its label:

> In August 1913 a judge convicted Jewish factory owner Leo Frank with dubious evidence of the murder of Mary Phagan, a thirteen year old girl employed in his Atlanta factory. Frank's four month trial ended in a conviction and the death sentence. Judges denied all of his appeals and after an unsuccessful hearing before the Supreme Court April, 1915, his supporters moved to obtain an executive grant of clemency. After a prolonged and contentious struggle, Governor Frank Slaton altered the death sentence to life in imprisonment. The governor's

> actions did not end the clamouring for Frank's death. On the evening of August 16 1915, 25 men abducted Frank from his prison hospital bed where he was recovering from a near fatal stab wound. The mob drove to a grove just outside of Marietta and hung Frank at dawn. Two Supreme Court justices, one ex-sheriff, and at least one clergyman were among those in the mob that murdered Frank. Commenting on Frank's lynching historian Lucian Lamar Knight unashamedly wrote "No finer Ku Klux Klaning was ever known in Georgia." The state of Georgia posthumously pardoned Frank in 1986.

DIFFERENCES IN EXHIBITION DESIGN

Given the above sketch of the differences in exhibit layout, I am now in a position to address more precisely what is meant by the claim that each institution gave very different weight to the visual history manifest in presentation of photographs of lynchings. At the Chicago Historical Society, it was decided that the exhibition would require substantial narrative in order to provide a historical context for the limited number of photographs presented, many of which would serve as evidentiary documents rendering of personal stories of victimization. In this respect, the curatorial project reflected Siegfried Kracauer's assessment "that behind a photograph of a human being, his history is buried as though under a blanket of snow."[26] In regard to photographs, Kracauer polemically argued, "the image chases away the idea" and thus functions as "a means of attack on knowledge." Indeed, Kracauer took the position that "when the world becomes photogenic in this way, history is mortified, rendered impotent, and reduced to 'indifference toward what things want to say'" (quoted in Didi-Huberman, 173). As will be elaborated in chapter 3, this concern with the mortification of history through images was central to the curatorial project of the Chicago Historical Society exhibition. Images were chosen where there were stories that one could tell. There are very few photographs in the Chicago Historical Society exhibit where there is nothing known about the person who had been lynched. This curatorial approach attempted to lessen the likelihood that the photographs would be engaged as fetish imagery, encouraging them instead to be engaged traces of facts to which one might bear witness.

In a different vein, at the Andy Warhol Museum the decision was taken to minimize explanatory historical contextualization in order to maximize the potential to engage in closely looking at the photographs. The assumption embedded in this curatorial project was that reducing labeling and other explanatory text would intensify the affective experience of confronting the actuality of the photographic images. The worry was that in relegating the photographs to the sphere of the document, one would severe them from "their phenomenology, from their specificity, and from their very substance" as images (Didi-Huberman, 33). The museum did experience criticism that they did not provide enough contextual information for the images, yet it was argued that too much information created barriers to the intense visual experience they wanted to create. As will be elaborated in chapter 3, the curatorial project at the Andy Warhol Museum was not so much an effort to promote a specific knowledge and understanding of history as it was to excite feeling, crystallize emotions, and direct commitments through the discursive frame of the exhibition's supplementary sections documenting and encouraging antiracism activism.

The tension between the varying assumptions embedded in these different curatorial projects is symptomatic of each institution's attempt to avoid the problems inherent in the challenge of curating an exhibit of images of violence and suffering. On the one hand, curatorial practice at the Chicago Historical Society attempted to mitigate rendering the photographs into icons of horror that would be subject to the desire to see everything in them. On the other hand, the concern at the Warhol Museum was to avoid reducing the photographs to no more than documents of horror, as images that principally provided information and evidence regarding the perpetration of deadly violence.[27] Despite these differences, the aspiration held in common by each exhibition was the creation of a mise-en-scène that would foster an encounter that would elicit the imperative to look headlong at catastrophe and bear witness to its fact and intolerable place in the human community in which one is a participant.

As outlined in the previous chapter, at stake in the contemporary exhibition of lynching photographs is the very basic question of how such exhibitions might reframe a selected set of images so as to contest the very purposes for which they were taken in the first place, purposes no longer acceptable but conceivably still resonant with aspects of contemporary life. In negotiating the problems just mentioned, each institution recognized that the contemporary exhibition of lynching photographs was importantly, but not only, a matter of the public presentation of historical documents. Additionally, they initiated practices of rendition that attempted to return to the historical present the arrival of a presence felt as a heteronomic force that would be difficult to ignore. This was the explicit justification for the exhibition at the Chicago Historical Society. As the director of the Chicago Historical Society explained in his statement that formed part of a wall text, his intent was not to "embarrass, cause pain, or be unpatriotic" but rather to recognize that these "shocking, unimaginable images reveal much about the terror and lawlessness that shaped race relations in America in the 19th and 20th centuries," thus "*forcing us* [my emphasis] to confront a shameful part of our history, a part many of us would rather forget."[28] This notion that an exhibit could enact a *force* was central to the curatorial projects at both the Chicago Historical Society and the Andy Warhol Museum. Yet the question remains: How is one to conceive of this force and its consequences?

All versions of the *Without Sanctuary* exhibitions attempted to render these moments of suffering and dying as demanding a witness that commanded one's attentiveness and claimed one's acknowledgment. These public displays of lynching photographs endeavored to bring forth a spectral presence that was exposed and embodied through the rendition of a disfigured human singularity subjected to the violent hands of those pictured as celebrants at the scene of death. As Jean-Luc Nancy put it, rendered here "is not . . . presence pure and simple . . . *not* the immediacy of the being-posed-there but is rather that which draws presence out of this immediacy insofar as it puts a value on presence *as* some presence or another."[29] The value exposed through the presence rendered by these images is not just that grasped in the moment of recognition of an objective depiction of suffering, but was to include the tactile impact or force felt as the sensation that accompanies the exposure to the rendition of a person undergoing extreme degradation and pain. In this sense, the photograph exhibitions under discussion were intended to be as much transactive as they are communicative. As Jill Bennett helpfully observes, "Images have the capacity to address a viewer's own bodily memory, to touch the viewer who feels rather than simply sees the event" depicted.[30] In this respect, the photographic image of a lynching has the potential to register more than it is meant to denote. This "more" is not just a felt loss (of individual life, of the adequacy of a known history, of a trust in the uprightness of the nation), but a felt responsibility that one cannot remain indifferent when faced with the pain of another. In this sense, such a photograph is not just to be understood as a representation of the world but a visual perlocution that registers and produces sensation. This is affect, not as opposed to thought, but as a possible means through which a claim is made on a viewer to both acknowledge the pain of another *and* begin the thought required to come to terms with the felt presence of that pain in the present. The affective force brought forth in the violent images of lynching does not simply interpolate the already morally predisposed viewer as a particular kind of subject (expressing horror at the act of racial violence, sympathy for the victims, and outrage for its perpetrators), but rather it instantiates a tactile connection that, *despite who we are,* bodily impacts on us. In saying this, I do not mean to suggest that all viewers of such images respond to the pain of another with the same empathic concern. Clearly, issues of identity and personal history will be implicated in this response. No doubt, such a response will be structured by the dynamics of identification and transference. However, it would be a mistake to too quickly move to the problem of accounting for individual audience responses. It is important to understand that the response to the images of suffering addressed here is not limited to the dynamics of identification with people now dead, but exists at that moment when the rendition of the disfigurement of another is felt bodily as a deep disturbing anxiety. To respond to this presence is both to acknowledge past injustice *and* the continuing affective heritage of the lynching photographs. On such terms, *the consequences of seeing the lynching photographs cannot be determined in advance*; it is uncertain as to the substance of the thought that will be provoked. Nevertheless, central here is the realization that violent images of lynching are not just "shocking" but also compelling in that they require an acknowledgment of another's pain that might lead to some yet to be decided thought and action commanded by the felt experience of viewing the photographs. Provoked by the rendition of historical documentation, this thought and action can be performatively understood as a continuous negotiation with and in the present in regard to an indeterminate link to the past.

If the sensory intensity initiated by the experienced image (experienced in the event-bound act of looking) is to be reflectively attended to by the one who looks, how this intensity is brought into consciousness, how it is named, understood, and assessed as to its significance has much to do with the curatorial judgments that have concretely composed and framed an exhibition as an image-event. The exhibitions at the Andy Warhol Museum and the Chicago Historical Society were events that attempted to couple affect, thought, and action while endeavoring to restrict the indeterminacy of this relationship within the terms offered through specific curatorial projects. At the Chicago Historical Society the force of the image was restrained (but not finally contained) by the extensive text offering both a historiography of lynching in America and a series of *petites histoires* that rendered intelligible individual narratives of racial violence. The extensive text employed by the Chicago Historical Society made it possible to read one's way through the exhibition, enabling visitors to both look and look away at the same time. The risk taken at the Chicago Historical Society was manifest in the creation of a visual event in which the photographic images could fade into historical knowledge, channeling the affective force of the images on to an unreflexive memorialization of those subjected to a tragic injustice. The possible jeopardy was the disregard of how the visual composition of the images themselves might give pause to consider the contemporary significance of the circumstances of the production and circulation of the photographs as photographs. If such were the case, it would be all too easy to place the violence rendered in the images as firmly in the past, affirming oneself and one's society as predominantly postracist.

Arguably, at the Andy Warhol Museum the affective force of the images of lynching was heightened by the minimal historical context provided. Standing in the photograph gallery at the Warhol implicated one in a double bind in regard to what might be accounted as a "decent" regard. Within the mise-en-scène of this exhibition it was much more difficult to both look *and* to look away. Yet it was quite clear that much work was done at the museum to restrain the indeterminacy of the affect provoked by these images and to channel these sensations into affirmations of the struggle against racial discrimination. Inadvertently, the attempt to restrain this indeterminacy also produced the risk that enjoining individuals to virtuous behavior might result in a looking away from the singularity of the photographs and a shift in focus to the personal actions one might take to fight racism. The possible unanticipated consequence of this would then be a short-circuiting of the thought provoked by attentiveness to "the way of seeing" offered in each photograph as well as images displayed being taken as a series of "repetitions."[31] The photographs of lynching from the Allen and Littlefield collection are not only documents of events that have happened in a certain place and time, but also bear witness to modes of encountering the world that are deeply problematic. While these archival photographs may seem to offer a practice of looking that appears foreign or even unimaginable, what is worth considering is if, in their appearance at the Andy Warhol Museum, they are more closely related to ordinary, contemporary positions of engagement than their contents seem to suggest. This consideration would have us reflect on the interests served by the particular "machinery of witness and identification"[32] inherent in this curatorial project. Mobilized differently, the affect-thought coupling consequent with viewing the lynching photographs might otherwise consider how seeing such "inconceivable" ways of seeing resonates with modes of perception complicit with the reproduction of the relations responsible for much of the present-day problems of racial inequality.

The curatorial projects discussed above are inherently equivocal. While the consequence of much collective thought and deliberation, they have to be understood as forms of practice subject to quite specific contextual conditions and the uncertainty as to how any given exhibit might work as an event. The following chapter opens up a consideration how the museum staff in each institution worked through the problems of exhibition design, development, and implementation.

THREE

The Curatorial Work of Exhibiting Archival Photographs of Lynching in America

In his discussion of curatorial ethics, Hernández-Navarro insightfully argues that "every institution speaks and shows itself through its exhibitions."[1] On these terms, a curatorial project animates an institution to speak while also speaking for it. In this respect, a curatorial project cannot fully escape the demand that it is representing an institution and attempting to fulfill its desires (e.g., enacting its mandate, securing its legitimacy, maintaining its currency). To deepen the consideration of the different ways that the Andy Warhol Museum and the Chicago Historical Society faced the challenges of exhibiting the lynching photographs in a mode consistent with each institution's aspirations and commitments, I turn to conversations held with museum staff regarding the development and display of the exhibitions. Expressed throughout these conversations was a heightened appreciation for the particular responsibilities each institution bore in finding appropriate modalities for the presentation of their respective exhibits. This expressed appreciation took the form of an ethical regard that was central to the curatorial projects at both museums. This regard unfolded concretely in a series of questions, concerns, decisions, and rationalizations in relation to the purposes, practicalities, and process of creating an exhibit displaying photographs of lynchings.

The decisions and considerations necessary to produce an exhibition drawn from any given collection includes determining whether the materials in the collection are appropriate for public display; what professional and community consultations might be necessary to make this decision (and those that will follow from it); what materials from the collection should be exhibited and which excluded; whether the displayed materials should be supplemented with other images, objects, and sounds and if so how; what texts (if any) will be used to provide context for the material displayed; what concepts and aesthetics should drive the visual design; and how programming and dialogues related to the exhibition will be developed. Also important are decisions as to how an exhibition should be made manifest to different publics through various media. This includes decisions as to what images and text should be used to promote the exhibit. These decision points of exhibit development were used as a framework for structuring the conversations with staff at the Andy Warhol Museum and the Chicago Historical Society. In the context of these conversations, it became clear that the issues associated with such decisions were addressed at different levels of specificity and personal concern depending on organization role, specific occupational tasks, and the given level of responsibility of particular staff. Thus, it was quite evident that staff who engaged visitors in the context of daily educational programming had to negotiate the emotional weight and racialized specificity of the images quite differently than say, senior administrators who very rarely met visitors and engaged them in conversation.

Throughout this chapter, I will present a substantial number of excerpts from these conversations. My intent is not to critique the assumptions and ideologies expressed by individual staff members nor is it to judge one set of curatorial practices over and against another. Rather, it is to illustrate, in quite concrete terms, the problems and issues inherent to a specific institution's development of an exhibition of lynching photographs. The interview excerpts throughout are drawn from an extended discussion of the curatorial projects that animated this development work. In this respect, the text provides viewpoints of various Andy Warhol Museum and Chicago Historical Society staff in regard to (1) their conceptions of public pedagogy enacted by the photographic display of images of racial violence; (2) their understanding of their location and the location of their institutions in the contemporary racial formation of the United States; (3) their thoughts about the responsibilities of memory; and (4) the personal and museological significance of the affective impact of the images with which they were working. The perspectives of Andy Warhol Museum staff presented are principally drawn from conservations with the museum director, the assistant director of education and interpretation, four different artist educators who were responsible for various tasks related to the public facilitation of the museum's *Without Sanctuary* exhibition, the head of visitor services, staff from the marketing department with responsibility for promoting the exhibition, and a free lance researcher who was contracted to undertake an independent evaluation of the exhibition and its impact.[2] As well, I cite excerpts from a published text written by the assistant director providing her account of the exhibition and its development. The curator who was responsible for working with James Allen and selecting the photographs of lynchings to be exhibited had left the museum at the time of this research and consequently was not available for an interview. The perspectives of Chicago Historical Society staff are drawn from conversations held not only with the exhibition's curator but as well those individuals responsible for the overall design, the design of graphics, text editing, and public programming as well as the administrative head of public programs and exhibits.[3] The then-director of the Chicago Historical Society had left the institution just prior to the exhibition's opening and thus it was not possible engage him in conversation. For the most part, conversations held with staff at the Andy Warhol Museum and the Chicago Historical Society took place in small groups of three to five people, although individual conversations were held when possible.

PRESENTING IMAGES OF RACIAL VIOLENCE: THE PUBLIC PEDAGOGY OF MUSEUM DISPLAY

No contemporary museum or gallery could justify a display of lynching photographs if such a display were to be simply apprehended as the recirculation of the spectacle of white supremacist violence. Thus, staff at the Andy Warhol Museum and the Chicago Historical Society needed to have an idea of how to exhibit the photographs so that they rubbed against the grain of the intent of the photographers who took them, in effect granting these photographers a museological form of "undeserved grace."[4] This meant that the curatorial project in each museum needed to come to terms with the question of how presentations of historically racist photographs of lynchings might ethically and pedagogically function in the context of an exhibition to be held in their particular institution.

Pedagogical Perspectives from the Andy Warhol Museum Staff

Any given curatorial project has to take into account that it will be actualized within the shadow of the institution in which it takes place. Clearly, museums have particular histories that not only shape decisions as to what is shown, but as well, inform the intelligibility of particular practices of exhibition. There was a keen awareness among staff at the Warhol that presenting lynching photographs in an art museum raised serious questions regarding the relation between art and documentation and the potential risks of the aestheticization of imagery of deadly violence. Consequently, Warhol Museum staff had to publicly express a clear justification not only for showing images from the Allen and Littlefield collection, but showing them in an art museum. Since the Andy Warhol Museum did not have either the mandate or expertise to present exhibitions that centered on historical narratives, the museum had to articulate its own particular terms for exhibiting the lynching photographs. As one of the Andy Warhol Museum artist educators put it:

> The Warhol kept repeatedly saying . . . no, no, no, this [the photograph collection] is not art, we are not presenting it as art, we are presenting it as a large community project that draws on . . . the [Andy Warhol] Museum's experience of looking at and dealing with challenging and powerful images. It was a very, very clear distinction that was made. This is not art and we are not treating it as such. We are treating it as powerful objects and powerful images, but not putting the image of a lynched man up and saying this is beautiful art.

This concern that a display of lynching photographs at the Warhol might be misrecognized and hence misunderstood (or, at best, be taken as anachronistic) was not just a consequence of the Andy Warhol Museum being known as an "art museum." Additionally, this concern was grounded in the sensitivity of museum staff to the possible framing effects of the Warhol's previous and ongoing exhibitions and their respective diverse flow of images. As the head of visitor services said:

> I wonder how much we confuse our public when we do things like *Without Sanctuary* and then we have [publicity] pictures of our director blocking the genitalia of two naked people covered in gold standing next to him. You wonder sort of . . . [laughs] . . . how the public juggles all of the things the museum is doing and what we're capable of doing. It's interesting that we have such a range that we are capable of doing something from both ends of the spectrum.

The issue of the public perception of the museum's institutional legacy was not lost on the artist educators. This is evident in the following brief interchange:

> ARTIST EDUCATOR 2: Well we went from *Without Sanctuary* to the Farah Fawcett exhibition[5] and then Diane Keaton's clown paintings,[6] it was just so . . .
> ARTIST EDUCATOR 3: Schizophrenic.

The issue of the public reputation of the museum constituted in the legacy of its previous exhibitions was also reflected by the assistant director in her comments regarding efforts to develop a collaborative relationship with *The Pittsburgh Courier* (Pittsburgh's African American newspaper that was featured in the exhibition in regard to their strong anti-lynching advocacy during the 1930s).

> Remember going to *The Pittsburgh Courier*? . . . it was natural to work with them . . . how many times did we say "come, come, come". . . . Our director couldn't get them in, I couldn't get them in, the marketing and Development couldn't get them in. Eventually we went to their office and we talked about the project and it wasn't until they saw that we were sincere. . . . I think they had the sense of [Andy] Warhol as a sensationalist.

As I will extensively discuss in the section of this chapter addressing the racialization of the Andy Warhol Museum, Warhol staff in fact made a determined effort to make sure various community groups understood its intent in staging the exhibition and, reciprocally, staff listened to and attempted to take into account what members of these groups had to say about the prospect of exhibiting photographs of lynchings. As the director put it, this was to be an exhibition addressing important issues, "one that could have a lot of repercussions—good or bad." The assistant director underscored this concern:

> We had a strong sense of how we thought this [exhibition] was important to the institution. But we wanted to be really responsible about how we would move forward and so we would go to the community board and ask about their thoughts and ask what we should be thinking of in terms of programming, presentation. What are your thoughts? Etcetera. Etcetera. Etcetera.

As briefly discussed in chapter 2, the curatorial approach at the Warhol was to minimize the historical information accompanying the photographs. Instead of providing extensive labels for each photograph and a historical narrative explaining the rise of the practice of lynching in the United States, the museum's approach was to emphasize an emotionally heightened, reflexive visual experience that enabled a consideration of the personal and social implications provoked by difficult images of death and suffering. In a published commentary reflecting on the experience of developing the exhibition, the assistant director indicated that part of the mission of the Andy Warhol Museum was to explore "the discursive power of images in our lives, whether past or present, art or document."[7] Understanding that such an exploration was not without its problems, she recognized that any exhibition of lynching photographs would likely be criticized for exploiting the pain of those who suffered racist violence. Nonetheless, she defended the exhibition on terms similar to those expressed by Dora Apel, suggesting that perhaps "the only horror worse than looking, is not looking."[8]

To convey what she thought of as the potential inherent in the display of the lynching photographs at the Warhol, the assistant director drew on the assumption that the museum's practice of spatially relocating images and artifacts contained its own important pedagogical potential. The supposition inherent in this pedagogy is that once an image or artifact is disclosed anew in a radically altered context from its previous deployment, one's perception of it would be irrevocably altered. This perspective is manifest in her statement about the unique power of placing objects in an "art museum." In "The Warhol: Museum as Artist," she wrote, "It is perhaps the very public nature of collective looking that takes place within an art museum that ensures we truly do look particularly at what seems incongruously in the wrong place" (Gogan, 6). Furthermore, the assistant director emphasized the importance of exhibitions that enabled viewers to question how they were personally implicated in "the looking" provoked by the exhibition. Recognizing this as a complicated and difficult process, she stressed the importance of the museum's supporting the working out of one's own personal emotional responses and trying to understand what they may mean for oneself and one's culture.

The pedagogy of support for such thought went extensively beyond providing a space for personal contemplation. Rather than assuming that thinking through the implications of "looking" was merely an individual affair, the Warhol's curatorial project assumed such thought to be a social process structured through an extended dialogue and discussion provoked by viewers' responses to the images they had seen. The assistant director was acutely aware that contemporary life in North America had reduced the availability of communal, physical spaces where people could find a safe place to have a discussion, think about different things, and/or be exposed to different issues. In her view, museums had a responsibility to help revive such spaces. She wrote:

> Once defined as an "image bequeathed to posterity," collective memory implies collective sharing. The photographs are evidence of hidden memories and images, unshared for the most part and unacknowledged in the national consciousness. This shift from obscurity to newfound visibility requires an emotional processing—a collective witnessing and sharing that draws its power from specific experience rather than universal themes. (Gogan, 15)

Given the above commitment to a dialogic pedagogy provoked by an engagement with emotionally provocative visual imagery, there still remains the question of whether or not the Andy Warhol Museum should have provided more historical information about the photographs and the events they depicted. Given the contrast between the exhibitions held in Pittsburgh and Chicago, it appeared that the Andy Warhol Museum was less proactive in the selection and display of particular lynching images than the Chicago Historical Society. Yet it is important to note that Warhol staff consciously decided to minimize the information associated with specific photographs. As the director of the museum put it, "In terms of the imagery, other than labels that were really taxonomic, we didn't have a lot [of text] because we wanted you to look at the images." This emphasis on providing an intensely visual experience is also conveyed in his comments describing the "somber and elegant" color of the background walls and the strategy for mounting the photographs:

> We wanted to take out this cold, harsh analytical thing because while these were documents, we wanted to raise the heat a little bit. Also, we wanted people to get close to the images, and this was necessary because the images were so small. You had to step into the row and you really had to be close up. We felt that was very important.

As signaled earlier, the assistant director was quite aware that the minimalist approach to the image labels might be seen as problematic. However, in an interview with our research team, she defended this method as follows:

> We had a lot of discussions [regarding] what the labels were. They identified specific images; they weren't the full text labels that were actually in the [James Allen] book. There were definitely different perspectives around how the images were to be contextualized. . . . We definitely had criticism that there wasn't enough historical information to contextualize the images. And perhaps on one level you need that to be able to have a clearer sense of the story, to give the victim that kind of context to prevent them from be overly identified with the image. The counterargument to that, and one that I think is important, is that in a strange way, because we [at the Andy Warhol Museum] are in so many ways about looking . . . we bring that aesthetic context to whatever we do. It is a challenge. What we can offer in that way is a frame to look at things.
>
> I think one of the things that was good about the way we presented it is that the images were there for people to look at and experience. Sometimes the historical context creates safety buffers and so in a way, having that kind of very intense visual and emotional experience, I think, enabled that [experience of

> looking], perhaps . . . certainly, the whole context of looking became a very real one in the exhibition itself.

This emphasis on provoking an "intense visual and emotional experience" meant a particular mode of privileging the image. However, despite this very clear framework for the exhibition, there remained some ambivalence as to the degree of contextual information that the exhibition did provide. Reflecting on the exhibit at the time of our conversations, the assistant director admitted "a question mark" in regard to whether or not they should have so substantially edited Allen's commentary on each photograph. In conversations with frontline staff, there was also a degree of ambivalence expressed regarding the approach articulated above. Artist educators who participated in dialogue sessions with visitors acknowledged that people would often ask about "what was going on in a photograph." The approach taken in response to such questions was to try and steer people away from an "intellectual," historical consideration of the denotative specifics of a given image toward a discussion of visitors' personal responses to the imagery and their individual and social implications. As one of the artist educators commented:

> I think occasionally with the adults . . . they would try to intellectualize it [the exhibition] and just talk about it, but we're not historians. I found that adults in the dialogues hard to facilitate; it was hard enough getting enough people together, but also it was hard to sit and talk about these things.

An example of this approach is manifest in the following comments of an artist educator with experience facilitating dialogues with visiting school groups:

> The suburban schools would come in without one African American kid in the group. I feel like with some of those groups, at least it's opening a door or window for them to consider something in a way they never had before. I don't know how effective we were with that because obviously some kids didn't get [the idea of] institutional racism or privilege, but we did try to move it from the specifics of the photographs to where they are in life and in that community and why are

> there no African American kids in their school. . . . And just having them look at issues of how urban centers have been created. We were looking at some larger cultural issues that came out of it, but really we would go with where [a] kid's reactions went. So it was never guaranteed you were going to get to this great dialogue of these larger cultural issues. We always tried to end with "what can you do" and "what can we do" but even that, I always felt like it was lacking and that I was lacking and I wasn't giving people enough to work with.

The above comment speaks to the challenges of having the exhibition offer a sense of hopefulness. The assistant director explicitly spoke of this as one of the desires she had for the exhibition: "We wanted to have some sense of hope, this was very important. Dialogue, context, and hope were embedded in how we developed material and how we presented those opportunities." One of the manifestations of this desire was the degree of emphasis that many artist educators placed on using reflection and dialogue to name and commit to possible actions for change. As will become evident in chapter 4, there was some tension between the affective responses of visitors to the exhibition and the desires of those staff responsible for animating conversations among people who had just seen the images. One of the artist educators recalled how hard it was to move people, who had just come out the exhibition, immediately into a discussion of what actions visitors might take in the present to fight racism. As she recalled:

> We would try to move them into action . . . [but] it's hard to move people from this shell-shocked emotional place to where they can have a serious, deeper discussion on the larger issues that cause it. And I think with the art piece and the dialogues we started to do that.

Moving people to "action" was central to the efforts at the Warhol to engage the shared aspirations of civil society. The stress on a dialogic process that supported "collective witnessing and sharing" meant that not only was individual learning and insight a desired outcome, but so was the possibility that the exhibition might make a difference in the social and political life of the community. This possibility was consistent with what was then the newly revised mandate for the museum written in the context of strategic plan discussions conducted during 1999–2000 (just prior to the development of the *Without Sanctuary* exhibit). This aspect of the mandate was registered in a conversation with the museum director as he emphasized the importance of doing "politically and emotionally engaged exhibits" in an era when "museums have gotten to be so quiescent and so dull and they have just taken all of the juice out of what museums should be." In reflecting on his experience seeing a previous exhibition of photographs from the Allen and Littlefield collection presented in another city, the director provided a sense of the ways in which he wanted the Andy Warhol Museum exhibition to be different from the one he had just seen:

> We walked into this very substantial room . . . with a sort of hushed setting about it. Because these were all very little images . . . in this big room, it wasn't the most appealing exhibition layout. But there were streams of people looking over the shoulders [of] others and observing . . . one race to another, one age to another. What were people's responses to the imagery? And what should be people's responses to the imagery? [That museum] focused mainly on [showing] the photographs and [providing] a little information on the civil rights movement at the end [of the exhibit]. That was it. And when we did the exhibition, we wanted more programming than that and we also wanted to have a local effect.

Given that images from the Allen and Littlefield collection were laden with "the emotional intensity of America's problematic past and present regarding race," the Andy Warhol Museum set about to present an exhibition that might generate "community dialogue around race and related issues of bias and bigotry in the context of a local climate fraught with economic disparity and the tensions of recent racial violence" (Gogan, 4). Thus, for Andy Warhol Museum staff, the exhibition offered an opportunity to "contribute to the dialogue on race relations in the city and to explore the potential of its mission to be a forum for contemporary issues" (Gogan, 4). In this respect, central to the exhibition was the work of orchestrating conversations wherein people could explore what they understood to be the significance of the traces of history they had just seen. As is evident from the detailed description of the exhibition in chapter 2, the museum put considerable effort into developing a pedagogy designed to enhance visitor engagement and dialogue. The following remarks by the assistant director provide some insight into how this pedagogy was structured.

> So in that vein we were thinking we want to have something that encouraged people to reflect . . . one of my experiences has been about showcasing different points of view rather than taking different comments and just putting them in a box. You actually present them back to people and by doing that, you emphasize that there are multiple ways of doing this, and you have a large sense of participation. And there's also a sense of a kind of permission giving . . . oh, look at all these different voices, and I can add mine, but if you don't want to add yours, you can participate in the dialogues anyways because you see it visualized and you also see it valued. Which is another core point to presenting that, in the immediate context, your opinion is actually valued enough to be put on this wall here and so all of those kind of things kept constant—in my mind trying to find what is the right avenue, what is the right take. And then the idea of postcards came up. We wanted to send something through the mail to counteract the element of that and that's where it sort of arose. It was in conversations . . . you know what you're looking for and you don't quite know what it is . . . and then you have this kind of moment where everything kind of jells.

In an interview with our research team, the researcher hired to assess the impact of this programming[9] stressed the significance of the extensive space that the Andy Warhol Museum devoted to enhancing a communal engagement with the exhibit.

> They used the traditional signifier of space allocation in a different way . . . they said look at all of these rooms [devoted to] the process of engaging with the photographs . . . the use of the [multiple] rooms made it clear that the discourse was what the exhibit was about. And then there were all those resources put into managing all those activities [meant to elicit responses and discussion]. I think people absorbed that instantly.

Finally, it is important to note that the priority given to engagement and dialogue was underscored by the fact that there were no interpretive tours of the *Without Sanctuary* exhibition and that most of the "front end staff" were assigned to conduct dialogue sessions.

Pedagogical Perspectives from the Chicago Historical Society Staff

Whereas the Warhol choose to present close to one hundred images with minimal wall text, the Chicago exhibition aimed at "uncovering *the stories* (my emphasis) of more than forty of these victims through postcards and photographs from the collection of James Allen and John Littlefield."[10] This emphasis on presenting stories of people (as opposed to a display of photographic documents) was central to the curatorial project at the Chicago Historical Society. As the exhibition curator stated, "There are over a hundred images in the [Allen and Littlefield] collection . . . [however] we chose mainly those images where there were stories we could tell. There are very few images in our *Without Sanctuary* exhibition where there is nothing known about the person who has been lynched." The centrality of this approach was manifest in the placement of the account of the lynching of Will James within the introductory space of the exhibition. As noted in the detailed exhibition description in chapter 2, when entering the exhibit space visitors were prominently presented with images and text devoted to the lynching of James in Cairo, Illinois, in 1909. Shown were five framed postcard images taken at various stages of the James lynching. When the exhibition designer was asked about the decision to begin with the story of the lynching of James, he restated that the story of the James lynching was comprised of multiple images and text that conveyed a detailed account through a linear, sequential narrative. In this respect, it offered a sense of story quite different from many of the single image postcards where minimal information was available as to the event depicted. As a consequence, the particular details available in the presentation of the story of Will James gestured toward a vibrant absent presence of other stories unavailable in other individual photographs.

This emphasis on the notion of presenting stories was further underscored by the way the Chicago Historical Society exhibit employed the use of labels. The text editor for the exhibition noted that while it was a challenge for her, the curatorial team made a conscious decision to allow the labels to be as long as they needed to be. This was understood not only as pedagogically important but also as a way of honoring the victims. Nevertheless, she was still surprised by the visitor response to these labels. As she put it: "The thing that was incredible to me, when you go to exhibitions you don't often see people reading labels in galleries, but every time I came into [the *Without Sanctuary*] gallery every person was reading. It's unbelievable; it's astounding [the amount that people are reading]." Adding to this aspect of the conversation, the curator said that they didn't want the labels to sound just like words taken from James Allen's book. She emphasized the fact that she did her own research on individual images and at times found information not noted in the book. While the curator compiled as much information about each image as she could find, it was then the text editor's responsibility to take this information to write a readable text. Clearly, in doing so she broke her own norms as to how long a label should be. The graphic designer also added her perspective on this: "Yeah, we didn't have to cut the length. . . . I am usually a bit of a pain about keeping things to a certain length because it makes it really hard for me production wise . . . but this time I just felt like I needed to let it go and just let the text be exactly the way the curator and editor wanted it." This emphasis on creating the conditions for presenting stories that would engage visitors also encompassed aspects of the spatial layout of the exhibit. Commenting on this, the text editor expressed the view that "what was so effective about the design of the exhibition space is that the objects have enough room around them so that individual visitors (in their own personal space) can engage with one object at a time. I think that's really important. They're not too spread out in the gallery, but they're not so crowded that you don't feel like you can't interact with one personal story."

The notion of story so central to the Chicago Historical Society exhibition was not limited to specific accounts of the circumstances of particular instances of lynching. Rather, there was a quite explicit intent to have individual stories crystallize into a more encompassing narrative. When walking through the exhibit and gesturing to the images and text that portrayed the lynching of Anthony Crawford, the text editor suggested that this story was a good example of the exhibition's overall curatorial frame. "That was a [black] man who was too successful according to all these [white] people around him, and that's a whole different kind of victimization than people who were accused of assault or other things. The fact that this exhibit touches on different kinds of victims and different kinds of mobs, I think it offers a really powerful, fuller story." This emphasis on the "fuller story" was also conveyed by the curator. "You have to let people know that the murder of these people was not just a loss of an individual life, but a loss to family, to community, to larger society. It's not just that this was a loss for African Americans; it was a loss for the whole community. It's something that diminishes everybody involved." That the Chicago Historical Society exhibition intended to convey a sense of this more encompassing story of loss was underscored yet again when the curator was asked about the emphasis the exhibition placed on Emmett Till, particularly since images of the lynching of Till were not part of the Allen and Littlefield collection. She responded:

> [From] the beginning it was accepted that the Emmett Till story would be as important as the Allen-Littlefield collection. In a lot of ways they are very complementary. I am not sure that that was what Mister Allen had in mind but for us, and the more we worked with the images from the collection and with our audience, we found that the Till story really helps to make sense of the larger story because for most of the images, we don't have a lot of information about who they are, but with Emmett Till you have that, and his story also suggests a more detailed version of the other stories in exhibit. I think that for us that was really important.

Further expanding on why she felt that the Till story was complementary to the approach the Chicago Historical Society took to the presentation of the Allen and Littlefield collection, the curator added, "It just makes him [Till] a person to see, that's who he was and that's him with his mother. You know what I'm saying. [When you see Till as a person before he was brutally beaten and murdered], you can't just be okay with that. And nobody was."[11] In this respect, much like the reasons given for placing the narrative encompassing the lynching of Will James at the beginning of the exhibition, the Till story served as a key element in the pedagogical structure of the exhibit.

How the story of Emmett Till resonated with the other images presented in the exhibit is also evident in the following discussion. Given that substantially enlarged photographs of Till appeared both at the entrance and in the final section of the exhibition narrative (including the historical, well-circulated image of a brutally beaten Till in his open casket), the exhibition designer and other members of the design team were asked if they ever considered enlarging and presenting any of the quite small images from the Allen and Littlefield Collection. The designer said, "We thought that they [the images from the Allen and Littlefield Collection] were intense enough as they were, and we wanted to draw people in to look at the images and read the labels as opposed to amplifying the horror. It's a good point about the size and why we didn't go with the blow-ups. If you are going to see the image, it's because you're choosing to. It's not so big that you can't avoid it." The head of volunteers and public forums additionally offered:

> I think from the visual perspective, the fact that they were postcards . . . we've gotten a lot of visitors commenting on that. They just cannot believe that these were sent through the mail. But the fact that they were made into inconsequential, everyday objects, that you don't ever associate, you know, with a calamitous impact, it makes them all the more shocking. So, I mean, they were postcards, and they are here as what they were, not blown up into something that they haven't been. I think that's really important.

Both remarks suggest that the contrast between the shocking, diminutive postcards from the Allen and Littlefield collection and the amplified horror that comprises the images associated with the story of Emmett Till worked to pedagogically supplement each other.

In the context of pursuing the process of image selection with the curator, she also discussed how the notion of telling a story was circumscribed within particular limits.

> At first we were thinking about using more [images], but there was the space issue, but also there is the idea that you don't want people to become overwhelmed. . . . So I think there was a sense that [let's present] just enough where people get it, but we're not bombarding them or beating them over the head with this. . . . There were some [photographs] that we thought were going to be too much. In the Will James series, for instance, if you have the [Allen-Littlefield] book you know

> that there is one [photograph] where there is his head on a pike or whatever in the park. [The director of the Chicago Historical Society] felt really strongly about not using that one. . . . We wanted to give people enough where they would understand that this was an epidemic but not so much that it just becomes exploitative in the sense that you're just showing death to be showing death.

Beyond the priority given to images where something of the story of each person victimized could be told, the curator also stressed the importance of providing substantial contextual detail to properly historicize the events portrayed in the photographs. She said the Chicago Historical Society director (at the time of development of the exhibit) was insistent that the exhibit provide some material that referenced the larger historical context accounting for the rise of lynchings across the United States. Thus, the curatorial team chose to supplement the images with documents that gestured toward the circumstances that gave rise to the violence addressed by the exhibition. This was the reason for the segment in which were placed reproductions of the Thirteenth and Fifteenth Amendments to the United States Constitution, a map that indicated the patterned distribution of lynchings of African Americans in various states and counties in the United States, and artifacts of terror such as a Ku Klux Klan robe. While walking through the exhibit space discussing her curatorial decisions, the curator explained that the exhibit was trying to make evident that the rise of the terror of lynching began in the post–Civil War Reconstruction era. "[During this time,] there was an attempt to bring African Americans into the [civic] fold. That's really when [the time] of terror starts. We wanted people to know the moment right before when all of this happens. And what was it? It was really an attempt to try and curb African Americans. . . . This robe here [gesturing to a Ku Klux Klan robe], shows just one example of the types of ways this terror is reinforced."

The exhibition's provision of a historicizing context was not just limited to a representation of the eliciting conditions for the terror of lynching but also included the response to this terror. The substance of this response was considered important to include because it provided a narrative of activism and resistance (as opposed to one of passive victimization). This is why the curator chose to include sections in the exhibit presenting information about Ida B. Wells and the NAACP.

> [Ida B. Wells], she's so great for a couple reasons. Her activism spans a lot of decades, a lot of years. She was really the first to start writing about what's really going on. . . . She was a founding member of NAACP, too, which is something. We chose to focus on [her and the organization] for a couple of reasons. Their anti-lynching activism was most sustained and the longest. And they had multiple tactics. They were multidimensional and kind of spawned other groups. [This section of the exhibit] was just a way to really let people know that no, people are not dying without there being some response or without there being some sense of outrage over it. We had to put this here to create balance. We didn't have a lot of artifacts, but we needed the balance.

In significant contrast with the comments made by the Andy Warhol Museum director regarding the tone of the color scheme for the exhibition at the Warhol, it is interesting to note that the exhibition designer at the Chicago Historical Society wanted to create a consoling environment for the presentation of the images. Early in the development of the exhibition, the curatorial team considered the possibility of collaborating with an artist who was interested in large red walls and large full blow-ups of images. However, these design features were antithetical to the approach the designer was developing and thus the collaboration never materialized. When given the task of creating a graphic identity for the exhibition, the graphic designer faced the challenge of developing a plan for the color, size, and font of the various texts (e.g., wall texts and labels) appearing throughout the exhibition. She approached this challenge by reviewing the photographs in James Allen's book, a selection of which would appear in the space of the exhibit. Wondering how she was ever going to do a graphic identity for such an exhibit, she ultimately settled on a typographical treatment that she considered quiet and reverential. She offered her reasoning as follows.

> I didn't want huge contrast, which is why I chose the gray and the white. I wanted it to be a formal type, formal font, and everything about it I wanted to be still. So that's why the logo's identity is very symmetrical and the blend goes from a cool gray to white and the text is reversed out of that. I didn't want

> any black or white or color per se, I just wanted to make it as quiet and calm as possible. To blend in to white in Western, more Christian-based religions has an ethereal feeling. Usually the exhibits here, even when they are serious they don't feel like they have the same kind of weight [as the *Without Sanctuary* exhibition]. I felt a responsibility to do justice to the victims.

INSTITUTIONAL POSITIONING WITHIN THE RACIAL FORMATION OF THE UNITED STATES

The United States is a society riven with historical differences structured along marked racial distinctions. This racial formation, while obviously undergoing change, provided a powerful context that impacted on the way images of lynching were presented within the respective exhibitions held in Pittsburgh and Chicago. Given the obvious racialized character of the exhibition materials, it is important to explore the views of museum staff not only in regard to their own personal positioning in this racial formation but as well in regard to the racialized positions of the institutions within which they worked. As we will see, a racialized self-consciousness is quite explicitly discussed by the Warhol staff in regard to their attempt to explicitly develop a wider, more diverse audience in a city that was highly stratified within the interlocking relations of race and class. In addition to this, we will also see how this racialized consciousness impacted on the self-identified white staff members who were staging cross-racial dialogues associated with the exhibition. Differently, in conversations at the Chicago Historical Society, the racialized identity of the institution was a less explicit concern. The reasons for this I explore below.

The *Without Sanctuary* Exhibition and the Racialization of the Andy Warhol Museum

There was an appreciable degree of institutional sensitivity in regard to the appropriateness of presenting an exhibition of lynching photographs in an institution locally characterized as "white," not only with respect to the racial identity of the artist whose work constitutes the museum's primary collection (Andy Warhol) but, as well, in regard to the racial identity of the majority of the museum's staff, patrons, and visitors. In conversation with the artist educator who was one of the few African Americans among the professional staff at the museum, she acknowledged that questions were raised in the local black community as to why the exhibition wasn't in "an African American space." While she speculated that it was a matter of existing organizational capacity (Pittsburgh's planned African American Culture Center had not yet been built),[12] when asked directly if she had any concerns about the appropriateness of the exhibition at the Warhol she responded as follows:

> The first time that I saw the book *Without Sanctuary* and I heard it was coming here and I said this has to come here . . . because these images were so important and they were so meaningful and . . . this again goes to two different particular issues. In comparison to this subject matter of these images dealing with deaths in African American culture, the Warhol is the whitest place you ever saw in your life. [However,] one of the things that the Warhol and everyone here knows how to do well is tackle very challenging subjects and treat it with the respect that it deserves, which is great and that is why there was the whole big list of community advisors and community collaborators.

This sense of a racialized institutional identity was partly the reason why staff at the Warhol put so much effort into pre-exhibition community consultations. Indeed, in all the conversations held with professional staff, it was quite clear that while a priori the museum was committed to presenting images from the Allen and Littlefield Collection, staff took the view that they could not develop the exhibition without some discussion of their plans with representatives of community groups. This was evident to many staff very early in planning the exhibition. For instance, the assistant director remembers that when she looked at the images from the Allen and Littlefield collection for the first time, she immediately thought that "there is no way we can do this without extensive community-based consultations." While the exhibition was never an event specifically intended for an African American audience,[13] there was a clear acknowledgment among staff that the African American "community" would have a proprietary interest in the exhibition. This sentiment was clearly expressed by one of the artist educators: "We had to make sure the community was involved because it's the African American community and we were depicting them and their lives and it's their story. It's not our story."

These community consultations were therefore defined and instituted within a very specific set of differentiating, racialized terms. From staff comments, it is quite clear that these consultations impacted decisions in regard to the development of the content of the exhibition. Most importantly, as a result of these consultations, decisions were taken to include not only the timeline of African American achievements but as well, a section of the exhibition devoted to the history of anti-lynching activism. Staff members had been told by community leaders participating in the consultations that they wanted the exhibition to help convey to a younger generation a greater awareness of the historic achievements of African Americans. Expressing an unease that the history of African American struggles was being forgotten, they wanted the exhibition to not only mark the advances in social equality gained through the long struggle for civil rights in the United States but, as well, to underscore the necessity of ongoing commitment to civil activism on the part of the younger African American generation. Clearly, what was being asked for was content that mitigated the reduction of African Americans to passive victims of racism. As the museum director emphasized, "It was important not just to show the negative side [of history]." As he understood it, the issue was not so much the supposition that youth would be upset by the images and history they referenced, but rather that they would be upset by an exhibition that left the impression of African Americans as a degraded and victimized community with little hope for a better life. Thus, it was important to include in the exhibition content that, in the words of the assistant director, conveyed "the incredible strength and resilience [of African Americans] amidst a very difficult social climate."

While the consultations referred to above had an impact on content of the exhibition, they also had an effect of enhancing the racialization of the identity positions of both the institution and its personnel. The assistant director provided several examples of moments in which she experienced not only the positioning of the Warhol as a "white" institution, but as well, her own reductive positioning on these terms. Offering an example of the way the museum was racialized, she recounted a conversation with one of the representatives of the NAACP who was on the exhibition advisory board. The representative had commented that "it was important to have the exhibition here [at the Warhol], [because it was important] to have white allies." This characterization of the museum as a "white ally" easily slipped into a discourse in which most of the museum staff members were seen by the community consultation committees on similar terms. Having to work within such racialized discourse, while not a surprise, remained a challenge and source of unease for the assistant director. In the context of a conversation on this topic, she recalled talking with the wife of a former African American journalist who together with her husband had been visiting with the director about the exhibition. "I was chatting with her after [the visit with the director] and she looked at me and said, 'That's the problem with the white liberals . . . you can be done being black.' So it's a very different state of consciousness. You just live in different spaces and you try to engage. It was really intense [and] exhausting."

As another example of a moment when she experienced this sense of living "in different spaces" and trying to engage across them, she told the following story about a brief interaction at one of the advisory committee meetings. A community member raised the possibility of informing the police that the exhibition was being programmed at the museum, ostensibly because of its potential as a resource for possible sensitivity training and antiracism education. The assistant director responded to this comment with a few supportive remarks. At this point, another of the community representatives intervened and turned to her and said "Why [should we inform the police]? Do you think there are going to be riots?" As a consequence she said, "I felt like I was being hit." At another time, she was talking to the committee about the structuring of the gallery dialogues and employing the dialogue facilitation expertise of the organizations Facing History and Ourselves and the National Council of Christians and Jews. In this context she was asked why there were no black organizations in this dialogue planning.

> And that's when you lose your voice. Because it wasn't actually true. . . . What was really being said was that those are Jewish organizations, when they are about truth and justice, anti-apartheid struggles and work around South Africa. . . . That was one of those things where sometimes whether it's sexism or racism you feel that you get hit by a truck; it's hard

> to fight back and say hold on a second. There is a lot of truth in the bell hooks statement that in the realm of racism, people just forget how to know. It was a very complex emotional environment. . . . I felt that I was in the situation where I was the blonde white lady leading the discussion and that this was both a race and a sexist issue.

An issue that became interwoven with the racialization of institutional and professional identities was the specific thematic focus that would frame the pedagogy inherent in the public presentation of the lynching photographs. The concern was the degree to which the exhibition would specifically focus on the long history of racism in America (and efforts to confront and overturn various forms of racial oppression and discrimination). Indeed, it was reported that a number of members of the Advisory Committee expressed some concern that the museum might "take our history away from us" by placing the history of lynching within the context of other historical events and forms of oppression (e.g., the Holocaust).

Not everyone at the museum saw the purpose of the exhibition requiring a limited focus on history of discrimination against African Americans. For example, when discussing the overall intention of the exhibition, the director expressed his view that as much as the exhibit was predominantly about the lynching of African Americans in the United States, "if this is just about racial issues I don't think that's appropriate for the moment." In elaborating on this, he argued for the importance of linking the exhibition to events such as the then recent and nationally known 1998 torture and murder of Matthew Shepard as consequence of Shepard's sexual orientation. This question of the exhibition's primary pedagogical narrative was also of concern to front-line educators. The African American artist educator mentioned above considered her work in dialogue groups "an effort to present [the exhibition as an aspect of African American] history in as full a light and strongest light as possible . . . and really try to keep [the dialogues] to topic." She was quite clear that there was something quite specific about this history that needed to be told. In her view, even though in the dialogues people brought up other violent events (e.g. the attacks of September 11, the Holocaust, the Native American Trail of Tears) it was important to frame the conversation about these in a way that related the "lynching of African Americans to larger issues of hatred while exploring what was really happening [in regard to the history of U.S. racism.]" Thus, for her it was important to register that the exhibition was functioning to help fill a gap in "the way history has been told." As she argued, "People are often very familiar with Holocaust history . . . it's been told, and told and told from multiple sources and in different formats, books and magazines and then movies and television." Such history is more extensively known than "our own African American history." She continued, "I think that's what we were trying to do . . . make sure this aspect of African American history was told very fully . . . but also acknowledge all these different others things that were happening and really make this about a history of racism and what is happening now."[14]

The assistant director expressed a different version of the same point, but one inflected with the sense of responsibility to an audience perhaps unfamiliar with the events depicted in the lynching images. She hoped that by presenting images in a way that provoked critical reflection the exhibition might "open the mind to be more tolerant, more understanding, and more aware." This did not require actions such as joining a social justice organization as a consequence of seeing the exhibition. Rather, she argued,

> One of the things that you find out is that a lot of white people don't really understand that they're white. . . . I know that kind of sounds slightly bizarre but this awareness of race, awareness of perspective, and awareness of the certain kind of privileges that you have by the virtue of the fact that you are white, it's one of those things that being aware shifts your perspective to the degree that it opens your mindset to hopefully entertain difference in a broader way. We were looking to try to see this as an opportunity to engage people in these issues, to discuss these issues and to perhaps, affect change.

Certainly, the issue of the likely racialization of the dialogue sessions was very much on the minds of those preparing for and participating in front line staff training. The head of visitor services starkly stated, "We sort of prepared for the worst because that way you are prepared," while the assistant director suggested there were some people anticipating extreme responses based on racial stereotypes ("Blacks are going to go out and riot because of these images"). However, the most telling sense of the impact on staff of the racialization of the museum was expressed by the front line personnel. The following is an excerpt of the conversation with several museum educators wherein they expressed some of their concerns:

> ARTIST EDUCATOR 1: It's about the institutional level [but] it's also personal . . . I mean for myself, how do I go in and lead a dialogue about racism and I'm white. I'm a white person by myself in a group of all black kids. . . . How am I going to lead a dialogue about that? And because at the end of the day it happened, we tried to be prepared but it got turned around when they said things like, "White people did this to us and what do you feel?" It becomes so personal, you're trying to be a facilitator and yet you're part of it and you're not supposed to be involved . . . at the end of the day, we're the ones who had to be in those sessions and not the people who decided to have the exhibit, it was day in and day out.
>
> ARTIST EDUCATOR 3: That was hard, that was really hard.
>
> ARTIST EDUCATOR 1: They would get really pissed off at you and rightfully so, but day in and day out . . . it was so overwhelming.
>
> ARTIST EDUCATOR 3: I think our staff felt like they didn't have the tools . . . a lot of people felt like they didn't have the right tools.
>
> ARTIST EDUCATOR 2: We got training.
>
> ARTIST EDUCATOR 1: Yeah and it was so late in the game.
>
> ARTIST EDUCATOR 3: And it wasn't enough. I think that we ended up taking some punches personally . . . I mean . . . one—we're not paid enough to do that and two—we weren't prepared to take it [laughs] we weren't prepared to get in that punching ring. I remember at one point just being really fed up with my dialogues.

Clearly, the artist educators were expressing the affective aftermath of constantly being assumed "to be one thing or another." As artist educator 1 expressed it: "It hits you in places that are very personal and when you have to deal with that every day at work it's pretty hard. We're not therapists and we just weren't trained to deal with that."

While these frustrations were readily expressed, they did not represent the sum of the artist educators' experience of the dialogues. Artist educator 1 emphasized that this was only one side, "on the other, it was such an amazing experience." Artist educator 3 added: "And I think the great thing was that we were really trying to not just answer certain questions, we were trying to get people to look at institutional racism and history [behind the] images." There is no question that for some artist educators, participating in the dialogues was a key learning experience. Here is artist educator 2 reflecting on his experiences:

> I guess whenever I think about those dialogues [what was] impressed upon me is the need to ask people open questions and just shut up and listen. And there's so much judgment all around about racism and people. I felt I was being judged at some points and I know I judged people. It still brings up some uneasiness for me when I think about those dialogues and what went on and what that means for me, and for my kids and for my culture. I try to think well . . . I just really need to listen to people . . . I definitely learned a lot I hadn't learned in school in terms of the history of racism. My kids go to a Pittsburgh public school and it's fifty-fifty and I'm friends with some African American parents but not very close you know . . . I think there are still boundaries that I feel exist and so . . . how do you break this down? Is it necessary to? I question it a lot, but I think that's a good thing. I question how my kids relate to other kids and the extent to which they are privileged.

Also apparent in interviews with staff was the sense that the gallery itself became a racialized social space. As the assistant director reported:

> You certainly had different people talking about the nature of feeling white and feeling black in that space. Very often one had a feeling not knowing what to do if you were white and blacks were looking at the images . . . just feeling the intensity of that. There was a whole other layer of dialogue happening in

> the sense of a kind of the visual experience of being that space, which I think is very strong and important. [While there was at times] a definite air of discomfort, I think that this was also a part of it too, a part that was very important.

There were times when the use of this racialized space was confusing to some staff who could not quite understand what was going on. For example, based on the assumption that the material was not very suitable for young children, a white staff member commented that she was surprised that so many African American families brought young children to the exhibition. Yet when commenting on the extent of families visiting the exhibition, the African American artist educator expressed no surprise:

> I think it is because it is this history that doesn't get talked about much. When I think about African American history in the way that it is taught, it is slavery and civil rights . . . those are the two basic things. And even though the areas before, between and after are kind of talked about, the two main things are slavery and civil rights and that area in between is lost. And I think that this exhibition was a way of reclaiming what was lost and so I think that's why a lot of families came to the exhibition to say, "This is what happened, this is part of your history and don't forget it . . . appreciate what you have now because these people died for us."

When asked about the personal significance of the exhibition, this artist educator admitted, "It was very, very hard to be in that space." However, she also said that the exhibit changed her life, reaffirming and rekindling what it meant to be an African American woman in the United States. As she put it:

> This is something to be proud of. It has a lot of pain attached to it that I personally haven't experienced a lot of. I met some incredible people through the daily dialogues who were trying to work through social justice issues. . . . Some of the co-facilitators that I met were incredible. And I think it was just this sense . . . the potential for personal movement that could happen in any part of the exhibition whether you were seeing

> these terrible images, or talking in your dialogue session or reading information in the *Pittsburgh Courier* about what they were doing with the campaign against lynching or viewing this art piece or listening to Billie Holiday.

Despite her understanding of the deep emotional difficulties of the exhibition, she chose to focus on "the movement" she could "see going on with people."

> In the daily dialogues, we asked three things—how the images make you feel, why do you think this happened and, what can you do to make sure this doesn't happen again. I was leading a group of people . . . and I remember there were three people sitting next to each other, it was a white woman. No . . . it was an Indian woman, a white man, and a black woman. I don't remember what was said but they all started hugging one another and I said that's it! That's what needs to be done. . . . So I guess all of that was a result of the exhibition and that was one of the big things that I felt. But it was hard. It was very difficult.

The *Without Sanctuary* Exhibition and the Racialization of the Chicago Historical Society

In striking contrast to the Andy Warhol Museum, there was virtually no concern expressed among the staff regarding the legitimacy and/or desirability of presenting a *Without Sanctuary* exhibition at the Chicago Historical Society. While there was some local debate as to whether the Chicago Historical Society was the most appropriate venue for this exhibition (as opposed to the DuSable Museum of African American History, also located in Chicago), there was little such discussion among the staff. Given the location of the Chicago Historical Society within a wealthy, predominantly white neighbourhood of Chicago as well as the racial demographics of the museum's visitors, one might have expected that the staff at the Chicago Historical Society would have been sensitive to the racialized identity of the institution in which they worked. The likely reason why this was not a concern can be traced to the presence of two key African American personnel at the Chicago museum. The then-director of the Chicago Historical Society (who left to become the director of the African American Museum in Washington) initiated the idea of holding a *Without Sanctuary* exhibit at the Chicago Historical Society, and this director also hired the curator who was also African American. As well, the lack of concern for the position of the museum with the racial formation of Chicago was likely reinforced by the lesser importance the Chicago Historical Society gave to consultative relations with community organizations as well as to dialogic encounters among visitors and staff.

This did not mean that the Chicago Historical Society did not do any community outreach prior to the opening of the exhibition. As the head of exhibitions commented:

> [The director] was here, and there were certain givens in him being here, not only in regard to his role as an African American leader but just as a very seasoned museum leader. . . . He did do a certain amount of shoring up relationships in the community . . . there were several meetings. . . . There was some people from the church community, there were certainly some people from the more secular influential African American community. It was important to just reach out to them and make sure they knew this was coming and why it was going to come here because not everybody wants history like this out there. There are people who say we need to move on, it's not in our interest to keep digging up stuff. So, I think a certain amount of work that the director did with the community was on that level of reassurance, providing an understanding of why the greater good is served by doing something . . . a lot of relationship building . . . fell to him.

After saying this, however, the head of exhibitions made it clear that these community meetings were conducted in a quite different vein then the advisory process set up at the Andy Warhol Museum. She underscored that while "there was outreach; nobody brought the community in to ask what should we do with this topic." She continued:

> I mean, we knew what wanted to do, we knew what we had to do with it. [Community] connections are one thing, but [a consultative relationship] was not what it was about. There was some history to be told here and we had an expert. We had two

> experts, including [the director], but particularly the [curator he hired]. Actually, three, when you throw in the photo historian.

When the curator was asked as to whether the Chicago Historical Society had engaged local community groups in any formal consultations regarding the exhibition she succinctly confirmed that that the Chicago Historical Society outreach was a way of letting people know in advance what the museum's plans were for the exhibition. In her view, "We knew how we wanted to treat the subject and that what we were trying to do was precisely what [community groups] said was needed."

Even though community involvement with the exhibition process was minimal, there were some conversations with community groups where it became clear in what sense the exhibition would serve the African American community. As the curator stated:

> There is a kind of a gap in people knowing about this knowledge. There are folks that do know about it, there's the older generation that definitely knows about it, who are not willing to talk about it or not able to talk about it yet. From that we felt very strongly that we were serving a purpose, a community purpose and introducing this material to people who may. . . . You know, there are family members who may very well know about it, but have never discussed it, so this is really a way to get some sort of dialogue going.

Despite this recognition that African American viewers were likely a primary audience for the exhibition, the curator wanted to make it clear that the exhibition was not developed for this specific audience. As she put it:

> I think there was a belief that there would be an inherent interest in the [African American] community but the exhibition was larger than just that one community. The [intended] audience was really just our general audience, which is adults, although also we planned pretty early on to involve middle school to high school students. [Our purpose was] to bring this information to the public in a thoughtful way and to

memorialize those persons who lost to their lives in such a tragic way.

THE PRACTICE AND THE RESPONSIBILITY OF MEMORY IN EXHIBITIONS OF LYNCHING PHOTOGRAPHS

All exhibitions that reference specific past events enact a form of remembrance, yet this remembrance takes on a very different character depending on the substance and structure of any given public display of materials and text. It is virtually axiomatic that any public representation of suffering and death resulting from systemic violence creates a demand for ritual moments in which the victims of this violence are memorialized. It is how, and to what degree, these moments are acknowledged in practice that defines another axis of difference between the frameworks that structured the curatorial projects at the Andy Warhol Museum and the Chicago Historical Society. Both exhibitions opened with ceremonial occasions and accompanying religious rituals commemorating those killed through practices of lynching. However, there were distinct discourses employed by the staff in regard to how affect-laden significations of such remembrance might be seen as directly incorporated into exhibition design. In this respect, I now consider how staff understood their work as, in part, a practice of remembrance. I consider not only what responsibilities they bore but, as well, the ways these responsibilities were translated into decisions regarding the details of exhibition presented.

Perspectives on Memorialization from the Andy Warhol Museum

No doubt there were staff members at the Andy Warhol Museum that recognized that the public presentation of the lynching photographs would set in motion a desire for some form of memorialization. Although the museum held ceremonial programming at different times during the exhibition's presentation[15] and included a space for "quiet reflection" within the exhibition's spatial layout, in contrast with the Chicago Historical Society, the Warhol exhibition mise-en-scène did not incorporate an explicit form of commemoration. In fact, the desire for memorialization was seen as in tension with the museum's primary justification for presenting the exhibition. As an "art museum" the focus at the Andy Warhol Museum was on designing a visual confrontation with the images in order to create opportunities for a dialogic consideration of contemporary implications of race and racism in the everyday lives of Americans. In this sense, staff at the museum seemed to take the position that practices of commemoration would be in contradiction to their central aims: engaging in a dialogic form of antiracism education and, importantly, cultivating activism. It wasn't surprising, then, that in various conversations with staff there was little acknowledgment that elements of the exhibition itself might be come to function as a form of memorialization. Thus, when directly asked if the Andy Warhol Museum exhibition might have served in any way as a memorial to those tortured and lynched, the assistant director reflected on how, in an indirect manner, various aspects of visitors' experience could be interpreted as expressive of the desire for commemoration. First of all, she pointed to what many visitors sensed was a degree of reverence that pervaded the exhibition space, even more than that normally carried by the authoritative weight of the museum. Furthermore, she thought that the intended pedagogy of the exhibition served as a form of memorializing practice "which was about being reflective, looking at the past, learning the past, respecting the weight of that."

However, the most explicit commemorative activity that staff noticed during the run of the exhibition was in regard to how visitors were using the "timeline" that was placed in the exhibit. Recall that this list of African American accomplishments over the one hundred year period of 1885–1995 was placed in the exhibit as an explicit acknowledgment that much was struggled for and won during this period. As one of the artist educators reported, "There seemed to be a flow of people who would look at the images [and then] move out of that room . . . directly across from the gallery where there was the long timeline . . . and people would pour over that wall almost in the same way that they would look at the photographs." Indeed, the assistant director spoke of the "ritualized use" of the timeline. "You'd find people just walking along the timeline, feeling the words . . . it paralleled a bit [the way people relate to] Maya Lin's Vietnam Memorial Wall. You could see people walking, looking and touching [different points in the timeline]. It was just something you could see was happening." It is likely that for many visitors, the timeline was felt as a recuperative moment set against the personal and communal trauma traced in the lynching images. The assistant director summed up this position as follows: "If the legacy is anything, it is what African American culture has done and accomplished in this country . . . in spite of this ghastly history. This history of accomplishments was our memorial without having a fountain or a statue of someone because unless it's done brilliantly, it can be maudlin."

Perspectives on Memorialization from the Chicago Historical Society

The concern regarding memorialization was quite different at the Chicago Historical Society. When the scheduling of the exhibition was finalized and the director and curator realized that the fiftieth anniversary of Till's abduction and murder would occur during this time period, it was decided that the exhibition would in part serve as a explicit memorial to Till while linking his loss to the lynching of thousands of other African Americans. As the exhibition curator explained, from the moment she "first heard about it, the intent was to use the exhibition to memorialize the victims of racial violence and to use this [the Allen and Littlefield] collection to help place and understand Emmett Till better historically . . . [our purpose was] to bring this information to the public in a thoughtful way and to memorialize those persons who lost to their lives in such a tragic way." Indeed, as shown in chapter 2, the Chicago Historical Society devoted considerable exhibit space to the murder of Till. While it may have been a coincidence that the Chicago Historical Society exhibition took place in Chicago in the year of the fiftieth anniversary of Till's death, it was nevertheless deemed quite important to have an evening program at the museum remembering Till and the implications for the civil rights movement of his violent death.

In addition to the inclusion of content about Emmett Till, a further illustration of the extent to which the Chicago Historical Society exhibition included practices of memorialisation is the construction of the memorial space placed at the midpoint of the exhibition narrative trajectory. It was thought necessary to have a location where people could get away from the difficult and disturbing photographs. This space became the large light pond and adjoining wall on which were written the names of three hundred lynched African Americans. With respect to this wall of names the curator commented: "Of course, there could be more names, [but] to name people is critical. We have these numbers, however we don't ever hear any names, so that's something we really wanted to do." The light pond and memorial wall was precisely the kind of memorial space not considered at the Andy Warhol Museum. However, it seems there were no second thoughts about having it in Chicago although the head of exhibition and programs indicated James Allen expressed some concern that the memorial would turn into a form of spatial kitsch. As the curator said: "That was one thing Jimmy worried about. When he heard about that, he thought, 'People are going to bring their teddy bears; [he said] I don't want to see teddy bears.'"

In the context of an exhibit "walk through," the exhibition designer spoke of the light pool and memorial wall as a form of spatial sanctuary. He too thought there was a need for a physical buffer where visitors could experience some relief from the violence of the images ("It was very important to have a place where people could get away from the imagery"). As the designer elaborated on the development of the memorial space it was clear that considerable discussion had been devoted to what space should be like and what kind of symbols should be included. The following interchange illustrates some of the ideas discussed:

DESIGNER: Some of our ideas were more literal, because part of our challenge was to create a space that would feel contemplative, sacred, but not specifically religious. We didn't want it to reference any particular religion. We looked at the idea of a river. We toyed with having a river and a bridge that you go over.

CURATOR: We toyed with light, not twinkling, but lots of points of light. I mean all kinds of elemental ideas.

DESIGNER: And with numbers too. When we had the riverbed idea, we thought one stone for every victim. You know, some way to visualize that kind of number. So we went all around different kinds of ideas, and this [gesturing to the light pond] is the idea that we settled on. Everyone really liked the idea of the circle. Our graphic designer had seen this projection system used before and was really pushing that idea and so, we took the idea of a circle of the water, and we combined that with our quote concept that we have working throughout. We also knew we wanted to have a wall of names somewhere. So, we just took all those ideas and put them together.

EDITOR: Originally, we were thinking about having another half-circle here, to block the space off and really make it a memorial, but we changed our minds and I think that was a good thing, because it gives breathing space. It's good to be able to see it, to look in here and turn around and see it [the space where the photographs were displayed].

HEAD OF INTERPRETATION AND VISITORS: And it was really expensive to build another wall.

DESIGNER: I originally designed it so that that was a circular room that had an entrance here and an entrance over there. We couldn't afford it, budget-wise. But in the end I am glad we didn't go with it that way because I like it being open and part of the space. It would have segregated it from the rest of the space.

Another example of the pervasive concern for memorialization at the Chicago Historical Society was the thought that went into the choice of the colors for the exhibit walls. Here is the designer again:

> We knew we wanted to have some spiritual feeling, especially to the memorial area, but as well to the whole space in general, but what kind of spiritual feeling? There's the ethereal, kind of spirituality, but there can be also a very natural earth-based kind of spirituality, um, so we had some very interesting discussions about that. I would imagine any time that one does an exhibition of this type, that would be something that might pop up in the discussion. If you are going to have this reverential, spiritual tone, what kind? What are you going to reference?

Finally, as part of the memorial structure of the exhibition, it is important to mention the decision to set out the "takeaway" cards that included the names of persons that had been lynched. Commenting on these cards, the editor said:

> They have been popular beyond anything we imagined originally. All we really wanted was a takeaway element. This was

> another big discussion, what could it be? We were talking about bracelets, we were talking about ribbons. . . . I think budget really drove the cards idea. Originally, they were just going to be quotes but then people wanted to see names. The head of exhibitions and programs wanted to see names and dates and places . . . we printed two thousand of these and they were gone in less than nine days. And we printed another two or three thousand and they were gone in a couple of weeks, so we printed twenty thousand. And I would bet half of them are gone now. It's unbelievable. Every victim [named in the exhibition] has a card. . . . For Emmett Till we printed many more just because visitor services told us that his was the most popular.

The curator added to this: "I've had people call me and say that they've got most of the cards but can I send them the others, they want a full collection. I come here and take them often, just to keep with me at my desk."

THE AFFECTIVE FORCE OF IMAGES OF LYNCHING ON MUSEUM STAFF

For those who have at least glanced at the photographs in the Allen and Littlefield collection, it is obvious that these images demand much from their viewers. Most viewers who spend any length of time with the images recognized that the photographs emanate a certain force. As I have argued earlier in this book, this force is a power capable of provoking an indeterminate affect that cannot be solely accounted for on the basis of their historical significance as documents of racist violence. Many people who attend to these images for any length of time often begin to feel that they carry an appreciable emotional weight and contemporary import that needs to be registered in some way or other. While I will explore this in depth in the following chapter in the context of remarks left by visitors in the exhibition comment books, here I discuss the impact that working with the photographs had on those whose professional responsibilities included presenting the images for public display. There are two aspects of concern here in regard to how staff carried this weight: (1) how they registered the impact of the images on themselves as they attempted to work through the selection of images and overall exhibition design, and (2) the concern and sense of responsibility they felt in regard to the anticipated impact of the images on others (other museum staff and visitors). My intent here is not only to convey how staff spoke of the affective impact of working with these images and how they anticipated impact of the force of the images on visitors, but as well to consider how such matters influenced decisions regarding the exhibition mise-en-scène. This has partly been signaled by staff comments at both museums in regard to the need for some buffer in the exhibition space to relieve visitors of the affective impact of the violence of the images. The comments below go beyond the expression of this necessity.

The Affective Force of the Images at the Andy Warhol Museum

The affective force of the images as felt and anticipated by Warhol Museum staff was substantially intertwined with their own anxieties regarding the racialized standpoint from within which they worked. This meant the force of the images were personally felt not only in regard to oneself, but also as one began to anticipate the emotional texture of what it could mean to face the response of other people to the images. To begin to unpack this, consider the comments by the assistant director regarding the emotional difficulty of working with the materials:

> I remember I first started looking at the images in my office and there were lots of questions, lots of questions. There were such a series of "unburyings," of emotional journeys. . . . I used [the poet] Toi Derricotte's term *unburying*, a sense of just unearthing . . . and it helped me a lot. Not being American, being Irish and coming from Canada, this wasn't part of my history, but you become part of this unburying place and it taps into your own personal story. It opens up all sorts of drawers, such an intense level of consciousness and you just are constantly looking at these things. . . . It's easy to think, "Oh how could they do this," but there are these people [in the photographs] standing there smiling and looking at these hung bodies. You have to think if there is something that we are looking at and still smiling, something that implicates us

in our own consciousness, in our own lives, it puts you in this kind of live wire consciousness that may be untenable to live with in the everyday.

While *Without Sanctuary* was still in the process of development, as per the standard practices at the museum, staff members were to begin work on the next exhibition on the museum's schedule, an exhibit entitled *Possession Obsession.*[16] However, work on this exhibit was for a time disrupted by the emotional effort of completing the *Without Sanctuary* exhibition. As an example of the emotional toll of work on the *Without Sanctuary* exhibit the assistant director referred to a staff session on the content of the exhibition that fostered strongly felt emotions ("Everyone was talking about their experiences at that session, it really was a kind of a group weep, really intense"). This session was a key incident etched into the memory of many of the staff. It was referenced in various ways in almost all of our conversations at the museum. The assistant director had organized a full day staff training session. In the morning there was a presentation by an academic who gave an overview of the history of lynching in the United States and did a slide presentation of the photographic images that would be included in the exhibition. In the afternoon, there was a presentation by a local activist who was expected to speak to current racial issues in Pittsburgh. He was personally unknown to museum staff but had been recommended by an advisory committee member. He had his own radio show, directed school programs, and ran a history center. An account of what happened is provided by the following conversation held with the head of visitor services, the head of marketing, and the assistant director:

HEAD OF MARKETING: [It was decided to have a staff training session that began with] a historical overview of the images and the whole history . . .

ASSISTANT DIRECTOR: [The presenter] was great, she did a quick lecture and then we took a break. [After the morning presentation] the community group came to me and they were furious because they felt that [the morning presenter] had shown the images as if they were a vacation show. And it was absolutely in the exact way that we imagined an academic lecture would be and they were just . . . the whole emotion just got . . . I was trying to handle that and then [the afternoon presenter] came up and he gave this, he was supposed to give it in the Pittsburgh context and it was just . . .

HEAD OF MARKETING: Oh, awful . . .

HEAD OF VISITOR SERVICES: Yeah, I just remember it got very quiet.

ASSISTANT DIRECTOR: I just thought . . . Oh fuck, oh God! I'm so screwed.

HEAD OF VISITOR SERVICES: I mean we had a lot of gallery stuff going on too and press . . .

HEAD OF MARKETING: So well intended but so wrong.

ASSISTANT DIRECTOR: yeah and I just thought oh God . . .

HEAD OF VISITOR SERVICES: In a way, I mean, I can't speak for all the gallery attendants that worked for me but in a way it was a moment of realization that this was a very serious subject and that this was potentially a kind of discussion that could happen. And I think the gallery attendants were like, oh, we need this training and we need to kind of go through all of this and we need to think about what this exhibition is all about. I mean some people took it in stride and some were like . . . wow . . . this is going to be interesting . . . the goal of having a dialogue that is open for interpretation and points of view that are different and how to control that and at the same time not to control it.

This conversational excerpt illustrates staff members' concern with the level of emotional response that could be elicited by the images. The problem they had with the afternoon session was the way the speaker drifted into a rambling presentation during which it became evident that the images he had seen in the morning provoked a sense of his coming undone, especially when he began to tell stories of his own oppression as a black man. The same incident was reported in a separate conversation with the artist educators, the staff who had been in the gallery accompanying groups looking at the photographs and subsequently trying to engage them in open dialogue. In response to a query as to whether they ever questioned the appropriateness of presenting the lynching photographs at the museum, the following ensued.

> ARTIST EDUCATOR 2: Oh sure. They did a meeting where they showed the slides to the whole staff, which was really handled badly . . . I thought. Well, they had a historian from the University of Pittsburgh and they showed imagery from the exhibition and no one was primed properly and there was no facilitation after that meeting of the staff's reaction. Some of the African Americans on the staff were very upset and it just . . . it was not handled well and I think that kind of drove home the reality of like this is not something we can . . . am I right on this? I'm just thinking of the timing but it just really made us think about these dialogues and what we need to discuss in terms of witnessing the exhibition.
>
> ARTIST EDUCATOR 1: Whoever gave that talk was criticized because it was coming from this very, kind of very academic, cold kind of way . . . it just happened you know . . . it was just really tactless and it was not appropriate.
>
> ARTIST EDUCATOR 2: Yeah, there was a big backlash amongst some of the staff and everyone just felt raw . . . but it was prior to the exhibition being here, which was good because it you know . . . it did wake everyone up.

Despite the obvious importance of the above incident in the staff memories of the process of exhibition development, this was not the only moment that illustrated a concern over the potential force of the images. One of the artist educators put the matter quite straightforwardly:

> You know, what scared me is like right from the beginning when [the assistant director] was talking about [the *Without Sanctuary* exhibition held in] New York and people running programs there and how deeply they were affected. [Staff in New York] said that they would come to work every day and would have people crying on the steps. And that kind of reality

> . . . What was that? I was very resistant because it's not my strong suit to sit down and dialogue with people with issues . . . [laughs] . . . but then like the reality of it, having to witness the pain that has happened to people in this world and what we've done to each other.

This anticipation of what was needed to address one's own emotions and the emotions of others was also registered by the African American artist educator:

> I remember we did several large training [sessions] before the exhibition and we talked about the different fears we had about leading this exhibition. Wanting to represent things correctly, wanting to make sure we don't fall apart in the middle of leading tours because I mean . . . we probably spent, and people from visitor services probably spent, the most time with the images. Looking at the images . . . talking to them . . . looking at them and doing things with classes . . . I mean, we were doing so much.

Indeed, the head of visitor services admitted that "among the gallery attendants we had a couple who in the end of the time period just didn't want to be on that floor anymore" and that from the very start the museum administration had said that "everyone does this project at the level they feel comfortable doing. So for me, if a gallery attendant said they didn't feel comfortable on the floor then we didn't schedule them there." Aside from the anticipations expressed above it is also instructive to listen to the artist educators describe their experiences standing in the gallery while visitors were looking at the photographs. When asked about their experience in the space, artist educator 1 replied "I didn't look at the photographs after the first three times I was up there. Even when I brought groups up . . . I'd feel upset, I couldn't take the visual strength over, over and over again, so I would kind of pull back." Artist educator 2 added: "If you stood more in the middle, you couldn't really see [the images]." Artist educator 1 also observed that "people went to the photographs first but then would flee to the timeline to find something positive. And then investigate the other two rooms, probably the *Courier* room before the last dialogue room." The

African American artist educator noted that "some people would walk through and they would look at all the images and some would walk in and just be able to see a couple." She said that for her

> the burnings were difficult. The burnings and the castrations were the most difficult because they . . . those ones and there was one where . . . um . . . two boys are in a tree and there is one [man] pointing at them like this [gestures] . . . and there's one where underneath the frame there's a chunk of one of the boy's hair. Those were probably the most difficult . . . there was something else, I don't recall what, but that absolute, complete horrible devastation was there and it happened. And I mean even during the dialogues you certainly didn't pressure people to look through the entire thing to you know . . . if you want to stop and come out that's fine. And they did, people cried and we had tissues etcetera all around. We had a little quiet room for people to go in to if they wanted to just sit, be quiet and cry in there.

The Affective Force of the Images at the Chicago Historical Society

To introduce a sense of how museum staff at the Chicago Historical Society expressed the affective force felt when working with the lynching images, I begin with a comment by the exhibition designer:

> It was quite surreal at times to be sitting in a meeting talking very matter-of-factly about how we were going to display these images. A notebook would be open with the photographs and we were just flipping through it talking about "Oh, this should be such-and-such a frame-size" or whatever. Meanwhile, there are these people in the images who are being murdered and mutilated and you know, every now and then it would just suddenly dawn on me, the bizarre juxtaposition of having this very practical, everyday conversation about such horrific imagery. And that was hard and I had to stop sometimes, I know it was really hard on the curator to have to look at all that imagery. Over time, I really felt we had a big responsibility. This was

> a great opportunity for us to really do something good. I was really excited about the memorial space and about the take-away [remembrance] cards and I thought that this is exactly the way that an institution like ours can make a contribution to the society by talking about these things.

Other staff members also expressed experiences of having to work through the personal impact of viewing the lynching photographs while working with them as required by their professional responsibilities. And yet, once the exhibition was in place, they too felt a profound sense that they had accomplished something important. The text editor mentioned that the day that she was assigned to the project, she went home and cried. As she put it, "I was one of the people that didn't understand why we were doing this show. I didn't see a huge merit in it. [And besides] there are two editors on staff and our supervisor tends to alternate shows and it wasn't even my turn." Nevertheless, once the exhibition was up and receiving visitors, she had a different view. "In the end it was definitely one of the most rewarding shows that I have ever worked on, particularly in regard to the visitor response. People are coming to the Chicago Historical Society just because they want to see that show, they don't just happen upon it. It is probably going to be one of the best shows I'll ever work on. Some of the previous shows were great, but *Without Sanctuary* is on a whole different level."

The graphic designer added the following thoughts to this conversation: "In the beginning I always do a lot of research with fonts and images and historical context if there is any, and so I was spending a lot of time with these images. I read every single anecdotal description. I really didn't understand one hundred percent how much it was affecting me until I'd go to do a presentation and I'd feel myself about to cry or I'd feel my voice shaking and I'd think, 'Oh my God, I'm really about to lose it.'" Nevertheless, she felt that this emotional intensity helped her create something that better served the purpose of the exhibition. Reflecting on the experience of developing the exhibit, she made it clear that if she had not been willing to go that far emotionally with the materials, her graphic design would not have been as successful as it was. "Once I started designing stuff, it was much more about the practical tasks such as working with the curator's text and designing the font for the labels. But in the initial stages of developing the design, I really needed to put myself in that emotional place; I feel I needed to do it in order to get that far. And there were things . . . you just can never underestimate what you'll learn about yourself."

Acknowledging the impact of working day in and day out with images of torture and murder, the curator had this to say:

> I knew about this era in our history but when I first started to look at the images and read the stories, I was just like, that doesn't seem like it could have happened, the brutality, not just the brutality but the ritualistic character of the brutality. So, I would look and read a little bit and then I would put it down and do something else and then I would look and read a little bit. But then there came a point after Christmas, cause I was like, well, I'll wait till after Christmas to really get into it, where I was just under it. The one thing I did, because at some point I thought I can't do this job if I'm going to be thinking about these images [all the time], is that I just never took the images and stories into my home or my resting space. I really didn't think about the exhibition much after I left the building.

Adding to this, the text designer remembered a conversation she had with the curator about figuring out a way to "put up a filter between yourself and the content so that you can get your job done because it's not as if we were just visitors to the museum coming to see and experience this. I mean if I didn't hit my deadline it would have repercussions for others on the design team."

In addition to the problem of staff members working through their own responses to the lynching images, they were also fully cognizant of the possible force of the images on the gallery visitors. In explaining his choice for the color tone of the exhibit, the exhibition designer elaborated on why he chose a very subdued quality.

> We obviously went with a very subdued tone, subdued colors, calming types of colors. There were some people that were suggesting the use of intense colors, large blow-ups and things like. We decided that the images were intense enough, and so with the design we tried to create a sense of a calming environment. . . . There are odd juxtapositions and angles though that are mildly jarring I would say. You get a sense that something is not quite right, but we didn't want to hit anybody over the

head with any intense design because the content was already so intense.

The curator further elaborated on how the exhibition design was intended to moderate the shock of the image. First she echoed the thoughts of the designer, indicating that the design functioned as a space that promoted a sense of quiet, where if people needed solitude they could find it. She stressed the need to provide people with just enough in the way of images and information, but not so much that they felt emotionally bombarded by the exhibit. This balance wasn't entirely intentional. As with all curatorial projects there were some factors that were out of curatorial control including the space allotted for an exhibition, the time frame within which the development of an exhibit had to be completed, the cooperation (or sometimes lack thereof) from lenders. As she put it: "You know those are the kind of things that really can tie your hands but in this instance I think it was a good tying of the hands. By the time I saw the materials that had been shipped to the Chicago Historical Society, when I saw this, I was like, that's enough, that's just right. And now when I walk through it, I feel like I can make it through. But if there had been many more images, I don't know that it would have been as effective, quite frankly."

A final example of how the design team tried to incorporate elements into the exhibit mise-en-scène that would mitigate the force of the images and artifacts is the found in the following comments by the designer and text editor:

TEXT EDITOR: I'd love for [the designer] to touch on the standing window for you, because I believe that is such an important design element.[17] I remember the first time I saw the Ku Klux Klan robe, I panicked, I mean the energy that radiates off from that object is just so powerful, and it's good to have just a little breathing room. Without that window it seemed kind of claustrophobic.

DESIGNER: Yes, I thought the window was very important because, you can see the light pond and memorial from there and you can see the anti-lynching stuff and we wanted to make sure that you could see that [NAACP] cloth that says "A man was lynched yesterday." Even if people might not be aware at this early point in the exhibit

> narrative how intense their experience is going to be, we wanted them to see that there was this interesting, restful kind of space. There's a place to take a break if they need to and that there are other kinds of materials in the exhibition. We want them to know it's not just these photographs.

A BRIEF CODA

The discussions with museum staff pertaining to pedagogical structure of their exhibitions, concerns related to the degree of racialization of their institutions, and their curatorial modes of addressing the obligations of memory and the affective power of the images illustrate the ethical regard through which each museum defined its curatorial project. This regard was rooted not only in duty to do justice to the memory of those who were victims of lynchings but also in the realization that an exhibition's mise-en-scène was a way of mediating the transitive character of the images to be shown, a way of mediating the way visitors would experience and respond to their force. As mentioned in the exhibition descriptions in chapter 2, readers may recall that at the Chicago Historical Society the decision was made to place a sign at the entrance to their *Without Sanctuary* exhibit that read: "The exhibition includes graphic images and may not be appropriate for young children." While in the minority, it is interesting to note that there were personnel at the museum who thought such signage unnecessary and a symptom of the anxieties staff felt in regard to the images. As one person put it, "I thought it was a lot of fuss over nothing. There was no necessity for that warning, but some people needed the comfort of having it there. I mean, what does anybody expect when they see that that's what the subject matter is?" While this comment is a reminder that not all museum staff respond the same way to the challenges of presenting highly charged images of suffering and death, it is also an additional affirmation that images presented had a power to violently touch people in a way that ought to be anticipated by both museum staff and visitors. In the following chapter, I take up visitor responses to the *Without Sanctuary* exhibitions as these responses were mediated by the different curatorial projects in each museum.

FOUR

Public Performance in the Social Space of Museum Comment Books

Without Sanctuary Exhibitions and the Extended Conversation about Race in America

It's amazing how stupid and selfish we act. The human race, which is supposed to be the civilized one, acts like jungle animals and kills other humans. Not only is lynching inhuman but burning the bodies or digging out the eyes, cutting off other body parts, it makes me sick. Those who did the lynchings will burn for it, and those innocent lynched will not and cannot ever be forgotten. This exhibit is heartbreaking. At the same time, a great reminder of our past, and should be a teaching tool for the future.

—Comment written by visitor at the Chicago Historical Society

I sit here watching my friend Steve write in another book. He writes so easily. What words flow to him? I am blank, torn, crumpled into this wooden chair like a used matchstick. Folded and useless. What can I say? That these images are bound to repeat themselves in my dreams? It would be truth-telling. What can I say? I want to talk about how afraid I am daily as a female-to-male transsexual, that I will end up like those photos . . . S 11/24/01. Take a stand against transphobia. Sign the petition @ www.strap-on.org/mwmf.

—Comment written by visitor at the Andy Warhol Museum

In previous chapters, I have discussed the differences and similarities in the approaches taken by the Chicago Historical Society and the Andy Warhol Museum in their respective exhibitions of selected segments of a collection of postcards imprinted with photographs taken at lynchings held in the United States. Each exhibition presented these images in quite different ways, in both cases provoking wide-ranging, deeply felt, thoughtful responses. I now pose the question of how visitor experiences of these two very different exhibitions were reflected in differences in the remarks written in the comment books that the museums made available as a component of the exit spaces of each exhibition.

A familiar fixture at exhibitions both in North America and Europe, the entries in visitor comment books are often used as indicators of visitor engagement, and as such, are incorporated into accountability reports regarding the effectiveness of any given display. The most common way of apprehending remarks written in comment books is to read them as explicit views of an exhibition reflecting something of the visitor's subjective experiences of it, that is, as inscriptions understood as providing access to aspects of visitor meaning making. However, this does not mean that the remarks in a comment book should be assumed to provide a transparent window onto visitor understandings of their responses to an exhibition. This is not just a matter of recognizing that as with any source of data, one needs to take in account the context of its production and how this might determine and limit the information gathered. Quite differently from such concerns, as Sharon Macdonald suggests, "an exhibition's visitor book should, perhaps, be seen as an integral part of [an] exhibition—an interactive exhibit in which many visitors participate (either by writing or reading)."[1] This insight is pivotal in expanding our understanding of the expressive significance of comment books. Without a doubt, they can be useful as one tool in an arsenal of data collection methods that assist in the assessment of visitors' knowledge, beliefs, and attitudes, and consequently helpful in future exhibition planning and development. However, quite differently, if a comment book is a determinate medium within which visitors might participate in the production and hence the experience of an exhibition, we can then ask: Within the various formats, conventions, and competencies bound up in the activity of comment writing, how is this participation enacted differently by different visitors (and in relation to different exhibitions)? Even more importantly, we can also ask what such forms of participation do, or, more specifically, What do they achieve or accomplish?[2] This question not only turns away from the use of comment books to assess exhibitions in regard to what they "transmit" to learners, but as well, from the use of comments to assess what exhibitions facilitate regarding individual meaning making (including the motives, emotions, and prior experiences this involves). This turn to the question of visitor participation via the medium of the comment book means that rather than using comments to access the mentalities of visitors, I am asking after the social productivity of the cumulative acts of writing in public.

To elaborate on this idea further, I begin with the position that the provision of comment books embedded in or adjacent to an exhibition convenes a unique social space within which the various people who are attending an exhibition are able not only to register their own thoughts and feelings but as well to read and, at times, comment on the thoughts and feelings of others. In thus rendering the comment book as a social space, I need then to elaborate on what is meant by this in precise terms. What kind of a space is this social space, in what manner is it embedded in the larger social space of the museum, and what notions of sociality might be enacted at the moment when one writes within it? In her excellent article discussing the comment books from the 1962 Moscow exhibition *30 Years of the Moscow Artists' Union (MOSKh),* Susan Reid makes the suggestion that the genre of comment writing in exhibition visitors' books needs "to be considered in relation to other genres of popular response-writing such as petitions, letters to the editor, and complaints books," all forms invigorated during the post-Stalin period in the Soviet Union.[3] While writing in a comment book has some parallel with writing a letter to the editor of a newspaper or magazine, the analogy is not altogether helpful. A "Letters to the Editor" section is not an open access forum. Newspaper and magazine editors are often quite restrictive in regard to what they chose to publish of responses to any given previously published article. Furthermore, one rarely has the opportunity to write a response to a letter that comments on a previously published article (except when editors arrange for a specific exchange of views). A better analogy is another of Reid's suggestions that comment books are akin to the remarks left in the comments section of an Internet website. In the context of her discussion of the responses to the exhibition she studied, she writes:

> The visitors' books served as a kind of virtual public space, something like an Internet message board; [at the Moscow exhibit] they became a space for a disembodied public exchange and formation of opinion—or rather, of multiple, competing groups of opinion—in relative independence from the state. They are one of the few material records we have of Soviet society representing itself, talking to itself, and articulating its identities and divisions without the intervention of an editor. (680)

In Reid's view, once the visitor books were established as a space of vigorous, relatively autonomous exchange of opinion they then generated further debate. Thus, she concludes "in the virtual social space of the visitors' books, we see communities of shared values begin to coalesce and differentiate themselves from others" (680).

While I remain cautious in regard to the Internet message board analogy, it is worth staying with Reid's theorizing a while longer in order to make clear my view regarding the possible forms of sociality enacted in the writing of comments into a visitors' book. Reid first notes that "writing in comment books is a conscious, voluntary, and sometimes risky act" (683). This was certainly so in the context of the Soviet Union in the Khrushchev era. Importantly, Reid then asks, "What does it aim to achieve?" (682). Noting that a comment writer can hardly expect any concrete advantage from his/his intervention, Reid dismisses any possible functionality to the writing of a comment, rendering it as "symbolic or expressive gesture" (682). In this context, she then proposes we treat visitor comments as an "exercise in self-affirmation and posturing, a performance of individual aspirations, identities, elective affinities, and distinctions as much as [they are] about the art itself" (682). Here Reid is drawing upon Pierre Bourdieu's discussion of art consumption and the production of distinction.[4] While for Bourdieu, writing in regard to twentieth-century France, the primary concern is the reproduction of class distinctions, for Reid, the remarks in a comment book are to be taken as forms of social exchange in regard to taste and style through which people articulate and mark their distinct positions of membership in either existing or emergent cultural systems. The importance of the argument that the visitor book functions as a public space for enacting performances with particular implications for articulating cultural systems and one's place within them can be illustrated in relation to Paula Findlen's discussion of the visitor books of Aldrovandi's museum in the late sixteenth century.[5] As Findlen points out, the performance in the visitor books of this period was essentially the act of writing of one's name (and occasionally one's place of residence and profession). As Findlen notes, "Such visitors' books immortalized the fame of the museum and its creator by recording their connection to the social, political, and intellectual centers of power" (137). However, employing Reid's perspective on visitor book comments we can reframe Findlen's insight. More than just recording their connection to intellectual centers of power, commenters were remaking and further fashioning it. In the moment in which any given visitor wrote their name into such a book at the Aldrovandi museum, they were inscribing and distinguishing themselves as participants in a social formation in which they inhabited advantageous positions in regard to relations of power and influence. This moment of inscription was a way of articulating to each other a shared degree of social status and certain cosmopolitan frame of mind, as well as a practice that further socially solidified their status.

However, as useful as Reid's insight is in regard to the social expressive function of visitor comments, in following Bourdieu too closely and rendering comments as only "symbolic or expressive" (682) of one's self-affirming membership in a cultural system, we unnecessarily limit our understanding of the comment books and the sociality they may enact. Indeed, toward the end of her paper, Reid is quite articulate in regard to the importance of the "art debate" that rages in the written comments that she considers. As her own analysis indicates, in the context of the power dynamics of de-Stalinization taking place at this time in the history of the Soviet Union and Khrushchev's personal condemnation of some of the work in the exhibition as "filth and fecal messing, decadence and sexual deviance," much more was at stake in MOSKh's comment books than a posturing that positioned writers within a particular set of status inflected elective affinities (673). Reid concludes her paper thus:

> Far from the unitary voice of the people which neo-Stalinist demagogues continued to invoke, the public response to *30 Years of MOSKh* provides evidence that, a decade after Stalin's death, any appearance of public consensus there may once have been was gone. The audience was fragmented—and

> prepared to say so. In the absence of consistent demographic data to accompany their comments, we can only surmise that the division in the art public corresponded to other social and demographic stratifications and hierarchies—generational, geographic (metropolitan versus provincial), educational, occupational, or ethnic. The comment books for a major and controversial art exhibition allowed them not only to voice views on art but, through this medium, to express attitudes toward Stalinism and de-Stalinization and, at the same time, to find ways to articulate something like class distinctions in a supposedly classless society . . . the choice of Laktionov or Falk can be seen as expression of public, political identities and differences that go beyond questions of art. What we find is not a singular culture of looking, a stable and homogenous "legitimate taste," but an open battle among multiple cultures still dispersed and inchoate but staking competing claims for authority. The public, or rather publics, was ready to be entrusted with the responsibility it had been promised—to judge for itself—and was prepared, publically and in writing, to claim this as its right, even if this meant challenging the Party's authority. (715–16)

While Reid argues persuasively that social distinctions were articulated and made evident through an exchange of comments, as the above quote indicates, much more happened than this. As a medium of open exchange about particular paintings and the substance and purpose of art, the juxtaposition of the remarks in the MOSKh comment books accomplished not only a moment of resistance to neo-Stalinism, but in doing so, helped actualize concretely a new form of social existence that went well beyond the lives of those who attended the Moscow exhibition. This illustrates well the very conditions Roger Buergel has outlined as to what might be meant by a political exhibition, that it "should give the visitors the feeling that they are participating in the compositional activity of making the world. This means taking active responsibility for the world we live in—experiencing first hand that one has this leeway, and also taking advantage of it."[6]

In my view, Reid's conclusion suggests that comment writing cannot and should not be reduced to a form of role performance. Unfortunately, Macdonald does just this when she suggests that Reid's point is that we should read comments "as a kind of performance—be it of the compliant citizen, polite guest or opinionated individual."[7] Viewing visitor books on such reductive terms reduces the task of analyzing comments to one of identifying the voices that make their appearance in the books (e.g., the "compliant citizen" the "polite guest"). It is important to remember that the reading of and writing in visitor books structures the process through which visitors formulate their own position *in relation to others*.[8] The consequence of this is that comments have to be read far more dialectically. *This means considering what their juxtaposition to each other in any given context accomplishes beyond the serial appearance of views that exemplify various socially defined modes of commenting*. While I agree with Macdonald that "a key analytical task is to try to identify the kinds of socially situated performances that are entailed in making a certain kind of entry in a visitor book" (122), the question still remains as to what might this most usefully entail? To more fully consider this question I return to the question of the character of a comment book as a social space.

It is important to note that the comment book functions as a gathering space, an open space accessible to all who wish to write in it (subject to their financial and physical capacity to access the exhibition itself and their physical ability to write in the book). As with any institutionalized cultural practice, the space of the comment book is subject to social convention and thus the normalization of what might be understood as an intelligible and legitimate comment (hence enacting the exclusion of those remarks visitors feel it is inappropriate to write). These rhetorical conventions are not only those that visitors bring with them from previous experiences reading and writing in comment books in museums and galleries, but as well are established in the context of the actual leaving of remarks in a book, building up a conversation of sorts with its own rhetorical forms (although it is always possible to rupture them, e.g., one might chose to simply write obscenities). The act of writing in a book leaves orthographic traces addressed to any of the book's future readers. Inscribed on paper, in full view for anyone interested in turning pages and committing their time and attention to reading the comments, they are left for anyone who has access to the exhibition and who is able to comprehend what has been written. In this sense, such writing performs a limited and quite specific exposure of oneself to the mostly unknown future readers of the book. One consequence of this activity is that it referentially defines the exhibition as an aspect of "a world in common," that is to say, the comment book establishes a relation among strangers in regard to their varied responses to the common world of the exhibition. Given the historical individual and social specificity with which each visitor engages an exhibition, the activity that produces multiple written comments that collectively form a juxtaposition of texts functions to draw people together while separating them at the same time.[9] Within such dynamics, the moment of writing into a comment book accomplishes a reflexivity within which one self-identifies as a member of a social entity-in-formation whose members have marked their time-bound relation to each other through their responses to what they have just seen in the exhibition space *and* read in the comment book prior to writing their own remarks. In this respect, the comment book is not only a space of self-disclosure but also a space for what Hannah Arendt called "world making." It is precisely in this sense, that a comment book is a space that convenes a public as an imaginary relation among those who read and write; an imaginary relation with very real effects.

THE SOCIAL SPACE OF THE COMMENT BOOKS AT THE *WITHOUT SANCTUARY* EXHIBITIONS

The above remarks begin to sketch out a general perspective for investigating the comment book as social space. However, such a perspective has to be considered in the context of the specific substance of an exhibition and the demands it may make on its visitors. In the case of the multiple instances of the exhibition of the *Without Sanctuary* photographs and postcards, the common premise across all such exhibitions was not only the presumed importance of providing access to a significant history of racist violence in America but as well "to issue an ethical and political command to see and testify in the service of justice."[10] It is no surprise that many *Without Sanctuary* comments are orthographic/lexical performances that take up the relation of the content of the exhibition in regard to the contemporary experience of race in America. My queries regarding these performances begin with questions regarding how such performances are socially organized, what seems to be their underlying logic, and in what manner emotions and ideas are expressed within the bounds of the medium of the comment. But further to the concerns of this book, I am also asking after the extent to which, collectively considered, the comments written may be understood as a particular way of extending the "conversation" about race in America. In this regard, I will be concerned with how the content and tone of this conversation might be shaped by the substance and structure of any given exhibition and in what ways such a conversation might influence the perspectives and future actions of a public-in-formation. Furthermore, I will consider how such conversations differ between the comments made at the Chicago Historical Society and the Andy Warhol Museum given the variations between their respective exhibitions previously documented and discussed.

Whether as a singular contribution or a remark provoked by a previous entry to the visitor book, each comment may be understood as a letter, or, better, a *note* written to a presumed unknown reader (or multiple unknown readers) of the comment. Sometimes it is evident that these presumed readers are museum staff members; however, most of the time the presumed readers are simply those who have also had access to the exhibition and are now reading the comment book. While these future readers remain unknown to the comment writer, implicit in the inscription of a comment is that its future reader will be someone like the writer who was interested and motivated enough to come to the exhibition. In this sense, the comment books at the Chicago Historical Society and Andy Warhol Museum gather the remarks of people who minimally share a common concern with the topics of their respective exhibitions. One implication of this is that the social relations of cultural production inherent in the exhibition itself constitute a medium for the formation of a public. In this respect, comment writing is part of the work of public formation.

But I still need to more specifically consider what is at stake for writers of comments at the *Without Sanctuary* exhibitions. As Reid put it, "What does it [the written comment] aim to achieve?"[11] As this detailed analysis will show, in writing a comment, the writer often assumes a position in which one is accounting for oneself as someone addressed, subjected, and affected by the exhibition and the issues it raises. The presence of the comment book in the exhibit space clearly does not actually require that a visitor provide such an account; however, it does invite, or perhaps more strongly, request that a visitor furnish an account of oneself as someone who just witnessed something emotionally resonant that has possibly registered as personally and/or socially significant. While at times, comment writers have understood this invitation as a request for an appraisal of the exhibition (e.g., "great exhibit!" or "strong content lacking in context"), much more frequently, what is understood as requested are comments meant to publicly record the substance of one's nonindifference to what one has just seen.[12] On these terms, comment writers seem to be proceeding from an understanding that they are to publicly express an aspect of what they are feeling and thinking as a result of seeing the exhibition.[13]

For many writers this extends to expressing not only how these thoughts and feelings impact on prior held conceptions of race in America but as well, provoked by the demand to face a violent past, to consider what possible actions one might take in the future. In this respect, in various ways, many comments indicate an encounter with images that have an affective force that implicates writers in questions of their social affinities, identifications, and future commitments. One obvious question that might be asked in relation to the comment books is whether there was a distinct quality to the comments from visitors who self-identified as belonging to a racialized group. As a corollary, one might also ask what differences existed among racially self-identified visitors at each exhibition. These two questions are important for thinking about how the conversations in the comment book extend an ongoing conversation about race in America, and I will return to them at various points in this chapter. At the outset, however, I want to stress that much more is at stake in the comment books than the display of responses traced to a writer's established sense of self constituted within the shifting racial formations of the United States.[14] As we will see, a considerable number of comments (presumably from non–African Americans) reflected the norms of a "good performance" wherein shocked, angered, and saddened by what had been seen, comment writers avowed their fundamental difference from the perpetrators and bystanders evident in the photographs. All too easily one might dismiss such comments as giving a superficial account of oneself as a moral person, disavowing any connection to those at the scene of a lynching. Equally, one might brush aside the significance of expressions of shame and loss offered by museum visitors confronted with (for them) a hidden aspect of American history, rendering these sentiments as narcissistic cathartic confessions that simply leave one feeling good about feeling bad. However, before foreclosing too quickly on the meaning of such comments, I want to hold open the possibility that the forms through which museum visitors gave an account of themselves might be understood on other, somewhat more productive terms. At the very least, it is important to consider the possibility that the invitation to comment allows for a self-reflexive productive performance in which the writing of a comment is synchronous with a movement of becoming someone who is somewhat different than one was before the act of written expression. If this thought has any currency, it means that for some visitors the exhibition may be understood as an event that took possession of the visitor and implicated itself in the constitution of the "I" writing in the comment book. As we shall see, at issue here is not just the question of the re-formation of self but the possibility that a museum exhibition might convene the formation of a public with the reflexive capacity to transform one's self-other relations.

The *Without Sanctuary* exhibitions held at the Andy Warhol Museum and Chicago Historical Society were designed around mise-en-scènes intended to provide sustaining conditions for ethical deliberation, judgment, and the rearticulation of future conduct in the context of an engagement with and acknowledgment of a central feature of traumatic American memory.[15] On these terms, the work of accounting for oneself through public written comments can be seen as a potentially productive moment in the actualization of such conditions. This work of accounting for oneself involves the internalization of a demand that takes the form of a desire to write, that is, to register one's "response-ability" for others, in front of others, offering a version of a self that one is becoming (and that one is not) through one's response to the exhibition.[16] This said, it remains very much a question as to the various ways this responsibility is played out and with what consequences. While this question will be centrally addressed in my examination of visitor comments from both museums it may be helpful to signal a few basic considerations. First of all, in the request to comment, visitors are being asked for an account of themselves facing images of another's subjection to lethal violence, something that they likely can only partially narrate. Second, to register their witness, visitors have drawn on particular vocabularies and codes, sets of discursive norms within which accounts of oneself (the "I" who has experienced the exhibition) are made manifest (and their limits encountered). This is what Judith Butler calls "the rhetorical condition for responsibility" ("while I am engaging in a reflexive activity, thinking about and reconstructing myself, I am also speaking to you and thus elaborating a relation to an other in language as I go").[17] Given both of these points, it is important to stress that my concern is not primarily with the adequacy of these accounts as a true rendering of postexhibition subjectivity nor am I concerned to diagnose the comments as symptomatic forms of identification or ego defense (i.e., as expressions of melancholia, denial, disavowal, aggression). Rather, what is of central interest is that established within this scene of address (exhibition/comment book) is the discursive work of the making of a public. Thus, I ask: Are there different forms of "publicity" (in Arendt's sense of this term)[18] evident in the comment books that developed in the wake of the two exhibitions?

Of particular concern in this regard will be questions regarding the relation of affect and thought in each of the respective publics-in-formation. In other words, I will be addressing the concern: Toward what does the affect provoked by the encounter with images of lynching propel viewers?

COLLECTING THE COMMENTS

There were substantial differences in the material conditions for the writing of visitor comments at the Chicago Historical Society and the Andy Warhol Museum. In Chicago, in a small space just before the exhibition exit, two comment book binders were placed on a podium next to piles of takeaway remembrance cards, each containing the specific name of a person who had been a victim of a lynching and was identified in one of the photographs in the exhibition. Also present was a box of tissues. Accompanying these items was a wall text citing Martin Luther King Jr.: "The arc of the moral universe is long, but it bends towards justice." Visitors who wished to write comments did so standing. This meant that at times several people were lined up behind those writing in the comment books, much like what occurs during signing the register at a funeral viewing. Once full, the book was taken away and replaced with a fresh one, as is done with visitor books in many museums and related places. The comment sheets were eight by eleven inch unlined single pages; printed on the top of the page was the phrase "Share your thoughts." This typically limited comments to one or two per page (with one page being the maximum length).

In Pittsburgh, before exiting the exhibit one entered a space designed to enhance comment and reflection in multiple forms. In contrast to the Chicago Historical Society, the Warhol provided a space for writing comments that was large enough to accommodate tables and chairs. Thus, comments were typically written sitting down and entered into hardcover sketchbooks found on the tables. Multiple books were left out on these tables for visitors to read or comment in leading to what staff thought was as much reading as commenting. In any given book, the comments were erratically arranged rather than sequentially written. It seems that visitors entered comments wherever they wished, or in reaction to other words on the same page, or wherever they perceived the comments before them to end. Most of the comments are arranged one per page, with some taking more than one page, and others are placed on the same page as another comment, often in order to respond to the comment already there. As well, many pages contain doodles or full-scale drawings, which often spill onto more than one page of a given book. Sometimes entwined with text, and other times left to stand alone, these drawings have been counted in the Warhol samples as comments on par with comments done with words.

At the Andy Warhol Museum, photocopies were made from eight different books comprising approximately eight hundred comments in total. At the Chicago Historical Society, comment sheets were removed from their binder, photocopied, and sent to the University of Toronto research group. These sheets comprised approximately two thousand different entries. This process meant that it was not possible to be sure of the original order of appearance of the Chicago Historical Society comments or to determine how any given comment was situated in a particular relation to others. However, the photocopied comments were packaged into sets with the approximate time frame for their collection marked on each bundle.

While specific comments in the samples[19] collected at both institutions did, at times, directly refer to other visitor comments, as one might expect from the differences described above, this happened more frequently at the Warhol. Sometimes these interactions were contentious engagements, such as the following exchange in one of the Andy Warhol Museum comment books where one person wrote, "Let us all remember that suffering *is* a common bond around which we can relate to each other, unify, and find strength [Initials]." This is followed by a short reply from another visitor: an arrow drawn to point to the previous comment and the word: "Bullshit." Often comments would simply suggest that the writer wanted to reflect on the general tenor of what others had already written. For example, at the Chicago Historical Society one visitor wrote: "People keep writing [in the comment books] about how terrible it was back then but let's not forget that these injustice [*sic*] remain today, just not so much in plain view. Hate continues to breed. Let's not just *remember* but also continue to look and listen. It's not enough to just remember if it's still happening. End the hatred today. Educate and stop it [Initials]." At other times, the interchange could be a bit more complex. Below is a sequence of three comments from the Chicago Historical Society that were written in close proximity on a single page:

> I feel sorry for the black people because life is very short. And I feel sad because I'm a black person to. And if I were one of them it probably happen to me to. [Elaborate drawing]. [Signature] Age 8 Nov. 2001

> It is really sad that people come to these events and become racist b/c the point is to remember those tragic events, it to have them not be repeated! Not all whites are the same in their beliefs. Please don't characterize us all as those beasts capable of what they are doing.

> [Arrow pointing to the first comment] This is what really hurts. I felt this way at age 8 too. And now I'm 35. Will things ever change? *BLACK IS BEAUTIFUL.* [Signature]

In order to do a detailed comparative analysis of the comments from both institutions it was necessary to sample from the sets of comments provided us by each museum. Given the need to balance representativeness and the sheer time it takes to initially code and then recheck individual entries, it was decided to draw samples of two hundred entries from each of the sets available. In the case of the Warhol, twenty groupings of ten comments each were gathered from the eight books of comments collected by the museum. Sampling across these eight books allowed a consideration of comments across the entire four month run of the exhibition. The ten comments in each of the twenty samples are almost all consecutive; a comment was passed over only if photocopying or handwriting made it completely illegible. I elected to include a few comments that were partly legible, so as to make the groups of ten as complete as possible—these illegible or partly garbled comments are part of what visitors would have read through before making their own contribution, and thus seemed important to include where possible. For the Chicago Historical Society data set, twenty groups of ten comments were selected at random from the various time-dated bundles of photocopied sheets. As with the Andy Warhol Museum, this ensured that the sample of two hundred comments spanned the duration of the exhibition.

ANALYZING THE COMMENTS: LEVEL ONE THEMES

Starting from the presupposition that any given comment is an improvised performance along a fixed set of limited themes, a coding system was needed for analyzing the samples that recognized that these performances were often complex, involving sequences of variations on multiple themes. Drawing on a musical metaphor, comments in effect enacted or performed as different movements in sequence, the entire sequence making up a composition/comment. Three members of my research group were responsible for the coding of the samples. An initial set of themes internal to each comment were inductively generated by each of the three reading through the entire sample set, proposing themes, and then revising these through extended collective discussion. The final set of what we deemed Level One codes consisted of eleven specific themes. In any given comment some subset of these themes were performed in different ways, each performance drawing on particular discourses influenced by contemporary community issues and historical antecedents regarding race in America, one's exposure to human suffering within history, and possibilities (or not) of a transformed future. The eleven themes are as follows:

A: The expression of (or struggle to express) explicit emotions (AFFECTIVE EXPRESSION)[20]
B: The explicit or implicit linkage of historical past and present events and conditions (LINKAGE)
C: The expression of a desire to redeem the memory of a terrible past in the name of a better future and some indication of how this might or might not be possible (REDEMPTION)

D: The expression of an interpretation or assessment of specific aspects of the exhibition just seen (ASSESSMENT)
E: The expression of knowledge gained through attending the exhibition or an indication of something already known that was recalled, reiterated, or reinforced (KNOWLEDGE)
F: A self-identification as a person who is writing from a particular historically defined, social position (IDENTIFICATION)
G: The expression of gratitude for presenting the exhibition (GRATITUDE)
H: The making the personalizing mark, often initials or a signature usually at the end of a comment (SIGNATURE)
I: Remarks concerning a particular aspect of the history presented in the exhibition (HISTORY)
J: The explicit or implicit comment on visual knowledge as an important feature of their experience at the exhibition (VISUAL)

There are multiple ways each of the above themes is "played" or performed in any given comment. As an example of how a specific comment might be understood as a sequence of different movements, each movement a particular variation on one of the themes above, consider the performative structure of the following comment written at the Warhol Museum. In order to make the complex coding system legible, I have included letters and descriptors referring back to the eleven Level One themes discussed above at the end of the comment.[21]

> I can't express what emotion I feel. Sadness, shame, a longing to make things right. These images from our past, our proud nation's past makes me want to sink to my knees and cry—what is wrong with humanity? How could this have gone on? How could people stand by and watch, let their young children watch, how could they do those things? I see so much pain in those pictures, but worse I see people who feel they are righteous. No remorse in the eyes of the onlookers, no pain or sadness, disgust or mercy. And I have to ask myself—are we really that different now? It seems like the normal thing to do would be to dismiss these things as coming out of an ignorant

cruel and distant past, but has humanity changed? The recent bombings? The hate and fear that is circulating in society. It scares me. People are beautiful precious things, but somehow that gets forgotten. Humanity must learn even if it means getting smacked on the face with our brutal past. I am sorry these things ever happened—my heart goes out to all in those pictures. I can say that I have love and compassion for them in my heart, even though it comes too late. Thank you for this exhibit. [Signature] [A—AFFECTIVE EXPRESSION; B—LINKAGE; C—REDEMPTION; G—GRATITUDE; H—SIGNATURE]

Here are several other examples. These were written at the Chicago Historical Society:

> The faces of the photographer's spectators—smiling and pointing—look out at us from the picture of Abu Ghraib as well. [A—AFFECTIVE EXPRESSION; B—LINKAGE]

> Bearing witness everyday is a small step forward in attaining world wide respect for all individuals. To the Chicago Historical Society, thank you for remembering and reminding us to remember. [C—REDEMPTION; G—GRATITUDE]

> Moving, tragic, regrettable, unforgettable exhibit. [A—AFFECTIVE EXPRESSION]

> There is so much I want to express about how this exhibit makes me feel. Anger Sadness, nauseous, deprived, grateful and so much more—to know that this happened makes me so proud to be a black woman—to know that after slavery, bigotry, lynching, and segregation we as a people still stand tall (And for those of you who don't lift your head high and be proud no body and I mean nobody will ever be like us). But in the same token it makes me angry and depressed to be an American to know that my "fellow human beings" (if they can be called that) could do such a thing to its neighbors, friends and family. We are all one people. We need to stand together.

> Because an Eye for an Eye leaves everyone Blind. STOP THE VIOLENCE. [F—IDENTIFICATION; B—LINKAGE; A—AFFECTIVE EXPRESSION; C—REDEMPTION]

TRACKING DIFFERENCES IN VISITOR RESPONSES

By coding the compositional structure of comments as above, I have rejected a coding that would render a comment as singularly thematic. Furthermore, the complexity of the coding scheme set the stage for a multilevel consideration of the differences between the comments written at the Andy Warhol Museum and the Chicago Historical Society. My interest here is exploring if there are any patterns of differences that suggest that the exhibitions presented at the two institutions resulted in differing public pedagogies whose consequences are evident in the form and substance of the visitor comments. This is in no way meant to suggest that the interests, knowledge, and desires that visitors bring to an exhibition are of minor consequence in relation to a specific design that overdetermines an exhibition's pedagogical consequences. Nor am I dismissive of the possibility that some of the differences in visitor comments may have been determined by systematic differences in modes of reception among the base of visitors willing to visit either the Andy Warhol Museum or the Chicago Historical Society. However, given the limits of a post hoc comparative study, the concern here is the question of how and why an exhibition design might matter when presenting "difficult" historical material of systemic violence. In this respect, I am interested in reading the visitor comments in ways that might draw possible linkages between the exhibition logics sketched in chapter 2 and chapter 3 and the remarks written by visitors impelled to express an account of themselves as having been touched by the force of the exhibit.

I began this consideration with the most basic question: Were there any systematic differences in the number of types of thematic units employed in the comments in the two samples? To calculate this I simply counted the number of comments that contained one or more instances of each of the Level One themes. The results allowed for an initial and somewhat simplistic analysis of how the different exhibition frameworks employed by the two museums were reflected in the comments gathered at each institution. At this stage, I noted, for instance, that although the Andy Warhol Museum comments tended to be lengthier, often with more internal contradictions, there were more comments written at the Chicago Historical Society that incorporated a greater variety of different thematic elements. This meant that the Chicago Historical Society comments presented more substantive internal variation despite the greater number of words and wordiness of the Andy Warhol Museum comments. In addition, the comments written at the Chicago Historical Society made much more extensive use of the opportunity to comment on how the exhibition was experienced as form of learning or reiteration of knowledge. As well, the above distribution strongly indicates that at the Chicago Historical Society there were more comments that expressed something of the specific history referenced by the exhibition. To further analyze the comments, a number of subthemes were developed within the Level One themes already mentioned. In the next sections, I will explore some variations within the Level One themes in more detail.

Affective Expression: Explicit Emotions and the Graphic Representation of Feeling

The first of the Level One themes identified above tracked comments wherein comment writers expressed or struggled to express explicit emotion. Within these comments a differentiation was made between comments that explicitly stated an emotion and comments that used graphics and other indicators to express an excess of affect. This was done to enable an analysis of the substance of the affect deployed within and across comments and to allow for a more detailed exploration of the variations within comment fragments coded on such terms. Many comments explicitly expressed some emotion or emotional state, and often expressions of a number of different and conflicting emotions were contained within one comment.[22] The number of comment fragments directly expressive of emotion was substantially greater at the Andy Warhol Museum. This difference seems primarily to be accounted for by a greater number of expressions of sadness, shame, and revulsion. However, it is also worth noting that more visitors to the Chicago Historical Society expressed gratefulness for having seen the exhibit. Perhaps this is related to the more explicit offer of historical knowledge implicit in the Chicago Historical Society exhibit as well as its acknowledgment of what many visitors considered a particularly shameful moment in United States history. It less likely that visitors would record gratitude for the emotional provocation of the Andy Warhol Museum exhibition, an exhibition more difficult to contain within the frameworks of the provided historical narrative and memorialization practices.

We also analyzed comments that contained an expression of non-denotative graphic indicators of affective intensity such as exclamation points, underlining, and profanity.[23] Analysis of this group of comments revealed that the expressive stylistics employed in the comments differed between those written at the two museums. At the Chicago Historical Society we found greater explicit use of words as a medium to indicate affective intensity. Hence, the greater tendency in these comment fragments toward capitalization (often entire words capitalized), profanity, and the citation of prayers and verse. At the Andy Warhol Museum, the comments made greater use of non-denotative techniques: underlining, exclamation points/question marks, drawings, nonnormative use of space on a page (the exception being the use of repeated words). What these differences suggest is that the visit to the Warhol exhibition aroused emotions that were less easily channeled into conventional expressions of affective significance. Visitors seem to be struggling more to express something of the force of the exhibit. Why this might be so is an issue I will return to later in this chapter.

PHOTOGRAPHY AND HISTORY: DIFFERENCES IN HOW IMAGES SPEAK TO US

As discussed previously, both exhibitions were justified as offering access to an occluded history, perhaps vaguely known but without a specific sense of the degree of complicity and brutality often perpetrated at lynchings. Comments wherein visitors referenced particular aspects of the exhibition through which they gained a new realization about the violent racial history of the United States or specific information previously unknown comprised Level One "E," which tracked comments that expressed "knowledge gained through attending the exhibition or an indication of something already known that was recalled, reiterated or reinforced." Also included in these comment fragments were moments when visitors expressed that, although they had previous knowledge of lynching in America, the exhibition reinforced and/or deepened their awareness of the events depicted. When comparing the written visitor comments at the Andy Warhol Museum and the Chicago Historical Society, the number of comments in which visitors expressed that the exhibition had been an occasion for learning and developing a historical awareness was far greater at the Chicago Historical Society than the Andy Warhol Museum. This greater degree to which Chicago Historical Society visitors wrote comments indicative of the educative significance of the exhibition is hardly surprising given the emphasis that the Chicago Historical Society put not only on an extensive text-based contextualization of the lynching photographs, but as well, on the provision of micronarratives that identified most of those people who were tortured and murdered by mob violence. Indeed, it is interesting to note that in the sample of two hundred Chicago Historical Society comments there were no unfavorable remarks concerning the level of detail the exhibition provided. At the Warhol, however, there were a small set of specific comments complaining about the confusing lack of information regarding what was taking place in particular photographs as well as the lack of framing information that might help explain how and why such brutality was in evidence. Two comments that expressed this point of view are as follows:

> While this exhibit is heart moving and painful what I never saw was information about the people who were lynched. Thousands of African American men were lynched for NO reason except they were black. You never said that. I only saw the government and society condoning the activity. While the intentions of the exhibit were good, try spending more time on research as to why, the conditions and political climate of the lynchings. (Andy Warhol Museum)

> Nov. 6 2001 I've seen pieces of this exhibit all of my life in history books, television, and magazines. This is not the first lynching exhibit that I've viewed it's probably one of the better ones. This exhibit sucks too because it lacks way too much information about the times . . . I'm not from the early 1900s so it's hard for me to understand why humans would allow other so called humans to treat humans so fucked up. This

> exhibit *is* a wake up call for me and others like me who don't feel like this shit will ever stop . . . (Andy Warhol Museum)

Within this thematic grouping, a small set of brief statements that expressed the educational significance of the exhibition in very general, nonspecific terms were included from both institutions. These included comments such as: "I had no idea" (Andy Warhol Museum), and "Thank you for this terrible/painful learning experience. It defies comprehension—man's inhumanity to man. It leaves me weak" (Chicago Historical Society); and: "Wow, it's amazing how much school books leave out I've learned more facts in the museum, then in high school" (Chicago Historical Society). Most of the comments that discussed gaining previously unknown information in each sample, however, indicated some explicit expression of a developing awareness or new learning regarding aspects of the history of race in America. As evident below, in many such comments, the racial self-identification of the comment writer is apparent; however, there was no overall relation between racial self-identification and the claim of new knowledge. Consistent with the overall difference in comments that expressed learning and knowledge for each institution, such remarks were far more common at the Chicago Historical Society than the Warhol and were in harmony with the exhibition's intent of conveying the "hidden history" of lynching in America. Examples of these more specific comments are as follows:

> When I first read about this exhibit I thought about how no one ever mentioned this in history class, like the Japanese concentrations camps. The ugly, shameful parts of our history are glossed over. As I thought more about it, I can recall my elegant little grandmother beginning a story—"And they was going to lynch a nigger." I'm shamed. (Andy Warhol Museum)

> Without Sanctuary had showed me, how hard it was to be black AND how hard they fought so that I can have a fighting chance. Thank you 4 the exhibit. I will never forget what I saw here today—[Signature]. (Chicago Historical Society)

> 10-16-05. It is unbelievable that we as human beings could be so cruel to other people because they are of a different race. It makes me feel ashamed. I pray my ancestors were never

> involved in such horrible brutality. [Signature]—Chicago. (Chicago Historical Society)

> 9/26/05 This is a powerful record of people's capacity for evil toward their fellow human beings. I'm afraid this country has still not come to terms for taking responsibility for it's past shame and perpetuated equally shameful acts on their fellow countrymen/women today—The poor and powerless always suffer in this country at the hands of the blindly self-righteous . . . Like now in New Orleans when people were threatened at gunpoint from seeking refuge in the nearby (mainly white) suburb across the Pontchartrain Express Bridge. It makes me sick to think that people will continue to forget and children will never be taught the true history of America so that someday we may live in a country where people respect life, regardless of race or societal background. Thanks for helping people remember—Korean-American woman 34 yrs. old. (Chicago Historical Society)

Given that the central artifacts of both exhibits were the photographs from the Allen and Littlefield collection, I wanted to know if there were any differences between the comment samples in regard to explicit remarks regarding on one or more of the photographs and/or the overall significance of the exhibitions as presenting a *visual* history. There were roughly the same number of comment fragments at both institutions that explicitly addressed these concerns. These comments were coded as a unique Level One theme, referred to in the list above as theme "J," comments that contained "explicit or implicit comment on visual knowledge as an important feature of their experience at the exhibition." Of the Chicago Historical Society comments, three-quarters of the comments in this category conveyed the importance of the photographs not only as a documentary record that provided visual evidence of a violent history but also as a medium that offered information that communicated beyond words, registering an unsayable dimension of the event rendered present in the image. Examples of such Chicago Historical Society comments were as follows:

> Without Sanctuary spoke to me in more ways than a textbook or newspaper article ever could. The story it tells should be seen and understood by all. (Chicago Historical Society)

> Thank you for sharing this with the rest of us. Only the pictures can truly speak to us. [Signature] (Chicago Historical Society)
>
> 11/11/05 Looking at these pictures lets me know how people was before I was alive. Although we come a long way since then it still makes me think about how some of those things still happen today. But I put them in my prayers. Because they helped me have rights. So I love them for that. I will always remember them. (Chicago Historical Society)
>
> Sadly, it was just yesterday. We can rub our eyes but so hard to erase these images. We can dress it in better robes, cryptic names, music & half-assed apologies—but it's here isn't it? As a woman of color, thank you for giving me the eyes to see clearer. [Signature] (Chicago Historical Society)

In contrast, only about one-third of the Andy Warhol Museum comments addressing the significance of the visual testament of the exhibition mentioned the importance of the photographs as documentary evidence offering a "truth beyond words." One such instance was the following text:

> I was deeply moved. Emotionally and mentally I will never be the same. A person can be told about an incident in history but to actually view something traumatic makes a person think. It was an excellent exhibit and I learned as well as many others about black history and how it affects all of us present day. I also really appreciated the talking to people other than my racial background about the exhibit, seeing my feeling as well as listening to their feelings. PICTURES SPEAK A THOUSAND WORDS, WELL THE LYNCHING PICTURES TODAY HAD EVEN MORE TO SAY! Lynching still exists today just in different forms. [Signature] Sept. 22, 2001. (Andy Warhol Museum)

If the above type of comment was relatively infrequent among those written at the Andy Warhol Museum, it is important to reflect on how the visitors to the Pittsburgh museum did register the significance of the images in the Allen and Littlefield collection. To address this concern, consider that the most common feature of the *Without Sanctuary* photographs mentioned at both institutions was the spectators who had posed to have their pictures taken along with the bodies of the people who had been lynched. But beyond registering their shock and disturbance seeing the smiling faces of the crowds (including the children present), did the comment writers do anything with this mode of attention, perhaps linking it to something beyond the explicit expression of affect? Most Chicago Historical Society comments in this regard simply register the affective shock of the image. A good example of this is the following:

> A powerful, disturbing exhibit; Even those of us who are familiar with the history of lynching in America, of which I am one, cannot help but be moved, shocked, appalled by the photos on the postcards. I especially noticed the faces of the mob, how joyful, happy or indifferent most of them seemed. I can pray, "May God have mercy on their souls!" [Signature] 9/26/05. (Chicago Historical Society)

The texts that visitors wrote at the Andy Warhol Museum included comments on the crowds that were more complex, often making apparent a degree of reflexivity not present among the Chicago Historical Society comments. Here are two examples:

> My god Fifteen thousand angry lynchers, crowded, shoulder to shoulder, head to head, a mass of citizens gathered together, packed tightly like corn kernels on the cob, facing inward. [scribble] The thousands of hats and heads focus inwards towards the center. The nucleus of this social force is a black man, naked, a rope around his neck lying sprawled over a pile of hay and wood that will be set aflame soon, to burn him slowly, but for now a man is beating him with a stick. The thousands watch, the man keeps beating him. Who will cry out for him? The fifteen thousand do not cry out for him. They watch [scribble], their spirits become knit together with the sweating red-faced man who raises his rod once again with a frenzied hellish self righteous ocean of justice gushing though his veins and the crowed presses onward for a better look at the criminal who is being killed. We are not far from these onlookers. We support [scribble] atrocious things by watching . . .

> watching watching watching watching watching WATCHING . . . (Andy Warhol Museum)

> I've read about it in books, I've seen it portrayed on T.V., but today I am awe struck at what I witnessed. It's something to look at the postcards and photos and to read the inscriptions. The looks on the faces of the onlookers (some of whom were smiling) really make me wonder how many generations removed one must be for such hatred to be removed from them. I, along with my husband and 10 year old son will discuss this exhibit at length. I am however compelled to commend the fact that along with all the grotesque photos were moments in Black History and how our culture contributes to this "land of the free and the home of the brave" [Signature] 22 Sept. 2001 p.s. Thank you for sharing and the work you do. (Andy Warhol Museum)

It is important to keep in mind that such comments as those above do not appear in the Chicago Historical Society sample. The primary difference between the Andy Warhol Museum and Chicago Historical Society comments in regard to the significance and implications of viewing the images was the greater degree of reflexivity exhibited in the Andy Warhol Museum sample where more than half of the comments linked the viewing of particular photographs to either their own viewing difficulties, their position within the racial formation of the society in which they were living, or to the way such photographs commented on contemporary concerns. Here are a few additional examples that illustrate this reflexivity:

> You walk through, and become numb. The bodies become dummies hanging from trees. And then you catch your own reflection in the glass of the frame. It's going to take longer than I thought to reconcile the two. These people were just as real as I am. I know that. It is just so overwhelming that I don't feel it yet. But somehow that's ok, because I know I am closer today than I was before. Thank you for that—November 17th, 2001. (Andy Warhol Museum)

> Scary !! Too graphic. It was hard for me to travel from scene to scene. Too hard! (Andy Warhol Museum)

While one might suspect that the above comments would be closer to what one might expect of visitors to an art museum as opposed to a historical society, it seems to me that the comments are an indication that the mise-en-scènes within which the selections of the Allen and Littlefield Collection were presented were implicated in how the photographs functioned within the totality of the exhibition. Even though the total number of comments in the samples that specifically referenced the pedagogical value of the photographs was not extensive, what is interesting is that at the Chicago Historical Society there was a consistent "reading" of photographs as documentary evidence of the events traced in its image. In this sense, it appears that the photographs worked in concert with the historical narrative and memorializing frame to become part of the historical documentation that rendered the truth of a violent American past, but in terms beyond what words alone could say. This might explain the difference found in regard to number of comments wherein visitors proffered moral judgments either about the actors rendered in the photographs or the character of the historical time referenced by the images. More frequent at the Chicago Historical Society than the Andy Warhol Museum, these comments registered explicit judgments as to the criminality of the perpetrators and spectators and/or the general immorality of period during which lynching occurred.

Of course, the staff at the Andy Warhol Museum wanted visitors to learn about the "hidden history" of lynching in America and to make evident its injustice. However, they also wanted visitors to experience the photographs as images that forced a confrontation with the very situated act of viewing them. The reflexive comments above come closer to this experience, certainly more so than the tenor of the Chicago Historical Society comments written specifically about the photographs themselves.

WHAT MIGHT BE MEANT BY A "USEABLE PAST"?

A major question for the practice of public history is how people formulate their understanding of the relation of past and present and with what consequences for historical understanding and thought concerning the contemporary moment. One index of how visitors understood what they were seeing as a "useable past" is the set of comments that explicitly or implicitly link the historical past to present events and conditions (Level One theme "B": "The explicit or implicit linkage of historical past and present events and conditions"). The total number of comment fragments that expressed a specific connection between past and present was relatively the same in both institutions. However, a closer look at some of the substantive differences as to how such a relation was articulated provide some marked contrasts between the two samples of visitor comments. The comments in this thematic grouping were coded under three subheadings: (1) comments relating the past and the present (including the expression of a need or desire for accountability regarding events depicted), (2) comments indicating the various ways in which history is a resource for thinking about present concerns, and (3) comments addressing the similarity or difference between the past and the present.

The first of these sets of differences concerns comments that gestured to a need or desire for the enactment of some moral, educational, or legal accountability regarding the historical events depicted in the exhibition. Although the number of times such concerns were mentioned is small, it is striking that all such comments were written at the Chicago Historical Society (with none appearing in the Andy Warhol Museum sample). These included comments such as:

> No one ever said I'm sorry and still the evils of hatred are still present even in this room as people view this terrorism. Please God help these people we are human beings Love ye one another 6-6-05. [Signature] (Chicago Historical Society)

> Extraordinary exhibit and one I am wholly familiar with. One need only see some of the photos to see that America has a debt to pay and until then there will never be a peaceful and fear-free co-existence between the races. What is especially troubling is that there appears to be no remorse from those reviewing [*sic*] the lynchings. [Signature] (Chicago Historical Society)

A second set of differences was found in comments wherein history is mentioned as a useful resource for thinking about concerns in the present. There were more comments where this was the case at the Andy Warhol Museum than at the Chicago Historical Society.

However, it is striking that when these comments were examined as to the concerns of the present that were linked to the history portrayed in the exhibition, there were a greater number of comments at the Chicago Historical Society that reference contemporary problems regarding race in America than there were at the Andy Warhol Museum. On the other hand, there were more comments in the Andy Warhol Museum sample that were willing to use the photographs of lynchings as a resource for thinking concerns beyond contemporary moments of racism. Comments from both institutions that illustrate the use of exhibition for thinking the contemporary situation of race are as follows:

> I have just had the chance, no the privilege of seeing one of the things that I am sure will change my life. I came to this museum with my class expecting and hoping to see some lame exhibit that my teacher requested I see. I just say that my whole perspective of the world in which I live has been changed. I have come to realize that the past is continuously repeating it's self, and until we as a Nation try, to do change, we will continue to go *downhill* and *not* evolve. I am, from this day forward, going to interact with other races and try to better understand myself and others. This exhibit has had a great impact on me. [Signature] Wilkinsburgh High School, Jan. 16th 2002. A day I will never forget. (Andy Warhol Museum)

> It's crazy how we as Black are called "animals," beast and other such names when over time unfortunately whites have committed more beastly crimes than any thug or gang member. I thank who put this together so that I may put away my so called beastly ways and realize the real beast around me. (Chicago Historical Society)

These comments are in contrast to the following where the exhibit is evoked as a resource for "illuminating" other concerns beyond race:

> 12/26/01 Being White, I feel ashamed of my own race. This exhibit really makes me appreciate the time that I live in. Would I have gone along with my fellow beings in the pursuit

of racism? Would I have been an activist for equality? Would I have allowed myself to be seen in one of those photographs? I am so grateful for my open mind and free spirit and exhibits such as this amplify that appreciation. "No Sanctuary" was a beautiful expression of how all peoples can rise up against this hatred and move on in peace. As the years have gone by "PC" has become part of every Americans vocabulary and this makes me proud. I feel proud because society, the media, and officials are actively making living in modern times easier for minorities. I think another exhibit should be dedicated to the discrimination of the mentally ill and homosexuals because these people are the African-Americans today. Think about this—when someone wants to insult another they say "retard" or "fag" and it hurts me to hear these. I am neither mentally ill or a homosexual but it offends me because people use a name of a minority as an insult. In the words of John Lennon, "IMAGINE"—[Signature] 16 year old Vincentian High school. (Andy Warhol Museum)

The faces of the photograph's spectators—smiling and pointing—look out at us from the picture of Abu Ghraib as well. (Chicago Historical Society)

I am reminded of my experience as a Lesbian and a Mexican simultaneously. While this focused and not unjustly on the experience of black/African American peoples lynching, it is impossible for me or any of us to think that this did not or does not continue to happen to blacks, Mexicans, Jews, gays, transgender individuals etc. Much of this exhibit, this being the historical society, points to past but ostensibly disregards the present. What we might call hate crimes today could be cosigned the modern counter part of a lynching experience. History is only valuable when holding the present accountable for its mistakes. [Signature] (Chicago Historical Society)

Despite the two Chicago Historical Society comments quoted above, there are more comments regarding issues of violent racial oppression and a consequent demand for justice at the Chicago

Historical Society, while at the Warhol there were more comments addressed to a wider range of issues associated with various forms of discrimination and inequity. This is perhaps expected as the less contextualized rendition of the lynching photographs at the Warhol makes them easier to "use" as examples of a generalized notion of hatred and intolerance. This then opens the question of what happens to and in conversations about race that are based on different historical narratives of racism. The mise-en-scène at the Andy Warhol Museum offered an engagement with a historical display of racism rooted in the visual manifestation of brutality and hatred. Within the mise-en-scène, there is little in the way of specificity of the events photographed to constrain the extension this history as a working framework for comprehending a generalized notion of hatred fostered on others. Thus, some viewers saw the example as an occasion of raising the problem of violence and discrimination perpetrated against gays and lesbians (thus reinforcing the equation of racism and homophobia). Certainly in Chicago, engaging an exhibition that narrated the history of lynching as a form of terrorism that was intended to prevent black upward mobility, made it much harder to have a conversation *only* about the generic problem of hate and prospect of love.

The third and final set of contrasts concerns moments in comments wherein the writer either gestures to the past presented in the exhibit and how it is similar or different from the present moment. The number of comments that spoke to this aspect of the relation of the past and present was roughly the same. However, when I separated comments into two categories, those that asserted that times were different now and those that suggested a greater continuity with the past, evident is a reversal of direction. There were a greater number of comments at the Andy Warhol Museum that suggested the equivalent continuity of oppressive racism while more at the Chicago Historical Society exhibit noted the present as fundamentally different from the past. Here are some comments that illustrate both positions, beginning with examples that expressed the idea that the present is fundamentally different from the past.

> Me personally I don't really care about what happen to us back then even though I should I just fill that yes this happened long time ago. But that was then this is now. I know there

> are still prejudice still in this world but I feel it is nothing to get emotional about. [Multiple signatures] (Andy Warhol Museum)

> I just wanted to say thank you for bringing this exhibit to Pittsburgh, I am so glad I got to see it. I guess I needed to see it to believe it. I never knew there were that many actual pictures of lynchings. I thank God that times have changed. I don't know how i would have reacted had i lived back then. I would like to think that I would have been disgusted just as i am now. Please thank God everyday that we live in a better time and pray that it gets better! Thank you, [Signature], Clarion Univ. of Penn. 11-10-01. (Andy Warhol Museum)

> I'm happy black and white people can be friends and not fight over slavery. [Signature] (Chicago Historical Society)

> Viewing this exhibit made me realize what changes we have gone through within a 200 year period. I am so thankful that we don't live in that kind of society. The "lynchings" were a disgrace and an intolerable act of racism. It needs to be a "MUST" to teach this stuff in schools to prevent these occurrences from reoccurring! [Signature] (Chicago Historical Society)

Examples of comments that suggest more of a continuity between past and present are as follows:

> Thank you for letting all see what most African Americans have known all along. This was a terrible time in history and unfortunately, things have not progressed as much as we like. Racism, bigotry still exists in this great nation. Hopefully there will never be another time like the one in the pictures. Learn from the past and move forward. [Signature] 12/30/01. (Andy Warhol Museum)

> 1/1/02 This exhibit is a horrible display of what humans are capable of. To see men, women and children at the site of these lynchings w/ smiles on their faces says a great deal about our society. The sad thing is that America is not far removed from

> that time. Today we still have hatred in our hearts. The hatred/racism that we have for each other is not overt as the pictures display but it is displayed in subtle ways which can be more detrimental in some aspects. [Initials] University of Pittsburgh. (Andy Warhol Museum)

> Thanks to the people responsible for putting this exhibit together. My biggest regret is not seeing it sooner, so I could then return with my nieces and nephews. I believe that there are a lot of things happening today that say or tell us that we as a nation have not grown that far from the days of lynching. I hope and pray that I'm wrong about that because no one should have to live in fear like blacks lived earlier in the last century or have to suffer the terrible death that the people pictured in the postcard here had to suffer. [Signature] (Chicago Historical Society)

> We as a Nation still have a very Long way to go; because modern day lynching is still going on today: [Signature] 9/29/05. (Chicago Historical Society)

And written in response to the preceding comment:

> This nation is not even headed in that direction. Still dragging black men toward the tree. 9/30/05 Let's go home, Love, [Signature] (Chicago Historical Society)

A set of comments that add nuance to the above discussion about the similarity or difference between past and present are those coded under the a category that tracked comment writers who claimed membership in a racialized identity group. These comments were tracked as a subset of the Level One theme "F," comments containing the "self-identification as a person who is writing from a particular historically defined, social position." This could take the form (and often did, especially in the Chicago Historical Society sample) of prefatory remarks that might be understood as establishing the writer's authority to comment, as in the statement, "As a Black man in America . . . " or "As a female white American . . . " Other forms of racialized self-identification were less explicit and were made through the use of pronouns ("we," "our") or "my people." Overall, the comments in this subcategory are consistent with the larger sample as a whole; however, in regard to the question of a usable past and the difference or similarity between the past and the present, it is interesting to consider what, if anything, can be said about how visitors who self-identify as belonging to a racialized group regard the differences or similarities between the past and the present with regard to race in America. Among visitors to the Chicago Historical Society and the Andy Warhol Museum who self-identified as racialized, there is a stronger sense that the present is different from the past, and a sense of progression or progress through history. This plays out differently in the comments written by visitors who self-identify as "white" versus those who self-identify as "black or African American." Whereas the comments that self-identify as white (at both institutions) tend to place lynching in the past and to pose questions such as "What would I have done?" the responses of the visitors who self-identify as black or African American are more varied. At the Chicago Historical Society, visitors who self-identify as black or African American in the comments tend to situate the history of lynching within a larger narrative of social struggle for civil rights in which they are personally implicated. In several of these comments, the comment writer is positioned as a direct heir to a better life because of the struggles of their ancestors. Similar ideas are also expressed in the Andy Warhol Museum comment sample, but not as frequently.

> Without Sanctuary had showed me, how hard it was to be black AND how hard they fought so that I can have a fighting chance. Thank you 4 the exhibit. I will never forget what I saw here today—Shana C. (Chicago Historical Society)

> I think today, Black people should remember, how we were treated back in the day, and stand together to change the world, and make the deaths of those poor people stand for something. (Chicago Historical Society)

> From my experience today it shows me how much I should appreciate my ancestors. (Andy Warhol Museum)

The greater frequency with which such comments were present at the Chicago Historical Society may speak to the stronger focus on presenting a historical narrative of lynching. This strong narrative component may have made it easier for visitors to identify with the people in the photographs. Among the Andy Warhol Museum comments wherein visitors self-identified as black or African American, some of the comments contained the viewpoint that the photographs acted as evidence for present-day racism. Examples of such comments that gesture toward a racism that is felt to be endemic to the social and political culture of American society include the following: "This is what America thinks of me because of the color of my skin? Really Sad . . . " (Andy Warhol Museum); and, "Whether it's physical, mental, or spiritual the breakdown of the black man will always be a part of what is America." (Andy Warhol Museum).

REDEEMING THE PAST: HOPE, ACTION, IDENTITY

A common presumption as to why it is justified to employ media such as museum exhibitions, film, and literary writing to revisit the scene of brutal systemic oppression and violence is the thought that through a disruptive force of "monstration," of *showing* atrocious events as a sight,[24] a terrible past can be redeemed through practices of cultural memory, practices that assist in securing a better future. While many scholars have posed questions about the ideological character of this notion of redemptive remembrance, there is still a strong sense that to justify the representation of images and stories of the degradation and murder of a particular group of people, such a practice must have some positive social or educative purpose. Clearly, what most public institutions have in mind is something quite different from Walter Benjamin's notion that a revolutionary spirit "is nourished by the image of enslaved ancestors rather than that of liberated grandchildren."[25] Rather, the pedagogical premise is the hope that images of a violent past, properly contextualized, will act as a prophylactic and prevent the repetition of such violence, both through the instantiation of moral norms and improved civic codes, as well as a better understanding of difference and an individual commitment to actions taken in the name of personal and social improvement. In this regard, it is interesting to consider the component of the visitor comments that spoke to the question of "what was to be done" after seeing the exhibition.

There is perhaps no comment in either of the samples studied that expresses both the affective disruption that accompanies the destabilization of habitual ways of seeing the world and the desire for thought or action promising a more secure framework for living in the present than the following text. This comment from the Andy Warhol Museum illustrates clearly the situation of a visitor to an exhibit being charged with affect but needing some direction in either thought and/or action that could contain and direct its disruptive force.

> I'm not really sure what I'm supposed to do when I leave here today. Things just can't go back to normal. I feel very sad when I look at the black faces hanging from those trees they look like my family, friends, people I see on the street everyday. What makes [me] more upset is to see those white faces, looking at the bodies with pride and accomplishment. Those white faces also look like the people I see on the street. (I'm very confused as what I should feel right now). Peace.

Reading this comment symptomatically, one can sense the spectral presence of the past commingling with the everyday surroundings of the comment writer. This seems to result in a loss of previously secured meanings and a deeply felt set of uncertainties as to how to negotiate this loss. The author's concluding comment, the underlined "peace," is a word written under subjection to the force of the exhibition and cannot be read simply as a conventional gesture of closing for a written communication. It is offered simultaneously as a relational posture, moral injunction, and a hope for oneself. The internal structure of this comment is exemplary of many other comments written at both the Andy Warhol Museum and the Chicago Historical Society that gesture to an attempt to resolve the affective disruption provoked by the exhibition. These attempted resolutions were collected together under the Level One theme identified above as theme "C," which traced "the expression of a desire to redeem the memory of a terrible past in the name of a better future and some indication of how this might or might not be possible." These fragments break down primarily into two subcategories: (1) moral injunctions that, if followed, would make for a happier, more just society; and (2) statements that expressed an avowed sense of personal responsibility to speak or act in a particular way. Most of the moral injunctions were comments that exhorted people to either remembrance or education, greater degrees of love, compassion, and acceptance, and/or the necessity of speaking out against injustice. Examples of brief comments that combine such injunctions are: "11-2-01 Stop hating, start loving. Learn from mistakes of the past. Don't use violence to fight for peace. Nicole from Germany" (Andy Warhol Museum), and "Lonnie Bunch [the then Director of the Chicago Historical Society] is to be deeply thanked for bringing this shameful part of American history to the Chicago Historical Society. We must never forget. In order for evil to succeed—as it did—it was *and is* only necessary for good people to remain silent. In a painful way, I am grateful for the time I spent here today. [Signature]"

A smaller number of exhortative comments at both museums invoked a return to explicitly Christian belief and values; for example, "The Devil is among us he takes many shapes and forms often times appearing harmless. Be a steadfast believer in Jesus Christ and everything will work for good in the End. God Bless. [Signature] 11/01" (Andy Warhol Museum). An interesting difference in the substance of the various exhortations and statements of personal responsibility between the Chicago Historical Society and the Warhol Museum was that there was a significantly greater number of calls for the importance of education about, and remembrance of, the past in the Chicago Historical Society comments as opposed to a greater number of calls to love and acceptance at the Warhol. Again, this is not surprising given the explicit emphasis in Chicago on the provision of a historical narrative and the explicit memorialization of the victims of lynching practices and the tendency in Pittsburgh to treat the exhibition as a moral injunction to broader conceptions of discrimination and injustice.

It is also interesting to note that the total number of exhortative comments written at both institutions was substantially greater than statements of personal responsibility, with a little over twice as many exhortative than personal statements occurring in each museum. At least half of the personal statements were a reprise of the hortative themes noted above, but were expressed in a register of individual responsibility. These ranged from the simple declaration, "I will never forget what I saw here today"(Chicago Historical Society), to "I will never understand, but I choose NOT TO HATE" (Chicago Historical Society), and "I will die before I become a victim of white oppression, which exists today in America" (Chicago Historical Society). Beyond the repetition of these themes, however, were statements that spoke of the exhibit as offering a legacy inspiring personal improvement and a commitment to activism.

> This exhibit inspired me to learn more about how my ancestors struggled for me to live a more free life. (Chicago Historical Society)

> I am greatly saddened by these photos but they have instilled in me a motivation to create change. (Chicago Historical Society)

> Without Sanctuary reminds me that I must consciously resist opinions that attack others. I must be brave enough to educate those with hatred and hopefully end our predispositions to joining the mob. (Andy Warhol Museum)

> This exhibit caused me to stop, Look, Listen. To take an inventory of my life, and to realize that I'm called to make a difference. (Andy Warhol Museum)

> This makes me want to work *harder* to raise my black boys to become educated and unstoppable soldiers . . . fighting in this war of racism. (Andy Warhol Museum)

It would be a misjudgment to simply dismiss such exhortations and statements of personal responsibility as empty, facile clichés symptomatic of popular discourse on issues of race and discrimination. What cannot be stressed enough about these statements is the propitious, reassuring function of such injunctions and how necessary they are in the moment of responding to one's (just prior) viewing of the exhibitions. In many of the comments, such statements were offered as a way beyond the crushing reality of racist brutality that visitors had seen in the photographs. The prevalence of these statements is testimony to the need to make some comment as to "what is to be done" so as to attempt to recuperate an ego whose integrity is under threat living in a chaotic, hate-filled world. Thus, these comments should be read not only as statements of belief regarding the foundations of a more just and peaceful world, but also as implicit statements of the necessity of hope when visitors publicly perform a statement of the impact and significance of what they have just seen. This is why academic judgments as to the meaninglessness of redemptive remembrance should not be made too quickly. Hope resides as a human need, however difficult it may be to come by. Poignantly paradigmatic of what is at stake here is also evident in the following comment written by a visitor to the Warhol Museum:

> 12/2/2001 I don't know what we need to do next and it makes me so frustrated. I do not understand how people can hate so much. I do not understand how any human being with a family, with a heart can take pleasure or satisfaction from doing such horrible things to the human body, to the human soul. Our history is so horrible, but we must overcome it. I *must* believe that there is something we can do to overcome it. We *must* overcome the distance that history has put between people. It will take so much love and so much time to overcome atrocities like these—and the distance we feel from each other. Can't we treat other people—all people—like they are our mothers or fathers or our brothers? We're all here together—we don't know how or why? Everyone's just trying to figure something out—to live, to love, to find happiness. Help others find happiness. Cause no pain. Fight for people in pain. *Love.* [Signature] (Andy Warhol Museum)

The structure of this comment was quite often repeated. Here is another version, this time paired down to its simplest form: "I could cry I could cry (I have cried over days). It is really time to love each other." (Andy Warhol Museum)

Of course, some degree of critical skepticism is warranted in relation to the overabundance of comments that seem to instantiate a performance of hopefulness in the face of the despair wrought by the lynching photographs. Certainly, we need to ask if such expressions are more often a becalming wish than an indication of hopeful imagination, that is, something of an impoverished dream rather than the need to imagine an alternative human world and to imagine it in a way that enables one to act in the present as if this alternative had already begun to emerge. For this reason, it is important to register variations in the source of hopefulness called upon by comment writers as well as the degree to which hopefulness was seen as possible in the face of realities of racial division in the United States.

First of all, when the comments that expressed a desire to redeem the memory of a terrible past in the name of a better future are examined as to the source on which their hopefulness was based, most statements expressed the importance of the teaching of and learning from history combined with the embrace of universal moral values that give priority to the dignity and sanctity of the "human" as an inclusive category that subsumes racial (and other) differences. Overwhelmingly, these sources of hope account for the majority of comments coded under this theme at the Warhol. While the same sources of hope were equally prevalent at the Chicago Historical Society, additionally cited in Chicago were the need for a critical self-consciousness, affirmations of the importance of black or African American solidarity, and a substantial number of comments that looked to God for help to redeem a violent past.

However, perhaps more important for understanding the implications of the different exhibition frameworks of the two presentations of lynching photographs are the differences as to the certainty with which hopefulness was expressed. An example of a rather clear declamation as to how the past portrayed in the *Without Sanctuary* exhibitions could be redeemed is given in the following comment:

> What a brave, frightening and coldly real exhibit this is. How important it is not to forget our past. This has been very important to opening my eyes to the horrific past my ancestors have left behind. And such opening of eyes is critical to the progress of our society. Thank you for this. (Chicago Historical Society)

It is quite important to note that there were many more of this type of comment at the Chicago Historical Society than at the Warhol. Much more evident at the Warhol were comments that registered a degree of uncertainty and contradiction as to whether the suffering and death shown in the photographs could be redeemed. The following seven comments, all written at the Warhol, range from rather short statements to much longer, more complex comments that were rarely found in the comments written in Chicago. Taken as a set, they indicate why the Warhol exhibition seems to have provoked a much greater degree of ambivalence among its visitors than did the exhibition at the Chicago Historical Society.

12/4/2001 There is so much hate and fear in this world. We seem to keep making the same egregious errors against our fellow people throughout time. Perhaps someday, hopefully now, we will learn from history rather than repeat it. Blessed Be. (Andy Warhol Museum)

It's not something we think of everyday. It is however history that we *need* to learn from but I don't think so many people did: do? Appreciate difference and change . . . Pray. (Andy Warhol Museum)

Thank you for letting all see what most African Americans have known all along. This was a terrible time in history and unfortunately, things have not progressed as much as we like. Racism, bigotry still exists in this great nation. Hopefully there will never be another time like the one in the pictures. Learn from the past and move forward. [Signature] 12/30/01. (Andy Warhol Museum)

Overwhelming and somewhat depressing but necessary. In times like these it makes you wonder. I truly am an American and I think killing innocent people is horrendous wherever and whenever it occurs. Nonetheless this is a reminder that we still have work to do as a people or our young men could risk their lives and come back to a country that still treats them as second class citizens. I think there are two wars that need to be fought simultaneously. One external and one internal. [Signature] 9/27/01. (Andy Warhol Museum)

Oct 12 "Without Sanctuary" was an important exhibition for me to see because it reminds anyone of what humanity is capable of. Mob "mentality"—a phrase I first heard in a high school English class after reading *Grapes of Wrath* still rings true today. After Sept 11—how many Americans were quick to judge a person they saw with skin unlike theirs—how quickly "rag head" and "one-dot" were coined to poke fun at what so many Americans know nothing about? Hate is ingrained in "mob mentality"—Even in the 21st century—we can repeat this unspeakable behavior—we still grasp HATE—we still poke fun and attack people of different colors, cultures, religious backgrounds. "Without Sanctuary" reminds me that I must consciously resist opinions that attack others. I must be brave enough to educate those with hatred and hopefully end our predispositions to joining "the mob." [Signature] (Andy Warhol Museum)

How could anyone do this to anyone else? These are human beings just like us. Children under 10 were laughing at seeing an African American dying. Badly charred bodies were just looked upon by spectators. We see this now w/ the people of Muslim Descent. How we just smile and turn our heads when we see a Muslim person getting bombs dropped on them. It makes me sick to think about what 1 person can do to another. Love each other for who we are. [Drawing of a Heart] [Signature] Class of 2003, Charters, Houston, High School. (Andy Warhol Museum)

There are a number of factors that are implicated in comments such as those above being substantially more prevalent at the Andy Warhol Museum. As is obvious from the comments, the impact of the exhibition opening just weeks after the September 11, 2001, attacks on the World Trade Center and the Pentagon (and subsequently the initiation of the war in Afghanistan) is clearly present in the comments. As well, the period leading up to the exhibition's opening was a tense time with regard to race relations in Pittsburgh, particularly in regard to an extended controversy in regard to a police shooting of an unarmed black man and the several mistrials that occurred in the context of the attempted prosecution of officers charged with being responsible for his death.[26] Furthermore, the physical setting for writing comments at the Andy Warhol Museum encouraged more extensive writing. However, in my view the substance and form of the exhibition itself was centrally implicated in the tone and substance of the comments written by visitors to the Andy Warhol Museum. Given the minimal contextualization of the images presented at the Warhol, it was difficult for this exhibition to avoid the consequences of the spectacularization of death. In the production of spectacle, a world is offered "without background, a world in which things exist or mean in the way they appear."[27] While one can argue this is exactly the terms on which the lynching photographs should be shown, what is frustrated within such a condition of display is any effort to know who took these photographs, who looked at them, and who were those in the actions and subsequent suffering evident in the images. Consequently, what is eliminated is the particularity of death leaving one face to face with the horror of the sheer brutality traced by the amassing of such images, one upon the other. Indeed, despite efforts at the Andy Warhol Museum to contextualize the images in relation to forms of resistance to injustice and engage visitors in public dialogue as to how discrimination can be challenged and contested, the weight of the considerable number of images of death and degradation clearly is felt in the comments above.

IMAGES OF RACIAL VIOLENCE AND ANXIOUS CONVERSATIONS REGARDING RACE IN AMERICA

It is now time to step back a little from the discussion so far. At the beginning of this chapter, I indicated not only an interest in how the writing in the visitor comment books was socially organized and what range of emotions and ideas were being expressed, but as well, the way the written comments, collectively considered, might be understood as a particular extension of the public "conversation" regarding race in America. No doubt, this question rubs against the grain of the popular conception that sees museums as public spaces for private contemplation. Limited to this perspective, the *Without Sanctuary* exhibitions at the Warhol Museum and the Chicago Historical Society would be rendered as image-events provoking intense private encounters with traces of the past, encounters to be reckoned with through the explicit relevancies and unconscious transferences stemming from personal experiences of living in a deeply racialized society. On such terms event-reference is bent to self-reference, transferring interest from the event to the subject's (self-) representation.[28] If confined to such an understanding, the *Without Sanctuary* visitor responses would be solely self-referential, displays of various individual ways of attempting to come to terms with horror that racism has wrought. On such terms, one might justifiably wonder if such exhibitions unintentionally turn our attention away from grappling with a much-needed understanding of the genesis and political meaning of lynching in America (including the afterlife of such events as they are implicated in the social structuring of contemporary life). In *About Looking,* John Berger famously warned of such a result in his commentary on public display of war photography.

> The possible contradictions of the war photograph now become apparent . . . the most extreme examples . . . show moments of agony in order to extort the maximum concern. Such moments . . . are discontinuous with all other moments. They exist by themselves. But the reader who has been arrested by the photograph may tend to feel this discontinuity as his own personal moral inadequacy. . . . [T]he issue of the war which has caused that moment is effectively de-politicized. The picture becomes evidence of the general human condition. It accuses nobody and everybody.[29]

Yet the visitor comments we have been considering in this chapter seem to suggest that the exhibitions at the Andy Warhol Museum and Chicago Historical Society need to be understood as differently intervening in the public sphere. Enacting more than what Richard Sandell has referred to as the discursive "(re)framing" of conversations regarding social difference,[30] the exhibitions acted as relays between the singularity of individual responses and a form of sociality bound to the affect provoked by the spectacle of barbaric violence. In this respect, the exhibitions convened a public around the photographic depiction of the violation of human bodies (more specifically African American bodies). These scenes became a point of contact wherein the space of communication constituted in the activity of reading and writing in visitor comment books initiated a new public-in-formation, joining people to each other in ways not preestablished by relations of kinship, friendship, or economic partnership.[31] *Contra* the arguments that suggest the mass attraction of atrocity exhibitions collapses the public world into the private,[32] this process of public formation signified an attentiveness to an aspect of "the world itself, in so far as it is common to all of us and distinguished from our privately owned place in it."[33] The importance of such concerns was registered by James Allen in the context of a discussion of his decision to display his collection of lynching photographs. Allen suggested that Americans were not talking straightforwardly about racism primarily because they aren't aware of its severity, thus suggesting that, "Americans have to have a visual vocabulary of racism before they can talk honestly about it."[34]

The above considerations suggest that the *Without Sanctuary* exhibitions provided public spaces, spaces held in common among people within which they may present themselves in writing and/or speech and recognize others as they do the same. Indeed, the substance of the "publicness" of the spaces initiated by each exhibition lies between the responses of the various people who attended these events. It lies in the relations that take shape through the form and substance of what visitors said as they wrote or spoke of their experience of the exhibition. To consider how each exhibition was implicated in this process, we need to further discuss the implications of exhibitions that provoke an unspecified affective intensity experienced by at least some visitors as demand internalized as a desire to write public comments about their experience of that exhibition.[35] As mentioned earlier in the chapter, in writing a comment, the writer is assuming a position accounting for oneself as someone addressed, subjected, and affected by the exhibition and the issues it raises. As I have argued, this is as an opportunity to publicly record the substance of one's nonindifference to what one has just seen. Regardless of the different forms and individual psychodynamics through which this performance of nonindifference is acted out, comment writers are proceeding from within a need to publicly express an aspect of what they are feeling and thinking as a result of seeing the exhibition. In this respect, in various ways, many writers recognize the images as having an affective force that implicates writers in questions of one's social affinities, identifications, and future commitments. This extends to expressing not only how these thoughts and feelings impact on prior held conceptions of race in America but, as well, provoked by the demand to face a violent past, to consider what possible actions one might take in the future. However, if this is so, we still need to consider how the differing exhibition frameworks for presenting photographs from the Allen and Littlefield Collection were implicated in the substance of this process.

I want to initiate this aspect of the discussion in dialogue with Jacqueline Goldsby's speculations on why archival lynching photographs are so hard to look at today. Goldsby makes the point that the relation between the common and unique is most palpable in death.[36] In principle, the constructed representations of lynching should then be capable of turning our attention to the relation between the universal and the particular, the presumed and the unknown, and the unimaginable and the image. In properly doing so, they would instantiate the family and communal loss resulting from the murder of specific individuals as well as yield evidence that specifies "how the violence was particularly directed against African Americans . . . [and] why the practice perfected the aims of white supremacy" (230). However, Goldsby suggests that when lynching is represented in the medium of photography, it fetishizes such violence and makes it easier to disavow. This is because photography transforms the violence of lynching into a spectacle that paradoxically proves "impossible either to ignore or see" (229). To unravel this paradox she suggests the representational containment of the photographic image together with its public repetition leads to thinking that "since there were so many lynchings, often carried out in the same general locale and in the same way (or so we presume), there are no unknown 'sovereign contingencies' that we need to identify. There are no 'absolute particulars'[37] that still require definition and analysis [and hence] no existential questions that are worth raising about the deaths of African American people" (229). On such terms, terms instituted in the lynching photograph's spectacularization of death, Goldsby argues that the dead are figured as

> signs of pure abjection who radiate no thought, no speech, no action, no will; who, through their appearance in the picture's field of vision, become invisible. Failing to restore positive bonds between the viewer and the dead, lynching photographs do not as a rule seek to summon the dead back to an imagined life. Rather, a particular kind of "scopic aggression" rages in lynching [end of p. 231] photographs, thwarting any such sympathetic identification between the viewer and the black (dead) subject. . . . By purposefully seeking not to distinguish African American victims of mob violence as particular individuals, scopically aggressive lynching photographs figure black victims of white mob violence as emblems of modernity, or indistinct parts of an interchangeable mass. (231–32)

As she notes, by "[c]ongealing and concealing the labour that goes into the work of killing black people, the photograph figures the violence as a sight to be looked at instead of the choices and acts that the murder actually involved" (279). This in essence is a way of looking but not seeing the deaths of black people. Rather, Goldsby suggests that the scopically aggressive image "acts on us with a kind of awesome power" that compels attention and yet wills viewers into a collective silence (279).

Goldsby's position is particularly apt in relation to her analysis of the cultural logic of lynching photographs at the turn of the nineteenth century, a logic that was particularly evident the modes of their production and circulation. However, it would seem appropriate to temper this analysis somewhat in relation to the appearance of lynching photographs in the form of more recent exhibitions.[38] While the scopic aggressivity of a lynching photograph might both strip black people murdered by mobs of the sense they were, as Goldsby suggests, "fully sentient, visible subjects, whose suffering was worthy to look at and mourn" (246) and probe their bodies in complicity with the mob's power, it is possible to view the exhibition frameworks through which these photographs were exhibited at the Andy Warhol Museum and Chicago Historical Society as attempts to divert and constrain this scopic aggression. Certainly in chapters 2 and 3 we have seen that the curatorial premise behind the logic that framed the Chicago Historical Society exhibition was precisely the attempt to individuate those killed by lynch mobs while rendering an understanding of this violence as particularly directed toward African Americans and a quite specific enactment of the aims of white supremacy. Indeed, the pattern of comments written at the Chicago Historical Society runs quite counter to Berger's argument above that images of violence become evidence of the general human condition and hence accuse nobody and everybody. It seems clear that the exhibition at the Chicago Historical Society was founded on the attempt to relate the common and unique in the Allen and Littlefield collection of photographs, constituting each death rendered as what Goldsby terms "epistemologically discrete," thus "deflecting a standardization of death that confuses and conflates" (216). Certainly it might be argued that the Andy Warhol Museum exhibition (given its lack of contextual information) was complicit with a certain degree of scopic aggression. However, another way of constraining such effect is to offer a space for viewing images wherein one can position oneself so that one's own relation to the rendered scene can be marked and accounted for. When this occurs, one would be reminded that what one is seeing is a murder witnessed and recorded and as a consequence one is now participating in the function and fruits of that labor. This self-reflexivity is the space of a critical contemplation and discussion intended to shift thought to take the measure of an image-event that continues to constitute the appearance of these photographs in our own time. This is a movement of witnessing beyond the actual circumstances in which an event took place that seeks to coax a responsibility for determining the significance of the reappearance of such images within one's own space-time.[39] Specific material elements of an exhibition can enhance the potential for such shifts. Hence the importance of the following comment from the Andy Warhol Museum, in which the framing, lighting, and angle of viewing are implicated in a reflexive turn.

> You walk through, and become numb. The bodies become dummies hanging from trees. And then you catch your own reflection in the glass of the frame. It's going to take longer than I thought to reconcile the two. These people were just as real as I am. I know that. It is just so overwhelming that I don't feel it yet. But somehow that's ok, because I know I am closer today than I was before. Thank you for that—November 17th, 2001. (Andy Warhol Museum)

A different example also comes from the Warhol and illustrates that for this museum visitor the exhibition was definitely more than the opportunity to view the Allen and Littlefield photographs, but rather to engage the entire configuration of text and image presented in the exhibition, including those comments spoken and written by other viewers.

> I keep looking for ways to learn about culture/diversity. The more I learn the more I realize that as a white female I may never truly understand what it means to be black—from discussions that I've had [in the Museum dialogue forum] and reading responses in this [comment] book I realized how much race can impact someone on a day to day basis. Growing up I never thought about this—I took it for granted that I have never been pulled over for no reason, or gone into a neighborhood and someone immediately thought that I might steal something or maybe be selling drugs—Is it my "white privilege" that allows me to escape this? Today I have seen physical

> evidence of racism. I am determined to keep trying to understand the implications for today. I know it hasn't gone away—I can learn to intellectualize culture/diversity/race but will never directly experience what it is like to be an individual living in America who happens to have darker skin and a different type of hair. 11/17. (Andy Warhol Museum)

There is a danger in privileging comments like this in pointing to how the Warhol exhibition managed to provoke comments with a reflexive turn. The risk is falling victim to one's own good performance allowing the photographs seen, to become about us (our shame, our sadness). As previously mentioned, this danger is especially fraught to the degree that such comments move one's attention away from the systemic history of racism in American and what reparations such a historical record warrants. Nevertheless, the above response does show how elements of the exhibition itself were implicated in moving beyond the stupefaction that can be elicited by the viewing of an amassed series of images of unimaginable violence. Yet if we are to fully understand the character of the conversations emergent in the visitor responses to each exhibition and how these were impacted by the form each exhibition took, we still need to come to grips with what I sense is a deep structural anxiety embodied in the visitor comments taken as a whole. This is an anxiety that must be reckoned with if one is to understand what was emotionally and politically at stake as a consequence of the cumulative entries written in both comment books.

What is evident when reading through the entire set of comments written at the Chicago Historical Society and Warhol exhibitions is that the specter of an intractable racial difference haunts the public consideration of the facts and implications of the racial history depicted in the photographs.

Beyond categorizing and counting the various positions visitors took about the future of race in America, reading symptomatically across the diverse, divergent, and often contradictory samples of comments, both sets may be characterized as structurally "anxious conversations" that not only reflect contemporary perceptions and desires but whose expression is deepened and sharpened by attendance at the exhibitions in question. It must be emphasized that the anxiety in question here does not reside in the disquiet evident in any singular comment but rather is a property of the conversational structure that simultaneously makes evident the limits of one's agency to transform racial antagonisms and one's hope for doing just that. It is the structure of feeling present at that moment when a serious problem is admitted along with a felt uncertainty as to its resolution. This is, then, a conversational anxiety manifest in the simultaneous recognition of unbridgeable differences. These differences are rooted in historically legitimated feelings of suspicion and mistrust. Yet rather than a melancholic denial of racial difference,[40] there remains the hope for the transformation of social bonds so as to manifest new forms of transracial solidarity and cohesion. In other words, this *structural* conversational anxiety is symptomatic of instability of sociality across racial lines, one whose emotional intensity at any point in time may (through relations of transference) be imbricated in personal anxieties associated with the loss of intersubjective security.

What seems to underlie the various contradictory views expressed in the totality of the comments considered in this comparative study is the concern that there is a seeming unending, fractious racial divide that runs counter to the radical hope for a society founded on different terms. While many comments in both samples express the idea that society has progressed so that the era of systemic racial violence had passed, others were equally adamant that there were present forms of racial violence that were a continuation, albeit in a different form, of a persistent white supremacist society. As well, while some comments stressed the importance of affirming one's racial identity and/or the impossibility of achieving understanding of a racial Other's experiences, other comments fervently affirmed the possibility of the oneness of humanity as not only desirable but achievable both through love and struggle. In his deeply influential *Black Skin, White Masks,* Frantz Fanon suggests that the reified, Manichaean relationships between black and white that make up so much of our broken world are resolvable only alongside the anxiety that constitutes and determines such relationships.[41] This anxiety he sees as an expression of dissatisfaction born out of the protracted economy of self and other that views black and white as perpetually ranged against each other. It is this anxiety that pervades the publicness of space formed among the visitor comments studied; it is an anxiety lying in the relations formed through what various visitors expressed responding to their experience of the exhibition. On such terms, multiple, heterogeneous participation in the public spaces convened by the *Without Sanctuary* exhibitions confirmed the persistence of this anxiety, standing simultaneously as evidence of the interminable character of racial division and necessity for its transformation. This goes to the heart of the paradoxical problem that accompanied both exhibitions, how to address a history of deadly enmity that has put into place deep feelings of racialized suspicion and mistrust so that such feelings, rather than simply being reproduced, are transformed in the service of a progressive civic culture.

Each in its own way, the Warhol and Chicago Historical Society exhibitions provided knowledge and acknowledgment of a central, but now occluded part of American history. In publicly surfacing this history, both exhibitions may have elicited a contemporary anxiety rooted in the possibility that the racial distrust endemic to the United States may be unresolvable. If this is the case, the criticism that the exhibitions replayed (and hence reinforced) social conflicts might indeed have some warrant. Certainly, such concerns were stated in several instances of public commentary written about the exhibitions. Expressed was the worry that the exhibition would provoke a sadness and anger rooted in the pervasive recognition of the continuity of racial injustice and violence. Also voiced was the assertion that the public display and consequent emotional force of the exhibition of lynching photographs would dispel the desire to repress the long, violent history of racial conflict, although it was simultaneously recognized that continuing such repression would only guarantee this history remain unaddressed.

In his book *Racial Paranoia,* John L. Jackson Jr. explores what he terms the new reality of race in America, a form of "paranoia" that inevitably constrains the possibilities of cross-racial conversation due to an intuitive, unfalsifiable distrust of the Other's attention, motives, and interests.[42] If Jackson is correct in his diagnosis of racialized social life in the United States, the anxious conversations evident in the *Without Sanctuary* comment books might be understood as an extension of this paranoia, which sets up the paradoxical realization that "we don't want race to rule our lives, yet we can't seem to live together without obeying its calls" (20–21). This argument raises the question of how exhibitions intended to address ongoing societal concerns might be understood as convening public spaces and framing conversations in ways that either challenge or are complicit with contemporary discursive formations. In this respect, Richard Sandell's suggestion to think of exhibitions "as resources (among many others in the mediascape), which audiences can potentially dismiss or draw upon in their negotiations with, and interpretations of, cultural difference" is helpful (105). Thus, it would become important to ask after how the deployment of specific exhibitions either contests or complements existing discursive practices within a larger mediascape. In the following chapter, I consider the Andy Warhol Museum and Chicago Historical Society exhibitions in the context of the other museum and gallery-based presentations that have offered perpetrator-produced visual evidence of brutal systemic violence. In context of this discussion, I will return to the question of the public pedagogies of exhibition practice and how we might understand the various ways such practices might contribute to the form, content, and heading of public discourse.

FIVE

Curatorial Judgment, the Pedagogical Framing of Exhibitions, and the Relation of Affect and Thought

Moving beyond a consideration of the *Without Sanctuary* exhibitions at the Andy Warhol Museum and the Chicago Historical Society, this chapter extends the discussion to other exhibition practices that have rendered into the contemporary moment perpetrator photographs that index historical events of deeply disturbing, systemic violence and its consequent suffering, degradation, and death. As will become apparent, this broadened discussion will further the case for how and why the particulars of a curatorial project matter in regard to what constitutes a pedagogy of public history. After some preliminary reframing and discussion of the differing exhibition practices traced in previous chapters, I consider two further sets of exhibitions. The first set includes the 1995 exhibition *Vernichtungskrieg: Verbrechen der Wehrmacht 1941–1944* (*War of Extermination: Crimes of the German Armed Forces 1941–1944*) and its subsequent "correction" in 2001, in the guise of a new exhibition entitled *Verbrechen der Wehrmacht: Dimensionen des Vernichtungskrieges 1941–1944* (*Crimes of the German Armed Forces: Dimensions of a War of Annihilation, 1941–1944*). Following this, I consider several exhibitions of the archival collection of photographs of prisoners held at the S-21 Khmer Rouge detention and torture center in Phnom Penh, Cambodia. The photographs exhibited were a selection of the thousands of images taken immediately upon arrival of each person detained at S-21, an event that was a prelude to torture and subsequent execution.

There are obvious and important differences among the archival sets of photographs that provide the basis for comparisons and contrasts developed in this chapter. Lynching photographs were sold by professional photographers to those at the scene, whereas the *Wehrmacht* photographs were private "trophy" photographs taken by soldiers during their service in the German army, and the S-21 photographs were taken as documentation by a venomous government police bureaucracy. Yet despite these differences, what these sets of photographs have in common is that they comprise collections of images taken by photographers in direct complicity with the violence they index. In bringing together a discussion of the various ways in which museums and galleries have staged exhibitions of these differing sets of perpetrator photographs, I will focus on how those responsible for presenting such exhibitions have attempted to reframe a selected set of images so that they function to contest the very purposes for which they were taken, purposes perhaps still resonant with certain aspects of contemporary life.[1]

To further develop what is at issue here I return to the pedagogical and ethical problems inherent in exhibiting perpetrator photographs that "traffic in pain"[2] so that visitors might bear witness to the actualities of suffering and brutality and, as a consequence, act to prevent the reoccurrence of similar violations. What is particularly significant about all such exhibitions is that they are public presentations of images of violence that cannot be singly reduced to their function as evidence of crimes. As discussed in chapter 1, in every case where an institution has justified the public display of the perpetration of violence, it is assumed that the images exhibited have a "force" that might effect some alteration in those who encounter them. Staff at the Andy Warhol Museum and the Chicago Historical Society recognized that their exhibitions of lynching photographs were not just a matter of displaying historical documents, but also of returning a presence potentially felt as a powerful form of heteronomy, compelling a response. This is a position quite different from one that assumes the photographic image "does not, and cannot, in and of itself implicate us in . . . relations necessary to sustain a moral and compassionate existence,"[3] given that in exposing suffering, the image functions to isolate us from actual suffering. On the contrary, it implies a meeting with another's pain and horror well beyond the trauma-inducing psychic shock that renders events as "unclaimed experience."[4] Both *Without Sanctuary* exhibitions attempted to create an experience that would ask something intimate of the self, something regarding the sustainability of one's prior attachments and the consequences of the fracture of meaning confronted in images of violence. As well, each exhibition solicited what Gerald Bruns termed a degree of an "intimacy with the world,"[5] an intimacy enacted as a mode of dwelling within the relation of the past and present. Such an intimacy contains the possibility of an altered way of living with and learning from images and stories so as to critically engage a person's sense of limits and possibilities, hopes and fears, and identities and distinctions. Clearly, both forms of intimacy were central to the curatorial projects at the Andy Warhol Museum and Chicago Historical Society. As what was put on view in Pittsburgh and Chicago was intended to provoke something other than the experience of watching suffering at a distance, this brought a pedagogical seriousness to the curatorial task. This seriousness rejected the dismissive assertion that questions of pedagogy were irrelevant to the development of exhibitions since viewer responses were like cards drawn randomly from a deck, it being totally unpredictable as to what card will turn up.[6] While recognizing that the content and structure of exhibitions never overdetermine the responses of those who engage them, the curatorial projects at the Andy Warhol Museum and Chicago Historical Society presupposed that the power of an exhibition of particular images to move us depends on more than what various viewers bring to their encounters with these images.

Recall that in justifying presenting the exhibition at the Chicago Historical Society, the former director explained that his intent was not to "embarrass, cause pain, or be unpatriotic" but rather to recognize that these "shocking, unimaginable images reveal much about the terror and lawlessness that shaped race relations in America in the 19th and 20th centuries. They *force us* [my emphasis] to confront a shameful part of our history, a part many of us would rather forget."[7] Throughout this book, I have been exploring the question of how curatorial practice might conceive of this *force* and work to influence the movement and direction of its consequences. In posing this question, I am not simply entering the terrain of the affective agency of the photographic image (particularly images of pain, suffering, and death). More specifically, my concern is with how one might understand the way the mise-en-scène of an exhibition is implicated in the mobilization of the force of an image as well as its trace within its consequent trajectories. Thus, my interest is not the photographic image in and of itself, but how it might work dialectically within the design and substance of the milieu in which it appears. One possibility for framing such a consideration is to begin to think through the implications for curatorial practice of what it might mean that photographs were felt by visitors as a "shock to thought."[8] Arguing that the presentation of lynching photographs initiates a force to thought of course guarantees nothing. Yet given that an exhibition is constituted as a material social practice, it is still important to ask on what terms might such a shock be conceived as a force that compels thought rather than a traumatic disruption that leads to the extended abandonment of thought. Certainly, there is the possibility of a split between being affected by an image and being able to think and therefore comprehend what it is that one is seeing. It has become commonplace to describe "atrocity" photographs as arresting and immobilizing, as pressing thinking up against its limits encountered in images of suffering and death.[9] On such terms, one might say that the exhibitions of lynching photographs that I have been considering present images that ruin thought and leave one in a state of disillusionment and despair as to "what humans are capable of doing—indeed volunteer to do, enthusiastically, self righteously."[10] There is much in the previous chapter to indicate that visitors registered such affects. Yet as I have shown, this is hardly an adequate account of the complex visitor responses provoked by the *Without Sanctuary* exhibitions. While the affective force of images of suffering and death can be immobilizing, we need to hold open the question as to how the mise-en-scène of an exhibition might support and structure the movement of this affect into thought regarding the implications of the witness one bears. Given the antiracist pedagogical investments of the institutions that have presented exhibitions of lynching photographs, museum staff members were very much concerned to discipline the force of these images. Of particular concern was the containment of the reproduction of frameworks of racial superiority, and in a very different vein, feelings of shame and despair that while instancing moral norms,[11] would abort the thought necessary to a witnessing that might alter the continued existence of what it witnesses.

To further the exploration of how an exhibition might be implicated in the movement of affect into and through thought, I turn briefly to the Greek myth of Medusa and consider what of this narrative might be related to an encounter with a mise-en-scène incorporating photographic images of disfigurement and death. Medusa was the monstrous Gorgon whose visage, if looked at directly, was capable of turning one to stone. When Athena instigated Perseus to kill Medusa, she warned him not to look at her face directly, but only as it appeared as a reflected image in a polished shield. Following this advice, Perseus was able to cut off Medusa's head. Siegfried Kracauer insightfully linked film and photography (the modern technology of image production) to Perseus's shield.[12] On the terms of Kracauer's insight, the lynching photographs I have been discussing are analogous to images reflected in Perseus's shield. They are Medusean images that allow us to know something of the horror of racial violence without having to confront its immediate presence, an experience that would be too overwhelming, figuratively turning one to stone. This argument would have photographs understood as weakened reproductions, substitutions for what they resemble. This means that while they are useful as documentation that would facilitate a confrontation with systemic racial violence, one need not make too much of the force of these photographs, for after all they are "only images." However, such a formulation vastly underplays the gain in force that these images accrue when the mise-en-scène of their appearance encourages us to take them as something more than photographic reproductions of all too real events. How then might one account for this increase in the "dynamis of the image"[13] when it is encountered as an integral aspect of an exhibition mise-en-scène?

Let's start with Mieke Bal's rather obvious point (often forgotten in much writing on visual culture), that visual images are not autonomous objects that travel through space and time in selfsame identity.[14] Clearly, the particular circumstances for viewing any given set of photographs offer very different purposes for their contemporary presentation, hence altering their significance. As this significance is defined through contingent, socially situated processes of meaning making, an image must be understood as essentially connected to an event of its appearance, an event that always occurs in the world. To grasp the full implication of this position, let me return for a moment to Kracauer's invocation of the myth of Medusa. In a commentary on Kracauer's text, Georges Didi-Huberman suggested that the horror reflected in images appearing by means of Perseus's shield might yet be a wellspring of knowledge on the condition that they are explicitly encountered through what he called a "*dispositif*" of image production.[15] To translate *dispositif* as simply "apparatus" or "mechanism," as Shane Lillis has done in the English edition of Didi-Huberman's book, misses the rich set of references associated with this French idiom.[16] Most often connected with Michel Foucault's writing on governmentality, but also elaborated on by Gilles Deleuze and Giorgio Agamben,[17] a *dispositif* is a term set in the context of theories of subjectification. It refers to a specific complex of discourses, material practices, and institutions that orient, enable, but also constrain and limit particular ways of rendering a sensate world comprehendible and hence structuring consequent thinking, speaking, and acting. If we read Didi-Huberman's use of the word *dispositif* on these terms, exhibitions of photographs of suffering and death do not simply pacify the horror of reality or present immobilizing, shocking images. Rather, within such exhibitions, the force to thought lies within the substance of any given set of material discursive and social practices that define the mise-en-scène within and through which images not only reveal and occlude the atrocities they document, but as well, the gaze within which they are recorded. It is the articulation of the exhibition mise-en-scène through a specific *dispositif* that defines the notion of curatorial practice that has framed the discussion in this book. On such terms, curatorial practice is inherently pedagogical, with much of the substance of the pedagogy at work in any given exhibition determined by the exercise of the curatorial judgment that establishes a mise-en-scène.

To repeat an earlier assertion, beyond the presentation of historical documentation, the differing mise-en-scènes presenting lynching photographs were attempts to summon a spectral presence through the re-presentation of a disfigured singularity subjected to the violent hands of those pictured as celebrants at the scene of death. The force mobilized by these images cannot just be traced to the scandal of these racialized scenes of death. As I argued in chapter 2, the *Without Sanctuary* exhibitions rendered not just the immediacy of spectral presence, but in Nancy's words, "that which draws presence out of this immediacy insofar as it puts a value on presence *as* some presence or another."[18] The gain in force of the image within the *Without Sanctuary* exhibitions was not just that accrued in the recognition of unjustly inflicted suffering, but included that felt when visitors are exposed to images of a *particular someone* undergoing degradation and pain. While I have shown that this exposure was accomplished in various ways at the Andy Warhol Museum and the Chicago Historical Society, it is still important to consider two related root ideas shared by the different curatorial projects carried out at these institutions The first of these is the notion that images have the capacity to touch viewers who feel rather than simply see the events depicted. The second is that the force of an image has less to do with the experience of seeing something in it than the feeling that, in looking at an image (even when alone), one experiences a sense of being seen.

On the terms of these two root ideas, a photographic image of a lynching has the potential to register more than it denotes. This *more* is not just that of a felt loss (of a life, of the adequacy of a known history, of a trust in uprightness of the nation), but includes an uninvited (perhaps even unwelcomed), felt responsibility that one cannot remain indifferent when faced with the pain of another.[19] This notion is an acknowledgment that the pain and suffering depicted in images of lynchings is a part of one's world, just as much as it is a part of the past indexed by the image. On such terms, the response to images of suffering is not dependent on the dynamics of identification with people now dead. Rather, this response exists at that moment when the rendition of the disfigurement of another is felt bodily as a deep disturbing anxiety (sometimes reflexively signaled through an uncontrollable wince or cringe).[20] Such an argument implies that images work on an affective plane not just within coherent formations of signification. Brian Massumi has argued that images need to be understood as "the conveyors of forces of emergence; as vehicles for existential potentialization and transfer."[21] Justus Nieland helps to clarify Massumi's assertion. Nieland reads Massumi as distinguishing between "two levels of reception of every 'image-event'—discursive qualification and affective intensity. The former entails a conscious, sociolinguistic, and in many cases ideological fixing of an image-event; the latter marks the unconscious, sensual register of the image-event's phenomenological force."[22] It is this force that Deleuze and Guattari call "affect."[23] An unqualified sensory intensity that is felt straight away, affect is not always immediately nameable or understandable. This means that affect operates prior to the conscious articulation of specific emotions. The potential of such sensory intensity is its ability to place a disruptive claim on viewers and provoke the possibilities of new thought without guarantees as to its substance and movement. Thus, the affective force brought forth in the violent images of lynching does not simply interpellate the already morally predisposed viewer as a particular kind of subject (expressing horror at the act of racial violence, sympathy for the victims, outrage for its perpetrators, and shame that a world exists where such events are possible). Rather, within this force, a claim is made on a viewer to acknowledge the pain of another *and* begin to come to terms with the felt presence of that pain in the present. In other words, this is a force to thought not as form of contemplation about the world, but in regard to one's actions in the world given the transactive presence of the pain of others. This is a force to thought as to what is required in order to live one's life as if the lives of other people mattered.

To further grasp what is at stake in the design and development of a mise-en-scène that might include an affective force that could compel thought and why we need to consider this as a necessary component of a critical public history, consider what was likely one of the first public exhibitions of lynching photography in America. This event took place on the streets of Seattle on a Sunday afternoon in 1893. Jacqueline Goldsby offers this account of Samuel Burdett, who was a forty-four-year-old black veterinarian active in local politics and African American organizations, in her book *A Spectacular Secret: Lynching in American Life and Literature*:

> Samuel Burdett [was] "whiling away an hour seeing the sights" in the city he called home [when he] came upon a crowd "that was attending to some sort of entertainment." "Curious," he approached the group, threading his way to the front "where a man was mounted on a stand or platform of some sort." At the center of the circle, Burdett clearly saw that the attraction was . . . a carefully planned display of the newest technology America had to offer. . . . An exhibit "for civilized citizens to enjoy according to their individual relish for the awful—for the horrible," Burdett recalled in anguish, the presentation "consisted of photographic views, coupled with phonographic records of the utterances of a Negro who had been burned to death in Paris, Texas a short time before." Mounted on easels and placed in chronological order, the photographs tracked the Paris lynching from the discovery of Myrtle Vance's corpse to the capture, torture, and cremation of Henry Smith [Smith had been accused of raping and murdering the young child Myrtle Vance]. Adjacent to these images was a gramophone

> with several listening devices—what we would today recognize as headsets.[24]

Listeners could hear a recording of the confrontation between the dead child's father and the child's alleged assailant [Smith], as well as Smith's response to the torture imposed upon him and the responses of the large crowd who had chosen to witness all of this firsthand. Intrigued by this remarkable, totally new combination of sight and sound, Burdett "'like others who where there' on that street corner in Seattle . . . 'took up the tubes of the phonographic instrument and placed them to [his] ears'" (Goldsby, 14). Horrified by both what he saw and heard and the very public street scene of such a display, years later in the context of his anti-lynching writing Burdett struggled with the words to express an experience that was profoundly unnerving.

At the very least, the contrast between the scene described by Burdett and the previously cited curatorial project offered by the former director of the Chicago Historical Society graphically underscores that the frame of analysis for the discussion of the practice of exhibiting souvenir photographs of racist violence cannot be the unconfined photograph alone but rather must center on the event that constitutes a specific practice of photographic exhibition. The exhibition mise-en-scène described by Burdett clearly indicates that the particular contexts for viewing any given set of lynching photographs may offer very different purposes for their public presentation, hence altering the significance of the photographs as a social sign. But Burdett's account also indicates that it is not just the denotative and connotative aspects of the photograph that are altered by its rendition within a given visual event; altered as well is its affective force. The Seattle exhibition rendering the lynching of Henry Smith throws into relief the spectral character of the absence in the photographs that were on display, supplementing them with recorded sounds in attempt to fill in what remained hollowed out in the image. The sounds integral to this event attempted to draw the viewer nearer to what the photographs alone could not show. This attempt approaches Jean-Luc Nancy's notion of "super-representation," a regime of rendition in which what is aspired toward is the exposure of a world without fissure, without withdrawn invisibility, that can be placed right before one's eyes.[25] In super-representation, its object is "completed within what is manifestly present" (39). In such a regime, the image actually gives out an affective force that exhausts itself either in spectacle of the image and/or the trauma of its blow with the consequence that there is little provocation to thought. That is, in a visual event constituted as a super-representation, the encounter with images is clearly traumatic and as such is unable to be processed as experience. There is no impetus to meaning other than the conformity of the world to its awful representation.

The *Without Sanctuary* exhibitions at the Andy Warhol Museum and the Chicago Historical Society obviously presented images on very different terms. The curatorial projects at each institution required a consideration of not just the inherent inadequacy of photographs as representations of pain, but, crucially, the way an exhibition could take such visual limits into account. Exposed through the presence rendered in the exhibitions of lynching images at the Chicago Historical Society and the Warhol was a revelation that, in revealing, withdrew what it revealed.[26] Within the photographic image, suffering was transactively revealed and withdrawn at the same time. Thus, what was taken into account was a "hollowness" at the heart of such a presence rendered through the lynching photographs (Nancy, 38). This hollowness resulted in an occlusion of what happened that was at the same time an acknowledgment of an unimaginable horror *and* an opening to thought. This opening is not just a matter of the incomplete understanding one has as to what happened before, during, and after the murder of those photographed, but is also a consequence of the affective force of what Emmanuel Levinas calls the demand of the face felt in the hallowness of an image.[27]

Gilles Deleuze has urged us "not [to] count upon thought to ensure the relative necessity of what it thinks," but rather to count upon the contingency that "something in the world forces us to think. This something is an object not of recognition but of a fundamental encounter."[28] For those viewers who arrived at the *Without Sanctuary* exhibitions thinking that the answer to the question of what the photographs show is entirely known in advance, their viewing remained a relatively sterile ritual wherein one looks at a photograph without encountering its image (and hence is not seen by it). The challenge in viewing an exhibition of images from the Allen and Littlefield collection is to discover not simply what it is one already knows, but rather that which one has yet to know, and must yet know. Arguably, the curatorial frame for any such exhibition must attempt to facilitate meeting this challenge in order to avoid rendering lynching photographs as a spectacle of violence or simply a grotesque synecdoche that reminds viewers of where notions of racial superiority can lead.

In absolute contrast to the Seattle street exhibit, the exhibitions at the Andy Warhol Museum and Chicago Historical Society were image events that contained their own "forbidding," that were subjects of their own retreat. Rather than exhibitions intended to provide access to the past, each exhibition in its own way attempted to couple affect and thought while endeavoring to restrict the indeterminacy of this relationship within the terms offered through specific exhibition mise-en-scène. As discussed in chapter 2, at the Chicago Historical Society the force of the images was restrained (but not finally contained) by extensive text offering both a historical narrative of the rise of lynching in America and a series of short texts that rendered intelligible the individual stories of racial violence. This sizeable quantity of text made it possible to read one's way through the exhibition enabling visitors to both look and look away at the same time. However, at the Chicago Historical Society the risk was that the photographic images would be reduced to illustrations of the given historical narrative directing the affective force of the images to an undialectical memorialization of those subjected to a tragic injustice. Arguably, at the Andy Warhol Museum the affective force of the images of lynching was heightened by the minimal historical context provided.[29] Standing in the gallery at the Warhol, it was much more difficult to look and look away. Yet it was quite clear that much work was done to restrain the indeterminacy of the affect provoked by these images, directing such sensations into affirmations of the struggle against racial discrimination. Inadvertently perhaps, this produced the risk that enjoining individuals to virtuous behavior might result in an undialectical looking away from the singular photographs of lynching, focusing instead on the personal actions one might take to fight racism. The possible unanticipated consequence of this would then be a short-circuiting of the thought provoked by an attention to "the way of seeing" offered in the photographs. The photographs of lynching from the Allen and Littlefield collection are not only documents of events that have happened in a certain place and time, but also bear witness to modes of encountering the world that are deeply problematic. While these archival photographs may seem to offer a practice of looking that appears foreign or even unimaginable, what is worth considering is whether they are more closely related to "ordinary," contemporary positions of engagement than their contents seem to suggest. Mobilized differently, the affect-thought coupling consequent with viewing the lynching photographs might otherwise consider how such "inconceivable" ways of seeing resonate with modes of perception complicit with the foundational relations responsible for much of the present-day problems of racial inequality.

The above considerations demonstrate why critical thought about curatorial practice must become central to those invested in the exhibition as a practice of cultural pedagogy. It is curatorial practice that sets the terms for framing various possible relations between affect and thought. If the sensory intensity initiated by the experienced image (experienced in the event-bound act of looking) is to be reflectively attended to by the one who looks, how this intensity is brought into consciousness, how it is named, understood, and assessed as to its significance has much to do with the curatorial projects that have concretely composed and therefore framed the image-event itself.

TWO EXHIBITIONS ADDRESSING THE CRIMES OF THE GERMAN ARMED FORCES DURING WORLD WAR II

The argument above can be extended to other exhibition comparisons. Consider how the two risks articulated above in relation to the differing exhibition of lynching photographs can be further discussed in the relation to two recent exhibitions presented by the Hamburg Institute for Social Research. The first of these, *Vernichtungskrieg: Verbrechen der Wehrmacht 1941–1944* (*War of Extermination: Crimes of the German Armed Forces 1941–1944*), opened in Hamburg in 1995 and subsequently appeared in thirty-three cities in Germany and Austria until, in response to controversy, it was suspended in 1999. Based on archival photographs not previously shown in public, the exhibition presented evidence of extensive war crimes committed by ordinary German soldiers serving on the Eastern Front during World War II. The intention of the Institute for Social Research was to confront the treasured image of the German army as fighting a difficult war, but one guided by military—and not racist and inhumane—principles. For this reason, the exhibition offered many images that documented an army that was complicit, and often an active agent, in a program of extermination. While the exhibition gave rise to an extremely intense national controversy, my concern here is not the controversy itself and the larger question of postwar German memory, but the exhibition's particular use of photography. This first exhibition employed more than fourteen hundred photographs, many taken as personal mementoes. In a substantial number of these photographs, soldiers and their comrades were present in the images—laughing, triumphant, or businesslike and cold while fulfilling acts of humiliation, incarceration, and murder. The most controversial curatorial decision in regard to the display of these photographs was to place a large number of them in thematic groupings without labels for individual images. These groupings were labeled by the activities depicted in the photographs making up each group, for example: tormenting Jews, the operation of gallows, shooting operations, deportations, etc. Some of these photographs were placed on curved display walls whose negative space defined a large Iron Cross (the medal for bravery and honor awarded to German soldiers since 1813). The use of photographs in the exhibition can be seen as intending "to 'block the work of forgetting' and 'immortalize [the] death[s]' caused by the *Wehrmacht*'s extensive involvement in the Nazi war of annihilation."[30]

Bernd Hüppauf has argued that the visual power of the images in this Institute for Social Research exhibition greatly contributed to a process that was changing the German collective memory of World War II: "freeing its history from the isolation and disciplinary constraints of conventional historiography given a new concern with images, especially the photographic image."[31] But it was just on these terms that the exhibition was accused of irresponsibly creating the general impression that all German soldiers had been criminals. The controversy that ultimately led the Institute for Social Research to suspend the exhibition was centered on charges that the exhibit misrepresented (or as some suspected, even fabricated) the photographs on view. This charge crystallized in regard to a small number of photographs wherein the death of those murdered were incorrectly attributed to Germany army personnel given other evidence that these murders had been done by the Soviet Secret Police. While these accusations were directed at a very small number of the images, the public controversy engendered threw into question the credibility of the entire exhibit (and its sponsoring institution). Under these circumstances, Institute for Social Research Director Jan Phillip Reemtsma suspended the exhibition and appointed an independent commission to assess what errors (if any) had been committed in its production. While the commission absolved the exhibit organizers of forgery, they did criticize the exhibition for its intellectual sloppiness and lack of historical rigor. Faced with this report, Reemtsma ordered the exhibition redone. A new curatorial team was appointed and subsequently in 2001 a completely new exhibition opened entitled *Verbrechen der Wehrmacht. Dimensionen des Vernichtungskrieges 1941–1944* (*Crimes of the German Armed Forces: Dimensions of a War of Annihilation, 1941–1944*).

Taking up twice the space as the previous one, the new exhibition contained considerably more text but only four hundred and fifty photographs. Gone was the use of the Iron Cross as a display space; utilized instead were a large number of individualized glass booths presenting documents and text. Within the revised exhibition logic, the photographs presented functioned primarily as denotative illustrations of the principal message supplied by text. Only 10 percent of the photographs that appeared in the first exhibition were present in the second and all photographs were individually labeled and accompanied by a large amount of contextual information—mostly in the form of written documents. The smaller role ascribed to photography was a result of a more rigorous historiography that required extensive cross-checking in regard to identifying the content of any given image as well as the desire of the new curators to provide contextual information for all the photographs shown. A further shift in emphasis occurred so that the new set of documents and text presented narrowed the focus of criminality primarily to German officers, rather than all soldiers.

Both Institute for Social Research exhibitions argued that the *Wehrmacht* was involved as an organization in the crimes perpetrated in the course of the war on the Eastern Front and that the war itself, taken as a whole, was criminal. However, it is obvious that they did this in very different ways. Reemtsma has argued that the photographs in the first exhibition accomplished a great deal. Shortly after the first exhibition opened, he acknowledged "that the exhibition makes an appeal to emotions [and that] it was organized . . . with the intention both to document atrocities committed by the German army and to create feelings of consternation and bewilderment."[32] Much later, after the second exhibition had concluded, reflecting on the entire experience of presenting the two exhibitions, Reemtsma wrote that although the first exhibition showed much of the reality of the war of annihilation, forcing people to think and ask questions (about perpetrators and witnesses, about those who photographed what they saw), ultimately this exhibition could not answer the questions that were being asked. While implicitly acknowledging the affective force to thought of the first exhibition, Reemstma concluded that this force was problematic given that the exhibition could not properly channel the thinking it helped initiate. In his reflections on exhibition design, written in 2004, he noted that visitors were left alone with their queries, "since the first exhibition did not anticipate the extent to which photographs would be taken as a representation of complex realities, rather than as isolated segments of reality in need of interpretation."[33] In other words, in his view, the affective force of images of atrocities had yet to be contained by the demands of proper historiography. It is not surprising therefore that Reemtsma concluded that the second exhibition "took up the problem the first exhibit initiated and rectified it as far as possible" (12). Responding to the criticism that the second exhibition was tantamount to a "walk-in book," he wrote: "Is that really an objection? The only question is whether the book has, in fact, been walked into and read" (13).

What Reemtsma's remarks convey is that the redeployment of photographs within the exhibition logic of the second exhibit involved more than ensuring that the images shown could reliably be offered as documentary evidence in support of a particular historical narrative. As well, in the service of producing an exhibit as a historiographic argument, one that was as clear and well documented as possible, the redeployment of photographs was seen as a necessary attempt to contain the force inherent in the indeterminate affective legacy of the souvenir atrocity photographs. Given the intent of the second Institute for Social Research exhibit, this need not necessarily be construed as a problem. However, as at the Chicago Historical Society and Andy Warhol Museum exhibitions of the *Without Sanctuary* photographs, the Institute for Social Research strategy was not without its risks. As Hüppauf and others have helped us understand, one of the risks of the second Institute for Social Research exhibition was the fading of photographs into historiography. In such a circumstance, images are to be read as documentary evidence of criminal actions taken by the German army, forgetting the conditions facilitating the *dispositif* through which the photographs were first produced and shown to family and friends. There is little question that the second Institute for Social Research exhibition did its best to minimize not just the horror of the atrocities depicted but as well the horror of the gaze through which they were recorded and first seen.

Whether in the context of the public rendition of photographs of atrocities committed by the German army on the Eastern Front or of photographs of atrocities committed by white racist mobs in the United States, to reiterate an earlier point, when public history is practiced through such forms of visual pedagogy, it is crucial to consider not only what a photograph means, but as well, what the public presentation of a photograph may do. This requires not only a rigorous historiographic method for the treatment of photographs as documents, but a way of thinking that grasps how the visual perlocution performed by a display of photographs is structured by practices of exhibition through which their images come into view.

EXHIBITING PHOTOGRAPHS FROM S-21

To extend the reach of this argument a bit farther, let us now consider some of the various differing exhibitions of' "identity photographs"[34] of people arrested and taken to Tuol Sleng, the Cambodian Khmer Rouge detention and torture center that operated during the years 1975–79. Initiated by the regime headed by Pol Pot, the Cambodian Khmer Rouge revolution was a brutal, bloody attempt at radical social reform during which, out of a population of 7.2 million, at least one million people died. Located on the site of a former high school in a borough of Phnom Penh, "S-21" (as the Khmer Rouge referred to it) was an example of the paranoid fanaticism that fueled the excesses of the Pol Pot regime. The thousands of people brought to S-21 were charged with being enemies of the revolution and on arrival were tortured and forced to confess their crimes of disloyalty. If not killed on site, the vast majority of the men, women, and children brought to this torture center were subsequently taken to one of the Khmer Rouge killing fields and executed. It is estimated that between fourteen and twenty thousand people were imprisoned at S-21 in the four years 1975–79, very few of whom are known to have survived. For the sake of the regime's police bureaucracy, all prisoners were photographed as soon as they arrived.[35] As explained below, selections of these photographs have been widely circulated outside of Cambodia both in the form of a book publication and numerous public exhibitions of the images.

The archive from which these exhibitions of photographs have been drawn was established soon after the Vietnamese entered Phnom Penh in 1979. It was then that the Vietnamese army discovered the bloody walls of Tuol Sleng and evidence of its operation of a detention and torture center, including more than six thousand negatives of identity photographs taken of prisoners who had been killed subsequent to their arrival at the site. After this discovery, the Vietnamese decided that the buildings of the former high school should be converted into a genocide museum. No doubt this effort to expose the violent excesses of the Pol Pot regime was, at least in part, motivated by the desire to justify the Vietnamese assumption of power in Cambodia under the terms of a new People's Republic of Kampuchea.[36] In the process of establishing the genocide museum, a portion of the recovered negatives of the identity photographs were cleaned, cataloged, printed, and then exhibited on site. In 1993, two American photographers, Chris Riley and Douglas Niven, visited the Museum of Genocide and were invited to assist in the work of the museum's documentation center, where documents were still being organized, catalogued, and microfilmed. In the context of this work, Riley and Niven found cabinets full of mildewed negatives, original negatives for many of the photographic prints on display in the museum. With the permission of the Cambodian government they set up a nonprofit organization, the Photo Archive Group, to raise money to clean, catalogue, and make contact prints of the recovered negatives, close to six thousand in all. In exchange for this work, Riley and Niven were granted the rights to one hundred images that were chosen for "photographic quality, historical value and to present an accurate cross-section of Tuol Sleng victims."[37] They were also given permission to print six sets, to produce a book of the images,[38] and to exhibit the photographs outside of Cambodia.[39] In this later respect, the Photo Archive group in collaboration with the Photographic Resource Center in Boston facilitated a large number of exhibitions at various venues in the United States, Canada, and Europe. These included public and private museums and galleries, photography festivals, and university settings. While the Photo Archive Group facilitated the traveling of the images, often enough decisions were made at local venues as to which photographs to show and/or in what manner the S-21 images would be exhibited. These differing curatorial judgments meant that there were important variations as to how the images were to be supplemented by text, additional images, objects, performances, and historical lectures and discussions.[40] It is precisely this variation that is my interest here, a variation well illustrated in the contrast between exhibitions held at the Museum of Modern Art and Boston's Photographic Resource Center.

From May 15 to September 30, 1997, the Museum of Modern Art presented an exhibition entitled *Photographs from S-21: 1975–1979.*[41] Displaying just twenty-two of the one hundred images available for exhibition outside of Cambodia, this was the first public exhibition of S-21 photographs in North America. Each photograph was enlarged and presented in ten by ten inch black frames with white matting hung equidistant from each other at eye level on three walls of Gallery Three, a modest space within the museum's extensive photography galleries. In the middle of the space chosen for the exhibition were two small sofas, with a coffee table between them on which was placed several copies of the book of S-21 photographs published by Riley and Niven, other publications displaying photography from the Museum of Modern Art's permanent collection, and a comment book for visitor responses. There were no labels accompanying individual prints. Thus, the individuals portrayed in each photograph were left unidentified and the photographer was listed as unknown. Introducing the exhibition were several brief wall texts outlining the Khmer Rouge's purpose in operating S-21, Niven and Riley's work in Cambodia in aid of preserving the photographic negatives, and the funding sources for the image preservation project and the exhibition itself. Also on the wall was a brief statement of the aim of Gallery Three, which the museum explained as "a place where visitors may pause to sit and reflect, and where Museum curators may share their enthusiasms for particular photographs, their thoughts about particular episodes in photography, and their explorations of the Museum's rich collection."[42]

In marked contrast to the presentation at the Museum of Modern Art, from September 19 to November 7, 1997, the Photographic Resource Center at Boston University presented a differently entitled exhibition *Facing Death: Portraits from Cambodia's Killing Fields.* This exhibition presented all one hundred images available for display. Most important to note about this exhibit is what was added to supplement to the photographs. This included a map, which located Cambodia in

Southeast Asia; a brochure providing basic historical and geographic information about the country; and a bibliography that one could use to learn more about the events of which the images were a part. The gallery also continuously ran a British Broadcasting Company documentary video on Riley and Niven's photo archive project that had been produced when the work of cleaning and cataloguing the negatives was underway in Phnom Penh. Not only did this video provide an explanation of the origin of the photographs and how they had been preserved, but it also offered a narrative explaining how the photographs came to be shown in North America. The video included interviews with people who had worked at S-21 under the Khmer Rouge as well as the recollections of people who had lost family members there. Furthermore, in the gallery in which the photographs were displayed, quotations from an S-21 interrogators' manual were enlarged and printed as wall text. Also on the wall was a reprint of a newspaper story about Nhem Ein, the S-21 photographer. In this story, Nhem Ein offered an explanation of how he came to be the one who took the images as well as an account of his experience working for the Khmer Rouge. Conjointly with the exhibition, the Photographic Resource Center also exhibited large-format platinum prints of Cambodia's Angkor temples built between the eleventh and thirteenth centuries. As these two exhibitions were in close physical proximity to each other, this allowed visitors to move from the S-21 identity photographs to the serenity of the temple photographs. It is also worth noting that, unlike the Museum of Modern Art, the Photographic Resource Center contacted Cambodian community organizations in the greater Boston area to invite them to the show.

This comparison of the Museum of Modern Art and Photographic Resource Center exhibitions of the S-21 photographs is vivid illustration of the considerable variation in how the images have been supplemented by text, additional images, and objects. Much like the various *Without Sanctuary* and *Crimes of the Wehrmacht* exhibitions, the contrasting S-21 exhibitions offer much to think about as to how images produced by perpetrators of systemic violence and death might be rendered for contemporary public display. In this respect, it is the controversial Museum of Modern Art exhibition that has drawn the most commentary, much of it deeply critical of the choice of venue as well the minimal historical context provided within the exhibition's mise-en-scène. This commentary focused on two primary concerns, the first being the impropriety and orientalist bias of aestheticizing the images by placing them in an art museum. This commentary is made explicit in Guy Treblay's review essay on the exhibit. He quotes Jeff Yang, publisher of a national bimonthly of Asian American culture, who asks rhetorically, "If Holocaust photos were displayed without any real context in an art museum, would we find that morally acceptable?"[43] Yang's comment is a telling illustration of how an institutional history can at times overdetermine the work presented within it. In this case, Yang reasonably drew the conclusion that whatever the Museum of Modern Art shows is shown in the name of art (whether the word *art* is used explicitly or not) or at least, in the name of the generic and the formal aesthetic considerations integral to art institutions. Viewing the exhibition on such terms, Yang judged that placing the photographs within such an institutional frame was morally indefensible. Yet in defense of the museum's decision to exhibit the images, Susan Kismaric, curator of photography at the Museum of Modern Art, placed the exhibition in the tradition of the museum's practice of exhibiting "vernacular work."[44] She noted that in the past the Museum of Modern Art had displayed images such as criminal mug shots and photojournalist Giles Peress's documentary photographs of the Rwandan massacres. In Kismaric's view such images made evident "the power of the medium." In this context, Kismaric argued that the Tuol Sleng pictures "help tell the story of the history of photography [by showing] the photograph's ability to capture people who are terrified."[45] Nevertheless, as indicated above, in addition to questioning the choice of the Museum of Modern Art as venue for exhibiting the S-21 photographs, other strong objections to the exhibition was made on grounds that the presentation of the photographs failed to provide adequate contextualization for the images. As Lindsay French argued, "If the historical context of these objects/photographs is what gives them their particular power and significance, curators working with them ignore this at their peril. . . . The less the audience knows about a topic, the greater the responsibility the curator has to inform."[46] Within this perspective, and in specific contrast to the Photographic Resource Center exhibit, French condemned the Museum of Modern Art exhibition as an essentializing production that misrepresented particular people by distancing and universalizing their experiences through an exoticizing objectification. Her preference was clearly to emphasize the historical referents of the photographs understood as visual evidence of a history (and its contemporary consequences) that needed to be understood without trivialization and in its full contextual complexity.[47]

However, neither the objections to the Museum of Modern Art as an site that overdetermines visitor engagements with the image and objects presented in its space, nor a critical curatorial judgment admonishing Kismaric for not providing enough context so as to make apparent the full referential, evidential meaning of the photographs, can be left as the final word on the Museum of Modern Art exhibition. While it is clearly important to critique this exhibit in regard to its failure to place the photographs within a history that demands to be grasped in its full complexity, still to be reckoned with is the quite intense disturbing visual experience that the exhibition seemed to offer to so many of its visitors. There is little question that curatorial judgment in regard to designing an exhibition of the S-21 images must take into account the power of an exhibition of these images to disturb, to effect an agitation that provokes viewers to not only think about the circumstances of their making but as well to consider the significance of the fact that they remain deeply troubling today. Even Lindsay French recognized as much in her admission that the exhibition of photographs at the Museum of Modern Art did have the potential to elicit powerful affective connections with viewers without personal histories that tie them to the people of Cambodia, and that this seems possible precisely because the exhibition of images contained so little information and hence resisted reduction to the status of a document.[48] Thus, it is important to consider various exhibition mise-en-scènes devised to work with the affective legacies of these photographs, that is, to work with the force of these images while resisting their singular reduction to documents whose significance resides in the substantiation of juridical or historiographic narratives. The key questions about the S-21 exhibitions are not only what is disturbing about the photographs, but as well how any given image-event that locates and frames the presentation of these photographs is implicated in the mindful direction through which the intensity of this disturbance moves. This is particularly important if we can assume that the force of the images to disturb provokes viewers to think more about them, to want know more about the circumstances of their making and the implications of why they remain so disturbing today. The problem with the Museum of Modern Art show may not have been so much its aestheticizing and objectifying tendencies in and of themselves, but a curatorial frame that held a more or less directionless disturbance, leaving the thought provoked by this affect nowhere to turn except perhaps to reflections on one's sadness and felt impotence in the face of the suffering of others. This suggests a need to think more dialectically in regard to the relation between what one might call the "aesthetic" qualities of an exhibition and its historical subject matter, allowing for the possibility that the mise-en-scène of these photographs in a gallery or museum might ultimately enhance the referential meaning that the photographs accrue. The consideration of this relation between aesthetics and history is what knots together my discussion of the exhibition practices associated with the S-21 photographs, the *Crimes of the Wehrmacht* exhibitions, and the *Without Sanctuary* exhibitions at the Andy Warhol Museum and Chicago Historical Society. In regard to all of these exhibitions, it is quite important to not only ask as to what worlds of meaning any given exhibition creates, but rather how an exhibition stages an event in which the work presented provokes a particular relation between affect and thought. On such terms, we might begin a conversation wherein we explore how it is that exhibitions of photographs (and other documents) not only provide social signs but also elicit a nonspecific affective intensity with the potential to provoke thought. It is at this point that our conversation can begin to consider how the lines of movement of such thought are made and how such movement may be framed (but not overdetermined) by the curatorial judgments that fashion the concrete substance of an image-event.

To illustrate one possible conversation on this theme, consider for a moment what it is about S-21 photographs that further distinguishes them from the photographs previously discussed. First of all, there is no overt violence depicted in these images. Without the knowledge that each person in a photograph is soon to be executed, each of the S-21 photographs might be appreciated as one in a series of compelling, somewhat unnerving "portraits" (more than once they have been said to recall the portraiture work of Richard Avedon).[49] Second (and relatedly), there is little question that many viewers have judged these images to have an aesthetic aura not present in the abject lynching photographs or those taken as souvenir trophy photographs by soldiers in the German army. It is interesting to note that in an interview conducted at the time that he and Riley were amassing the photographs for exhibition, Douglas Niven remarked that "even though they were of horrible subject matter, with horrible histories," he and Riley saw "the possibility of making beautiful photographs" from the negatives they helped restore.[50] Niven is not the only person who has commented on the aesthetic character of Nhem Ein's photographs. Such a characterization remains deeply controversial and it is not my intent to enter into a full discussion of this controversy here. Rather, what I want to emphasize is the importance of not just acknowledging the aesthetic force of these images, but of thinking through how this force might be implicated in the affective intensity provoked by their public rendition in galleries and museums, and in what ways an exhibition mise-en-scène might work to discipline and orient such intensity.

Helpful here are Thierry De Duve's writings on the implications of the S-21 Museum of Modern Art exhibit as well as the exhibit of S-21 images presented at the 1997 version of the photography festival *Les Recontre Photographiques d'Arles*. Unhinged by the affective intensity he experienced viewing curator Christian Caujolle's presentation of the photographs at Arles, De Duve has been thinking through the implications of this experience for more than a decade. Given his clear awareness of the historical significance of the photographs, in an article in the journal *October* published in 2008, De Duve writes of the exhibition, "The moral responsibility I felt I had vis-à-vis these images entailed a refusal and a rejection of the aesthetic feelings they yielded. Of course, this couldn't be done, because aesthetic feelings are involuntary."[51] Of key importance to my discussion here, it was the impossibility of rejecting the aesthetic feelings evoked by the photographs that made the exhibition unbearable for De Duve. It was when De Duve figured out how to view the photographs in a way that embraced this tension inherent in what he called "the aesthetic . . . category . . . of genocidal images," that he found a way of coming to terms with his experience (15). Moving through a sense of individuality "draped in a generic humanism," he had to "address each photo, each person in the photos, individually" from within his aesthetic response before he could "acknowledge receipt of their gaze as if it were addressed to [him] in person" (22). In this respect, De Duve is echoing the discussion earlier in this chapter, admitting to a subjection to the force of the image in which this force references a moment in which the image sees more than it is seen. As he writes, "Only then did the people in the photos rise from the dead, and only then did this unbearably controversial exhibition acquire its true legitimacy," its specters inhabiting the present and dialectically entwining with his contemporary concerns (22).

To offset any notion that such thought was an idiosyncratic response to such difficult photographic imagery, consider briefly the remarks of Jenny Edkins, writing of her response to an exhibition of photographs taken by Sebastiao Salgado of migrant children living in poverty in refugee camps.[52] Edkins found these portraits, in technique and manner, to be uncannily reminiscent in technique and manner of British Victorian portrait photographs of the respectable working classes. Similar to De Duve, she found that traversing genres through the framework of aesthetic similarities somehow challenged her expectations in regard to her encounter with Salgado's images. While she entered the exhibition with the expectation that she would be staring at other people's misery and consequently would likely experience a degree of sympathy and concern, unexpectedly she found herself confronted with the singularity of an existence in each portrait that made her the focus of its gaze. In this moment in which the image sees more than it is seen, Edkins found herself confronted, positioned so that she was no longer in control, no longer the omniscient benefactor of sympathy or simply a sentimental bystander. She admitted to being moved, but in way that threw her off-balance and into thought. Thus, Edkins asks: "Who are we? Who are these children? So utterly distinct one from the other, are they in some sense the same? The same in their difference? And what is it about [these images and these children] that challenges us to rethinking our expectations so much?" (362).

What De Duve's remarks (and Edkins's comments and questions) might mean for the question of curatorial judgment is clearly indicated by the following exhibition framework offered by Mark Kramer, exhibits coordinator at the Weisman Art Museum in Minneapolis. Kramer was responsible for an S-21 photographic exhibition at the University of Minnesota in 2001 and he graciously shared his curatorial framework in an e-mail communication.[53] Kramer approached the task of curatorial judgment within the position that each face photographed "was a record—not a portrait—of a murdered person." In this respect, Kramer viewed the images as "mug shots" understood as identity photographs taken of criminals, and often of citizens too, as part of the procedures of control and administration of state bureaucracies. As Edkins states, "The mug shot produces the subject as object: as [what Giorgio Agamben called] 'bare life,' exposed only in its nudity and nakedness in the face of sovereign power."[54] Rejecting placing the photographs in a single line, what Kramer called "the dreaded 'bathtub ring' installation," Kramer felt that to give any power to the installation, the one hundred faces needed to be seen as a whole. Thus, he hung the photographs in five rows of twenty each, or a grid of five high by twenty wide. The photos were framed in black with white mats, allowing them to stand out in sharp contrast with a deep—almost black—gray painted wall. There were no spaces between the frames so the photographs created a solid rectangle of faces. Kramer explained his mise-en-scène as follows: "I thought the power of the subject was best portrayed by seeing all one hundred faces at once. It was possible to see them individually; the photos were large enough that it was still possible to see each face clearly. What my design provided was a chance to see each in the context of all. It was analogous to hearing one voice or a hundred at once." While not extensively contextualized as the Photographic Resource Center exhibition, the Weisman Art Museum supplemented the photographs with historical information in both English and Cambodian, printing the text directly on a wall of the gallery. In addition, they provided a platform for a small shrine that was created by the local Cambodian community, who were also extensively involved in the public programming created for the exhibition.

Kramer's exhibition mise-en-scène was remarkably similar to that presented by Caujolle in Arles, the exhibition that provoked De Duve's extended thought about his encounter with the S-21 images. In the context of various categories that articulated the "ethics, aesthetics, politics" theme of the 1997 festival, Caujolle listed the S-21 exhibition under the category "The Duty of Memory." As reported by De Duve, in installing the photographs Caujolle had arranged them in grid occupying only one of walls of the room in which they were shown. This enabled the visual grasp of what De Duve described as the collective, "shattering diversity of their appearances and the singularity of their address" (19). The scale of each of the enlargements were done to fit this precise arrangement, that is, all the photographs fitting on one wall and one wall only. A text explaining the reasons for presenting the photographs was printed on a sheet of plastic placed on the floor in front of the photographs. The text ran the width of the grid in such a way that one had to walk back and forth to read it. While Caujolle did not provide further contextualization, both Kramer and Caujolle provided a mise-en-scène that not only concerned what worlds of meaning an exhibition provided, but as well, how it might provoke indeterminate affect and its movement into thought. In doing so, their intention ran against the grain of a practice that would straightforwardly unbox the one hundred photographs sent to a museum, hang them in a double row running the length of the gallery walls, and place at the entrance to the gallery an explanatory text panel providing a brief historical context for the images. Such curatorial judgments, however, are not without their own thoughtfulness. In explaining the decision to exhibit the photographs within this mise-en-scène, Catherine Evans, curator of photography at the Columbus (Ohio) Museum of Art stated that her goal was to create "as neutral a display as possible."[55] This "neutrality" was intended to serve the purpose of presenting the photographs at the museum so as to raise consciousness about this period and to help avoid future instances of genocide.[56] Evans was certainly aware that the identity photographs she was presenting represented only a fraction of the people killed at S-21 and the majority of these were unidentified. Evans stated that she wanted to present the photographs in a "context that allowed for the individual people [pictured] to be recognized." In other words, Evans wanted the Columbus Museum's exhibition to support viewers in the recognition of the singularity of those depicted in each photograph. She wanted viewers to recognize that each portrait presented a discrete, particular human life, rather than a person whose identity was overdetermined by the fact that they were one of a large number of people who had been murdered. In this sense, Evans's curatorial objective was similar to, but clearly not the same as Kramer's. In each case, the mise-en-scène of the exhibition was implicated in the demand that viewers open themselves to the work of addressing images that addressed them first and foremost via affect.

In pointing to the very real difference in curatorial projects of Kramer's and Evans's mise-en-scène, my purpose is not to offer an assessment that would judge one as a better exhibition than the other. Rather, it is to underscore the need for a conceptualization of curatorial practice that would allow us to consider the difference between these two approaches without resorting to the claim that one approach was too "sterile" while the other was too "artsy." What I have been arguing in this chapter is that such a conceptualization needs to begin with recognition that variations in the mise-en-scène of an exhibition hold different implications as to the possible direction of the relation between affect and thought. Both Evans and Kramer attempted to refuse any dichotomy that would confine a response to the subjects portrayed in the photographic exhibitions as to either "what" they are—e.g., victims—or to "who" they are in their singularity. All exhibitions of the S-21 photographs I have discussed attempted to create an experience of flux between these two positions. Yet these exhibitions differed from each other in the relative emphasis each placed on these positions. Evans wanted to enhance of the force of an image through the singularity evident in individual portraits, setting a structure in place that provoked contemplation on the irreplaceable, non-substitutable loss of each individual portrayed. In doing this, she risked moving thought away from a consideration of the collective event of genocide and how one might be responsible to the memory of such an event, particularly when one has no immediate connection to the lives of those killed. On the other hand, Kramer thought that seen one at a time, the photographs would not convey the overall gravity of the event. As he put it, "One by one, each photograph did not add up to the totality of the systematic murder of these people but rather the real power was in the whole." Thus, Kramer chose to enhance the force of the image by emphasizing its status as document, a record produced in the process of incarceration and subsequent murder of not only a person portrayed in any given photograph but many thousands of others as well. What this mise-en-scène risked was a missed encounter with the loss of singular, non-substitutability of human life in the face of the massification of photographs into their collective identity as victims of genocide. The wager of this risk is that those who engage the exhibition will be decentered, that is, thrown into thought and not simply into the despair that results from an exposure to the brutal aspect of humanity or a congratulatory self-confirmation that one has gone to an exhibition that has left one feeling anguished over the suffering and death of others. At risk at the Weisman Museum exhibition was the possibility that viewers might not find themselves addressed, subject to an affective legacy that might force thought as to what it would mean to be responsible to the memory of those killed at S-21.

BEYOND A PEDAGOGY OF WITNESS

The consequences of the physical sensations that accompany the acknowledgment of the presence of bodies in pain rendered by photographic images of suffering and death are indeterminate. There is an affective force felt when viewing such images, though how this force is embodied and with what consequences cannot be specified in advance. Given this, the question remains as to what would justify a visual practice of public history on such terms. To speak here of the courage to (and responsibility of) witness is not nearly enough. To claim that we owe the dead our witness simply avoids the question as to what would constitute an adequate practice of witnessing and how such a practice might be encouraged and supported. Contemporary ethics would have us attempt to guard against reducing another's suffering to imaginative or quite real versions of our own by critically attending to the inescapable failure of comprehension that is always a component of ethical witness. Yet, as Theodor Adorno reminds us, "even the most radical reflection of the mind on its own failure is limited by the fact that it remains only reflection, without altering the existence to which its failure bears witness."[57] To witness in a manner that opens the possibility of altering the existence of that to which it bears witness requires a dialectical coupling of affect and thought, implicating the self in the practice of coming to terms with the substance and significance of history. Exhibitions are events that can stage such a possibility. Nonetheless, because the consequences of the affective force of an image are indeterminate, there are pedagogical (and political) risks associated with the practice of exhibition. With this recognition, we might commence a conversation wherein we explore how it is that exhibitions of photographs (and other documents) not only provide social signs but also elicit nonspecific affective intensities with the potential to provoke thought. It is at this point that one can begin to consider how the lines of movement of such thought are made and how such movement may be framed (but not overdetermined) by the curatorial judgments that fashion the concrete substance of an image-event. It is through these conversations that we might attain a better understanding of what is gained and lost in such pedagogies of provocation and containment, for it is such understanding that will determine much of what might be made of the affective legacies ingrained in the difficult visual histories of our contemporary world. In the following concluding chapter, I place the above argument in context of broad consideration of various curatorial frameworks that specify how it is that the past comes to matter in the present.

SIX

Some Closing Remarks on Curatorial Practice and the Pursuit of Social Justice

Hopefully, the previous chapters have illuminated some of the rich possibilities inherent in comparative studies among exhibitions. Not just different exhibitions of the same material, but different exhibitions more generally. We still seem to be in our infancy in regard to curatorial studies, particularly when it comes to understanding the issues faced by the development of exhibition practices that attempt a public rendition of traces of past violence and suffering. In this respect, there is much to learn through the study of prior exhibitions assuming there is adequate documentation as to the development of their mise-en-scènes. This book can be taken as a call for better documentation of exhibitions so that comparative studies such as those discussed here can be undertaken. However, such documentation efforts cannot be the sole responsibility of overworked and underfunded staff of museums and galleries. These efforts would require the commitment of scholars working and studying not only in curatorial studies programs, but as well in programs addressing public history and memory studies. Such a commitment no doubt requires some sense of the significant issues at stake when comparative studies of exhibitions are undertaken and in what sense such studies may be understood to be scholarship in the public interest.

In 2011, the Association for Canadian Studies commissioned a nationwide survey that indicated 84 percent of those surveyed expressed either "very strong" or "somewhat strong" levels of trust in the way museums present historical eras, issues, people, and events.[1] This was particularly striking in contrast to the 52 percent of the respondents who said they trust in Internet Web sites when it comes to information about the past. While this survey was welcomed by many museums as a validation of current practices, it also is a sobering study that underscores the serious responsibilities inherent in what I have called the *curatorial project*. As demonstrated by my discussions of exhibitions drawn from the same historical documents, the practice of public history is not simply about providing information about the past but also about proposing a framework within which the past comes to matter in the present. However, this said, it must be recognized that it is no longer adequate to simply state such well-worn clichés. What is required is a process of thinking through the different ways in which exhibition practices foster differing terms on which the past comes to matter, clarifying one's curatorial commitments as to what one anticipates a given exhibition might accomplish.

As noted in chapter 1, many exhibitions have as their purpose the articulation of a grounded, shared understanding of a particular past that is intended to help create a community of collective meaning. National museums have traditionally offered such authoritative renderings in an attempt to foster a sense of civic cohesion or at the very least recognition of the self as part of a historically formed collectivity. On such terms, an exhibition's curatorial project is to present a particular "reading" of documentation in a manner that facilitates some shared understanding as to the meaning and significance of specific past events. Such practices are clearly important to the civic consciousness of geopolitical entities (e.g., nation-states), particularly when instantiating the significance of particular past events that have been ignored in previous dominant narratives. Nevertheless, the question remains, beyond rending persuasive historical narratives integral to a collective's past, what can the practice of curating public history accomplish? Can it foster the enactment of a different type of relation between past, present, and future?

In taking up such questions in this concluding chapter my purpose is not to offer prescriptions as to how to curate exhibitions addressing "difficult knowledge"[2] drawn from traces of past events. Indeed, in any discussion of curating, it must be underscored that there are no universal rules or principles for curatorial practice. How a specific curatorial project is defined is always already being worked through in the situated context of the fourfold demands placed on curatorial decision making. These are felt as a set of multiple and often contradictory commitments to: the demands of institutions in which exhibitions appear, the historical integrity of the artifacts, images and texts to be shown, the public who comes to see an exhibition, and one's vision as to what is to be accomplished by the event of an exhibit. As Hernández-Navarro has emphasized, the task of curating is the infinite articulation of these often-competing demands.[3] Much of the differing *Without Sanctuary* exhibition practices at the Warhol Museum and the Chicago Historical Society resides in how these competing demands were met in each institutional context. This said, and as previous chapters have attempted to show, the situated character of curating does not negate the value of theorizing curatorial practice. In this respect, the following remarks are presented as a further set of questions, concepts, and thoughts that might inform the work of those involved in exhibition development as they define their curatorial projects and work through the multiple demands referred to above.

REMEMBRANCE AND THE PROSPECT OF HOPE

While it was addressed in the opening chapter of this book, it is worth reemphasizing that there is good reason to remain ambivalent in regard to the capacity of remembrance to serve the yearning for a better, less violent world. The pervasiveness of public remembrance in an era as violent and destructive as our own would seem to give little cause for hope, particularly hope grounded in the anticipation that the memory of past evil will help prevent its recurrence. Clearly, an unqualified notion of remembrance does not ensure anything, least of all justice and compassion. Yet those of us with commitments to the possibility of a more just and equitable society have to face the necessity of remaining hopeful. This condition of hope requires that we see the present as incomplete and thus open to the challenge of bringing about what is not yet present—a less violent, more just society still to come, in which human dignity is affirmed in all its diverse singularity. For those of us dedicated to this work, it is imperative that we pursue the question of the grounds on which we might bring about the tenuous linkage between the requirements of hope, the pursuit of justice, and practices of remembrance.

Arguably, the curatorial projects framing the realization of both the *Without Sanctuary* exhibitions at the Andy Warhol Museum and the Chicago Historical Society as well as the exhibitions discussed in the previous chapter may be understood as pedagogical events with the potential to consolidate various publics holding antiracist and antifascist commitments. However, it should be clear by now that the exhibitions of concern in this book have been realized through a more complex vision than that of the strengthening of particular communal identities. The exhibitions I have discussed are intricate examples of the fact that all forms of remembrance are not reductively conservative in their instantiation and maintenance of the regulating discourses of established historical narratives. Quite differently, these exhibitions have attempted to bring traces of past events into the present in order to create a fissure in one's historical consciousness, one that makes it possible for certain traces of the past to break in and indeterminately alter the present and its future possibilities. The prospect of hope embedded in these exhibitions lies in how they serve to make apparent the present's inherent incompleteness, holding it open and marking it as unfinished.[4] As a pedagogical and political event, when traces of the past break into the present, remembrance becomes a form of difficult learning. The intention of such learning is not to shock in ways that arrest thought or mobilize a set of psychodynamics that serve to defend against changes to existing relations and practices. Rather, this is learning that seeks affirmation as a radical necessity, as an opening to the recognition and requirement that the present must be rethought. This form of hopeful learning no doubt requires a particular way of reading, seeing, and listening, a way of facing the traces of the past that exceeds their idea in the present. On such terms, attending to traces of the past brings something new in the current moment in a way that helps remake it. In this sense, it is the separateness and alterity of the past that faces one, demanding both responsibility and a response. The past approached on such terms opens the present not merely to gaps in its knowledge, but to a radical reframing of what historical remembrance might accomplish beyond an awareness of things not previously known.

When fostering a hopeful learning, remembrance is integral to what Lauren Berlant has called the ongoing formation of the historical present.[5] This historical present is not something constituted in the idiom of pasts and futures. As Berlant notes, it is not about "the past's presence as revenant," a return of the past that haunts the present, but rather that such a historical present resides as core aspect of the "present's ongoing condition" and as such, is a thing being made and lived through (92). It is not only infused with particular interests, emotions, and desires but as well, questions pertaining to ethics and politics. In this sense, the *Without Sanctuary* exhibitions may be seen as attempts to reopen the past so as to enable a reopening and remaking the present as something yet to be completed. These have been curatorial projects that have sought in different ways to facilitate a certain type of *bond* that links the past, present, and future so as to inculcate a singular sense of responsibility in and for the unfinished state of the present and its possible forms of futurity. As Michael Rothberg has argued, without this bond, "there is no nexus within which to think justice," to think what constitutes justice and how it might best be pursued.[6] Yet to merely suggest the notion of such a bond and its concomitant responsibilities and possibilities is not nearly enough. We need to consider the question of what sort of bond this might be and how it might be related to exhibition practices. This means clarifying assumptions about the substance of the attachments that constitutes this bond as well as the desires and feelings that are tied up with the dynamics of living with it. These questions are crucial for advancing our understanding of what it means to curate "difficult knowledge" and how such practices might contribute to the pursuit of what one might call justice.[7]

It is important to be alert to the fact that there are a variety of ways to constitute this pursuit. Below I will consider three different frameworks for designing exhibition practices that attempt to constitute the bond referred to above. Despite their differences, what these frameworks share is the supposition that the political importance of any exhibition established within them does not lie in the confirming messages it might convey to a subject. Rather, the politics of these frameworks are dependent on an exhibition's potential to unsettle rigid forms of identities, affective investments in particular ideologies, and triumphalist fantasies of righteousness. An exhibition that simply advocates or argues a unified position is more likely to "reinforce a traditional and unhelpful notion of the political subject—unitary, pre-constituted, and self-possessed—one who enters an equally traditional public space of protest."[8] The radical hope that curating difficult knowledge encompasses does not reside in a reductive redemptive framework addressed to those who wish to count themselves among the righteous of the world. Alternatively, one can think of an exhibition as an essential pedagogical and political space wherein subjectivity is informed and complicated by the relationship between the self and others thus redirecting affect and thought, opening new possibilities for action in the present.

The exhibitions of concern here are in fact pedagogical events whose mise-en-scènes set images and texts in relationship with viewers, encouraging the possibility that subjectivity might be altered as part of the experience of such a relationship. This is precisely in tune with notions of what constitutes "the publicity" of a public sphere as put forward in the writings of Hannah Arendt and Claude Lefort.[9] For Arendt and Lefort, the public sphere is established through the demands of the ethico-political question not of how we appear (e.g., what identities we affirm, express, and enact) but how we respond to the appearance of others, and in particular, in what ways this appearance calls one into question. In other words, to be in public is to be exposed to and addressed by alterity. Curators who want to present exhibitions integral to a public sphere thus have a twofold task. Not only must they create events that help those who have been rendered invisible to make their appearance within public life, but as well, exhibition practices must be designed to help develop a viewer's capacity "to respond to, rather than simply react against, that appearance" (Deutsche, 64). This makes the question of what exhibition practices foster the pursuit of justice somewhat more complicated than an answer rooted in the prevalent but false dichotomy between thought and activism, a dichotomy that, more often than not, dismisses mere thought in favor of promoting the viewer's moral responsibility to take some action in the world as a consequence of the visiting of an exhibit.

However, it is also important to recognize that no one exhibit should be held accountable for either altering beliefs and attitudes or instigating action in the world. If one wants to consider the place of an exhibition in regard to how it contributes to the social pursuit of justice, we must open up the much underdiscussed question of how and why curatorial practices may come to matter. In this regard, what needs to be considered is the way any given exhibition is situated and participates in the larger social ecology of pedagogy and politics that encompasses a society. This ecology is defined by the relationships over time among a wide variety of sites wherein one may be exposed to information and ideas beyond what one already knows. It means that the images, stories, and ideas presented by any given exhibition must be understood in relation to those presented not only through other museums and galleries but digital social media, newspapers, film, and television, schools, and universities, as well as events held and conversations initiated in community meetings, religious institutions, union halls, and recreational facilities. For this reason, it is important to understand how the pedagogy of an exhibition might be impacted by the conjuncture within which it takes place. Particularly when one sets about to curate exhibitions presenting difficult knowledge, it is impossible to maintain a disjuncture between curatorial practice and other forms of cultural and political activities that are supposedly peripheral to it. This means that in considering curating as practice of pedagogy, one also has to come to terms with how such pedagogy is understood to function as a situated practice that is always in an articulated relation to other practices of cultural pedagogy operating within a particular conjuncture. In other words, there is a need for an understanding of how and why an exhibition might function as an extension, supplementation, and linkage with and to other practices. It is only through such thought that one might begin to grasp a sense of how and why any given exhibition might be an important pedagogical intervention in a public sphere. Thus, exhibitions founded on the three positions considered below are not to be considered self-sufficient initiatives. Rather, their force is defined within the complementary and contradictory terms that bear on the material relations and cultural practices from which people draw a sense of meaning and significance.

EXHIBITIONS AND VARIOUS WAYS OF LINKING THE PAST, PRESENT, AND FUTURE

To further clarify what is at stake in the comparative study of exhibitions, I want to consider three different exhibition frameworks that endeavor to foster a temporal bond that links the past, present, and future. The premise of this consideration is that exhibition frameworks that attempt to serve justice by publicly presenting difficult knowledge pertaining to past events are frequently based on varying assumptions that have quite different consequences not only for exhibition practice but, as well, for the pedagogy and politics of remembrance. The differences among the curatorial frameworks I sketch out below have significant implications for how one might conceive of and realize exhibitions addressing past events incorporating violence and suffering. This is not to say that one might not find elements of each of these frameworks at play in any given exhibit. The realization of exhibition practices consistent with one framework does not preclude the incorporation of practices consistent with others. It remains an empirical question for any given exhibition how various sets of practices might either be complementary or contradictory. The first of the frameworks discussed assumes the possibility of a temporal bond based on processes of identification with those subjected to violence and oppression. The second of these frameworks assumes such a bond is established by cultivating feelings of grief and shame regarding events that happened in the past. The third framework is rooted in the assumption that an exhibition can confront visitors with an insistence that they do what is necessary in order to inherit what they have just seen or heard within an exhibition's mise-en-scène. As will be argued, "to inherit" means to engage in a form of work that requires critical thought and judgment as to degree and substantive contemporary significance of various aspects of prior events.

REMEMBRANCE THROUGH IDENTIFICATION

A prevalent way of thinking about how images and narratives regarding past events become implicated in the ongoing formation of a present is through fostering emotionally charged attachments with specific people caught up in these events. Within the context of an exhibition, this often takes the form of an invitation to personal, affective engagements with representations of particular individuals and their stories. Within exhibitions, such representations are often presented via excerpts of oral or written testimony and sets of photographs providing visitors with an intimate visual reference. In an attempt to "make history come alive," such displays provide personal accounts of what it was like to live under specific, often oppressive historical circumstances. Engagements with such material are often presumed to give rise to investments in the significance of these narratives for illuminating stories of one's own. These dynamics are assumed to structure a form of identification within which one can empathize with people from the past, particularly those who have suffered the abuses of subjection and the violence it enacts.[10] Attempting to establish similarities between past hurts and present abuses, the curatorial projects animating such exhibitions aim to foster a deeply felt, compassionate understanding of past lives that can provide affectively inflected insight into the lived experiences of one's contemporaries as well as a commitment to mitigate their suffering and precarity.

Drawing on Alison Landsberg's notion of "prosthetic memory,"[11] Andermann and Arnold-de Simine have registered these dynamics of identification as a process of museum visitors "adopting" other peoples' memories of events in a way that alters a person's subjectivity and politics.[12] On such terms, forms of "prosthetic memory" are understood as artificial. When someone takes on such "foreign" memories following an engagement with representations such as exhibitions, this adoption is viewed as the collapsing of self with others from the past. Offered in the context of a warranted critique of the limitations of such forms of identification for museum practice, it nevertheless seems to me that employing the notion of adopting others' memories is a bit too cynical, serving not to only describe a cultural phenomenon but to also register what is assumed to be the superficial character of much of public memories. There is little question people find significance in representations of other people's lives through quite various and not altogether predictable forms of attachments. While curators interested in fostering identifications often rely on identity categories (e.g., gender, age, ethnic or racial identity, religion, etc.) or on assumed universal themes (e.g., childhood, the provision of basic life necessities, love and sex), compelling connections between the past and present can unconsciously occur in ways that remain emotionally powerful even if they seem potentially problematic. An excellent example of this is detailed in Laura Levitt's "Intimate Encounters: A Holocaust Lesson."[13] In this important discussion of issues related to psychic identification and making significance from historical narratives, Levitt draws the fraught connections between her own experience of sexual trauma and representations of the devastation of lives caught up in the Holocaust.

Her essay is exemplary in that it makes clear the force of the often-uncontrollable dynamics of identification and the necessity of a critical turn of thought that clarifies the problems with and limitations of such identifications. The point is not to dismiss instances where the temporal bond is constituted within the dynamics of psychosocial identifications; rather, it is to understand both the productivity and limits of this way of forging connections between past, present, and future.

As Levitt makes fully evident, a central concern in regard to temporal bonds built upon the dynamics of identification is that the specificity and particularly of past events is attenuated as one reduces such events to accounts recognizable as thematic versions of one's own stories. In his magisterial work *Memory, History, Forgetting,* Paul Ricoeur argued that the "duty of memory is the duty to do justice, through memories, to an other than the self."[14] Ricoeur was clear that the virtue of justice necessitates turning toward otherness. At the very least, what this means is being attentive to the degree to which the temporal bond forged in practices of remembrance might incorporate a regard for the nonequivalent singularity of others. If exposure to others lies at the heart of democratic public life, exhibitions consistent with Ricoeur's "duty of memory" have to confront the problem raised by Rosalyn Deutsche, who asks, "With what kind of vision shall we meet the appearance of others?" (64). Thus, the question as to whether a curatorial project can help establish ways of seeing that do not seek to reduce the impact of exposure, that on the contrary foster a nonindifference, an answerability, or what Levinas calls a "response-ability." For a curatorial project to accomplish this it would have to incorporate practices that foster a truly public vision, "one that undoes narcissistic fantasies that blind one to otherness, either rejecting it or assimilating it to the knowing ego as the Same" (Deutsche, 69). Such a vision would seem to be necessary in order to limit the placement of the self at a too-comfortable distance from insights that might illuminate one's own complicity in sustaining relations of violence and oppression. If one is unable to explore the possibility of such complicity, the force of memory for rethinking one's life in the present is considerably weakened.

However, the problem of the collapse of self and other within the dynamics of identification is not the only problem with this mode of establishing the temporal bond. As is evident from the recurring systematic malevolence within many societies around the world, forming sympathetic affective attachments and forms of identification will not suffice to prevent the recurrence of violence. Remembrance, at least on such terms, is not the secret of redemption. Andermann and Arnold-de Simine put it well when they state that the problem with such a way of defining a curatorial project is the false assumption that feelings of empathy based on identification can "produce new memory communities and political alliances across divides of gender race, ethnicity, and nationality and that this empathy [in and of itself will] foster ethical thinking which is then transferred to topical conflicts for which it elicits tolerance and deeper understanding."[15] Their key point is that in such a process there is little room in our understanding of past and current events for the necessity of historical contextualization, analytical examination, and critical reflection. It is certainly arguable that for an exhibition to contribute to the pursuit of justice it must foster more than affective attachments. Rather, it must help visitors recognize and engage with the material relations that continue to structure individual and collective identities and in doing so help think through what actions might come to bear on the political relations structuring the present.

REMEMBRANCE THROUGH GRIEF AND SHAME

Let us consider another curatorial framework responding to the question of what sort of temporal bond might inculcate a responsibility in and for the present and its possible forms of futurity. Of concern here are curatorial projects that attempt to foster a temporal connection rooted in feelings of a deep sense of grief and shame regarding the occurrence of events distant from one's immediate existence. It is in no way straightforward to speak of a curatorial project that would foster such emotions as a progressive force integrating traces of a past into a historical present and its future prospects. While grief reasonably signifies a felt sense of loss, what of the sense of shame invoked in this context? Shame is a complex state, emotional and evaluative, reflexive and yet social. It is an emotion that comes in many forms, each with very different implications and consequences. It is an emotion rooted in critical judgments and their consequent feelings of inadequacy and unworthiness. Central to the formation of a temporal bond based on grief and shame is the realization of intense feelings of disgrace not only in regard to oneself, but also in regard to previously idealized particular assemblies and collectivities within which one is felt to be implicated. Such an extended notion of felt humiliation and disgrace is a consequence of judgments that render shameful actions that have been taken by some members on behalf of the larger collective of which they were or are a part. Writing in the wake of the Nazi genocide of European Jewry, both Primo Levi and Hannah Arendt broaden this idea of extended ignominy by advancing a sense of shamefulness in being human in world in which genocide was a historical and still is a present reality. Levi and Arendt made it clear that they each experienced a sense of elemental shame at living in a world in which evil, pain, and suffering exist and are part of human potential.[16] Clearly, this is a shame grounded not solely in what one personally did or did not do. It is also grounded in the discreditable, irrevocable actions of others that bring about internalized felt judgments as to one's worthiness, judgments that often carry a sense of failure, deficiency, and diminishment (doubling grief to include not only the realization of the loss of others but also in the process a loss of self). In fostering this shame the intent is obviously not to provoke immobilizing feelings of distress or despair but rather to cultivate an emotional state dependent on our grasp of a standard that has yet to be met and by which we may be judged by others and by which we might judge ourselves. The assumption is that shame can be transformational, a productive force for destabilizing and consequently altering our relationships with others, ultimately altering who we are in relation to what we aspire to be both individually and collectively. It is assumed to be a way of awakening moral inertia and rekindling actions aimed at minimizing the unequal forms of violence and precarity that exist in the world.

Clearly, the curatorial mobilization of shame that is most relevant here is not just that assumed to accrue from the public exposure of perpetrators and their reprehensible acts (e.g., it is not only to present an exhibition in order to cast shame on those who participated in acts of lynching and/or who reveled in viewing photographs of such acts). More to the point is the assumption that concrete exposure of the factual realities of past acts of violence and oppression (including their resulting multigenerational personal, familial, and communal devastation) will foster affect that resolves itself as a personally felt, collective shame that embodies an essence of hope for yet a better world. As Berenice Fischer has argued, such shame needs to be understood "not as a mark of our inadequacy but as a sign of our commitment to act, as a mark of the tension between the present and the future, as a touchstone for understanding what we expect to achieve and how."[17] Rather than an emotion associated with a humiliation that fuels one hiding from the view of others or conversely expressing a storm of anger and defensive aversive behavior, Fisher maintains that shame needs to be worn differently—in public and with dignity.

This curatorial framework does not require visitors to identify with those who suffered in the past, nor do they need to feel a sense of personal culpability for this suffering. Exhibition visitors are not antagonistically indicted for acts they did not do or could not have personally prevented. The basic aspiration for exhibitions attempting to foster feelings of grief and shame is to constitute the mise-en-scène of an exhibition as a cognitive-emotional space where one might experience the affect associated with a collective failure to live up to one's ideals or at least to what is intimated that these ideals should be. While there is obviously no prescription on how to foster such emotions, exhibitions designed within this framework will most likely highlight visual evidence of wounding and death as well as emotionally rendered narrative accounts of what it meant to be subjected to such violence and how this has impacted on living on afterward.

Despite the arguments above, it is important to register that there are considerable risks associated with the attempts to foster grief and shame. As soon as one realizes that shame is an emotion that seeks to nullify itself by negating what gives rise to it, it becomes evident there are various ways of doing this that are not transformational. As Michael Morgan observes, "We may seek to avoid shame or dispose of it by forgetting, treating the past as dead and gone, by closing the past from the present or by allowing the present to cover over it as though the past is its own world separate from ours."[18] Another response to shame that enacts such a nullification is the provocation of an affective storm of anger directed at others. Such reactive feelings function as a form of ego defense against the self-abjection shame can foster. In addition to such forms of nullification, the experience of shame can disrupt ongoing activity through producing a sense of confusion and an inability to think or act clearly.[19] This may be so especially for those people who experience a pervasive lack of authority and influence. On such terms, whatever one does seems inadequate to the challenges of making a difference in the world beyond the survival of oneself and one's immediate family. In such a situation, the shame of existing in a violent and unjust world is a condition in which one lives. This is reinforced by continual exposure to suffering without insight into its genesis and reproduction. This pervasive sense of shame and consequent disempowerment remains virtually remarked, unfelt, and unseen and cannot be drawn upon for the clarity of thought required to rework how one might yet be in the world.[20]

This is a crucial problem for a curatorial project hoping to form a temporal bond on such terms, since the presumption of hope embodied in the fostering of shame in regard to what has happened in the past is not only the transformation of a moral inertia but the conversion of this feeling of shame into knowledge and thought. As Kathleen Woodward has pointed out, while affect may serve as the catalyst for thought, "it is not affect itself or by itself that carries the potential for transformation."[21] Indeed, the extended forms of collective shame considered above may be constituted on terms that block the thought necessary to the substance of a reworked, historical present. One likely requirement of such thought is the necessity of working through and beyond the reifications of groups of people that one often finds in rituals of remembrance. Giovanna Borradori has argued persuasively that when "others" are grouped and objectified into a "them" (as, for example, in the schemata of victims, perpetrators, and bystanders), needed is the recovery of the multifaceted reality that constitutes our shared humanity, vulnerability to suffering, and constant exposure to risk of loss. But this said, the same reification haunts the "we." As Woodward put it:

> The founding obligation of both showing and seeing the suffering of others is to disrupt any collective actor's claim of a fixed oppositional identity, such as "we" and "them," since a group, a nation or a culture is not only delimited by other groups but also internally differentiated into singular unique individuals whose identity is crafted and re-crafted constantly by their relations to others and themselves, by the forces shaping the context in which they live or which they left behind; and finally, by all the discursive framings and their distinct effects on each human subject. (171)

REMEMBRANCE THROUGH PRACTICES OF INHERITANCE

Kant famously posed three questions as central to human concerns. "What can I know? What ought I to do? For what may I hope?"[22] These questions remain central to practices of remembrance, particularly as the hope inherent in a temporal bond between the past, present, and future is dependent on what one would judge as a just world that is still to come. However, such judgments alone are insufficient. Hope also requires the possibility of thought that might deepen an understanding of the never-ending production of the historical present and hence the possibilities leading toward its transformation. Different from the dynamics of identification and/or the inculcation of feelings of grief and shame, such considerations take us to a third curatorial framework within which to foster a "hopeful" connection between past, present, and future. This is a temporal bond rooted in a felt sense of obligation to inherit what one has seen and learned so that it becomes a locus of difference in the way one lives one's life. To inherit is never a passive condition, never simply a transfer of title of some material goods or symbolic heritage, never just a felt sense that the violence of the past weighs on one's psyche. Rather "to inherit" is to engage in a particular form of work that intertwines thought and affect. Following Derrida, one's inheritance is never simply that which is given, "it is always a task."[23] When considering what it is that exhibitions might actually do, one response is to view exhibitions as initiating the task of inheritance. In this sense, exhibitions may be understood as a form of gift, one that interpolates its intended receivers in a manner that demands a thoughtful response (even if that response is ultimately to ignore the bequest).

To take up the work of inheritance within this response requires maintaining a fidelity to the singular specificity of historical events while simultaneously embracing the license one needs to truly inherit. Derrida argues cogently that if the legibility of a historical legacy "were given, natural, transparent, univocal, if it did not simultaneously call for and defy interpretation, one would never have to inherit from it" (16). Without the critical thought intrinsic to the work of inheritance, one would be situated in relation to history as a nonmediated, determinative cause. Thus, within the work of inheritance one must have the opportunity to filter, sift, criticize the elements of gift one has been given. This is the ongoing effort of sorting out the possibilities that inhabit the "injunction" to inherit (Derrida, 16). It means that what one inherits is never a fixed entity, but is always in the process of something to be made.

This remembrance forged within the work of inheritance is inescapably a complex interrelation of the contextualized physical and expressive practices that bring such traces into presence (e.g., the mise-en-scène of a specific exhibition), the various discourses for interpreting these practices that are available to visitors to an exhibition, and the individual and social determinates of the psychodynamics that mediate the possible significance of "the gift" offered by an exhibition. As I have noted previously, curatorial judgments cannot be said to be responsible for the impact of any given exhibit. However, there are exhibition practices that can encourage and advance the centrality of the work of inheritance within a practice of remembrance. Examples of such practices include (1) making clear that a given historical narrative contains inconsistencies and contradictions not easily resolved by the information currently available about a given event; (2) providing visually compelling image/texts that are not easily reduced to illustrations of a given narrative and thus provoke a degree of surprise, concern, and query as to what is shown and how to respond to it; (3) creating a layered structure of text, images, and recordings so that visitors with the time and interest can interactively pursue issues they are curious or uncertain about; and (4) providing access to a variety of visitor responses to the exhibition as well as an opportunity to add one's own views to the dialogue spawned by the exhibit. Each of these practices is consistent with a curatorial project aimed at not simply representing past incidents but, as well, creating an event that has a certain obligating force to thought. This is a force that sets thought into motion so as to respond to the question of what it means, in light of the experience of the past, to be who one is in the present moment—a thinking person faced with a myriad of decisions as to how one might act in an world in which the consequences of one's actions are not always predictable.[24] Such affectively charged thought is a mode of attunement to the tensions intrinsic in the formation of the historical present. As such, it is integral to the very possibility of hope, that is, to the possibility that the future might be different from the present and past. Within such thought, public history is something other than a practice that places us is in the midst of a social formation we did not choose. Alternatively, the curatorial projects that further the work of inheritance as integral to public history foster the recognition that our present is not only permeated by inconsistency and incompleteness but also troubled by a lack by which we are addressed and in some fashion answerable.[25]

No doubt some degree of risk associated with such a curatorial framework accrues from the possibility that the work of inheritance may require too much of the museum visitor; too much time, too much thought, too much alteration in ideas and attitudes that have grounded one's sense of self and relation to one's community. While particular constellations of curatorial practices such as those mentioned above may help ameliorate the problems posed by these issues, there can be no curatorial practice that will ever resolve these concerns. Such problems, however, are not the only source of risk associated with exhibitions framed through "remembrance as inheritance." The work of inheritance initiated by an exhibition will unavoidably risk producing public memory as a field of individuating and isolating difference and conflict. If this happens, public memory devolves to a conjoint remembrance of a particular event by people without overlapping histories and/or a shared place or project.[26] Such a form of public memory is defined only by each member's acquired relation to a definite event and a marking one's position within a field of difference in regard to the significance of past events. Such a risk, however, offers its own opportunities for furthering public history as praxiological and not just reproductive. The concern is not so much how public history functions to maintain the continuity and coherence of a social unit and more a matter of the possible consequences of any given practice in regard to if and how people might deem it necessary and/or desirous to forge new relations with one another. Here, curating is not only a practice that instantiates social relations but possibly transforms them through the ongoing interchange of thoughts and affects, opinions and beliefs, attachments and antipathies. On such terms, the social realm does not entirely preexist exhibition practices, but is constituted, in part, in the possibility of various modes and methods of curating as forms of social praxis.

SOME LAST WORDS

Exhibitions addressing the rendition of past violence and suffering face the persistent pedagogical question of how to represent the death and anguish of others so as to provoke sustained attention, concern, and corrective action rather than a few days' sensation that is soon forgotten. All such exhibitions embody the hope that they and the history they are attempting to bring into presence, will matter in regard to both present existence and future forms of social life. It is often taken for granted that such exhibitions are invaluable because they bear witness by revealing what happened at a particular time and place. Consequently, such revelations are taken as important information essential to rethinking our present and opening new possibilities for a future beyond the repetition of the forms of violence depicted. Understood on these terms, the main requirement is to simply look at such images and artifacts, or, more charitably, to work through and overcome our resistance to looking and thus no longer look away. However, as I have argued throughout this book, neither the provision of information about past events nor simply registering this information through one's acquisitive gaze can satisfy what is required in practices of remembrance that support the pursuit of justice. If the remembering instigated by public history simply devolves to the act of refusing to turn away, of looking straight-on at events that are difficult to face, what constitutes an act of remembrance remains relatively impoverished. This certainly would be the case if any given exhibition of violence and suffering were to be grasped as a "sad past," but one that has no currency in the present. Curating exhibitions that address a difficult past requires the development of a concept of a cultural pedagogy capable of bridging past and present without reducing one to the other nor dictating the terms on which this is to be accomplished. In this respect, curatorial projects should not and cannot prescribe what viewers see and comprehend, but they can be understood as implicated in the possibility of modes of apprehension and thought that might be occluded through a too-quick settling of what is felt and understood in regard to one's encounter with an exhibition.

Unfortunately, there is ample evidence that an awareness and moral assessment of previous unjust violence and brutality does not automatically constitute a bridge for linking the past and present. This leaves us with the still quite salient project of envisioning a curatorial practice as an ethical force, opening the way to a political discourse with some contemporary currency. To accomplish this we will need a curatorial project rooted in the notion that exhibitions of difficult knowledge must attempt to retain that which does not expend itself as information. Certainly, this pedagogy must be cognizant that the transmission and condensation of the past events through thematically mediated concepts structure the readability and effective circulation of the primary narratives that underwrite the significance of an exhibition. However, as the exhibitions previously discussed in this book have made it clear, curating not only involves judgments as to the presentation of images and artifacts to be interrogated as to their status as evidence that supports truth value of specific narratives. Curating difficult knowledge also requires judgments that establish a mise-en-scène within which images and artifacts act as petitionary perlocutionary signs, embodying an affective force provoking thought and action. In other words, curating must ultimately be concerned with the question of how exhibitions might be presented so as to serve a *transitive* function that could open up an indeterminate reconsideration of the force of history in social life. In evoking the necessity of fostering the transitivity of an exhibition, needed will be a conception of pedagogy that can help us identify the curatorial judgments necessary so that exhibitions that trace the lives of those who have lived and died in times and places other than our own may yet have some force that enjoins our capacities and felt responsibilities.

NOTES

CHAPTER 1. EXHIBITING ARCHIVAL PHOTOGRAPHS OF RACIAL VIOLENCE AS A PEDAGOGY OF WITNESS

1. James Fisk, quoted in Dora Apel, *Imagery of Lynching: Black Men, White Women, and the Mob* (New Brunswick: Rutgers University Press, 2004), 13–14.
2. Avery Gordon, *Ghostly Matters: Haunting and the Sociological Imagination* (Minneapolis: University of Minnesota Press, 2008).
3. Robert Gibbs, "Messianic Epistemology: Thesis IV," in *Walter Benjamin and History,* ed. Andrew Benjamin (New York: Continuum Press, 2005), 197–214.
4. Walter Benjamin, "Theses on the Philosophy of History," in *Illuminations: Essays and Reflections,* trans. Harry Zohn (New York: Schocken Books, 1968), 254.
5. Roberta Smith, "An Ugly Legacy Lives On, Its Glare Unsoftened by Age," *New York Times,* January 13, 2000, para. 13. http://www.nytimes.com/2000/01/13/books/critic-s-notebook-an-ugly-legacy-lives-on-its-glare-unsoftened-by-age.html. Further citations to this work are given in the text.
6. Ruth Wodak and John E. Richardson, "On the Politics of Remembering (or not)," *Critical Discourse Studies* 6, no. 4 (2009): 231–35.
7. Of course, exhibitions may incorporate other sensory possibilities such as sound. As recorded oral and video testimony has become important for practices of public history, the relation of sound, text,

and image has become increasingly important. However, as the exhibitions discussed in this book were limited to images, objects, and texts, these issues will not be discussed here.

8. Photographs from the Allen and Littlefield Collection appear in James Allen, ed., *Without Sanctuary: Lynching Photographs in America* (Santa Fe: Twin Palms Press, 1999). Also available online at http://www.withoutsanctuary.org.
9. See for example, Bettina M. Carbonell's discussion of the differences between the exhibitions held at the Horowitz-Roth Gallery and the New York Historical Society. Bettina M. Carbonell, "The Afterlife of Lynching: Exhibitions and the Re-composition of Human Suffering," *Mississippi Quarterly* 61, no. 1–2 (2008): 197–216.
10. Early in the twentieth century, photographs of lynching began to appear in anti-lynching publications, particularly in the African American press. See Jacqueline Goldsby, *A Spectacular Secret: Lynching in American Life and Literature* (Chicago: University of Chicago Press, 2006), 11–41. For an important discussion of the multivalent circulation of such photographs see Shawn Michelle Smith, "The Evidence of Lynching Photographs," in *Lynching Photographs,* ed. Dora Apel and Shawn Michelle Smith (Berkeley: University of California Press, 2007), 11–41.
11. Jacqueline Goldsby, *A Spectacular Secret: Lynching in American Life and Literature* (Chicago: University of Chicago Press, 2006), 33.
12. Winthrop Sheldon, "Shall Lynching Be Suppressed, and How?" *Arena* 36 (1906): 227, quoted in Goldsby, *Spectacular Secret,* 20.
13. Ann Louise Wood and Susan V. Donaldson, "Introduction: Lynching's Legacy in American Culture," *Mississippi Quarterly* 61, no. 1–2 (2008): 5–26.
14. William D. Carrigan, The Making of a Lynching Culture: Violence and Vigilantism in Central Texas, 1836–1916 (Urbana: University of Illinois Press, 2004).
15. There are obvious exceptions such as the murder of Emmett Till (1955), Michael Donald (1981), Matthew Shepard (1998), and James Byrd Jr. (1998).
16. For a discussion of the concept of "difficult knowledge," see Alice Pitt and Deborah Britzman, "Speculations on Qualities of Difficult Knowledge in Teaching and Learning: An Experiment in

Psychoanalytic Research," *International Journal of Qualitative Studies in Education* 16 (2003): 755–76.

17. Jill Bennett, *Empathic Vision: Affect, Trauma, and Contemporary Art* (Stanford: Stanford University Press, 2005).
18. The position taken here is quite different in its implications from the stance offered by those who employ Roland Barthes's mediation on photography to avow that the *studium* is all we have since the *punctum* operates at the level of the unconscious and thus is beyond control. For an excellent recent set of discussions regarding the function of the *punctum* see Geoffrey Batchen, ed., *Photography Degree Zero: Reflections on Roland Barthes Camera Lucida* (Cambridge: MIT Press, 2009).
19. Pitt and Britzman, "Speculations on Qualities of Difficult Knowledge," 755. Further citations to this work are given in the text.
20. Roger I. Simon, "The Terrible Gift: Museums and the Possibility of Hope Without Consolation," *Journal of Museum Management and Curatorship* 21, no. 3 (2006): 187–204.
21. Deborah Britzman, *Lost Subjects, Contested Objects: Toward a Psychoanalytic Inquiry of Learning* (Albany: State University of New York Press, 1998).
22. Stanley Cavell, "Knowing and Acknowledging" in *Must We Mean What We Say*? 2nd ed. (Cambridge: Harvard University Press, 2002), 238–66.
23. Emmanuel Levinas, "Useless Suffering" in *Entre Nous: Thinking of the Other*, trans. Michael B. Smith and Barbara Harshay (New York: Columbia University Press, 1998), 91–102.
24. Hagi Kenaan, "What Makes an Image Singular Plural? Questions to Jean-Luc Nancy," *Journal of Visual Culture* 9, no.1 (2010): 64.
25. Jean-Luc Nancy, "The Image—the Distinct," in *The Ground of the Image* (New York: Fordham University Press, 2005), 1–14.
26. Edward Said, "The World, the Text, and the Critic" in *The World, The Text, and the Critic* (Cambridge: Harvard University Press, 1984), 31–53.
27. Kenaan, "Facing Images," *Angelaki: Journal of the Theoretical Humanities* 16, no. 1 (2011): 145. Further citations to this work are given in the text.
28. The institutional context in which images appear elicits its own form of supervision. This is discussed further in chapter 3.

29. Mark Reinhardt and Holly Edwards, "Traffic in Pain," in *Beautiful Suffering: Photography and the Traffic in Pain,* ed. Mark Reinhardt, Holly Edwards, and Erina Duganne (Chicago: University of Chicago Press, 2006), 24. Reinhardt and Edwards are here referencing Alan Sekula, *Photography Against the Grain: Essays and Photoworks 1973–1983* (Halifax: Press of the Nova Scotia College of Art and Design), 62. For further details about the exhibit *Beautiful Suffering: Photography and the Traffic in Pain,* which ran from December 28, 2005, to April 30, 2006, at the Williams College Museum of Art, Williamstown, Mass., see: http://wcma.williams.edu/exhibit/beautiful-suffering/.
30. The one exception to this practice was the very first exhibition of seventy-eight images from the Allen and Littlefield collection held at the Roth Horowitz Gallery, a small art gallery in New York City entitled "Witness: Photographs from the Collection of James Allen and John Littlefield," January 13 to February 12, 2000. For a further discussion of this issue see chapter 2.
31. Judith Butler, "Introduction: Precarious Life, Grievable Life," in *Frames of War: When is Life Grievable?* (New York: Verso, 2009), 1–32. See especially 9–10.
32. Mieke Bal, "The Pain of Images," in *Beautiful Suffering,* 93–115 (see ch. 1, n. 29). Further citations to this work are given in the text.
33. Joseph Jordan, "Truth as a Way to Reconciliation," *Atlanta Journal-Constitution,* April 28, 2002, quoted in Apel, *Imagery of Lynching,* 14.
34. There is a genre of scholarship that considers the photograph as a form of visual testimony. See for example, Sharon Sliwinski, (2010), "Visual Testimony: Lee Miller's Dachau," *Journal of Visual Culture* 9, no. 3 (2010): 389–408. However, I am proceeding from the assumption that the communicative, transitive act that defines the practice of giving testimony requires the integrative consideration of the terms and circumstances on which a photograph makes an appearance. Thus, the time and space coordinates of the display of a set of images as well as the mise-en-scène in which they are situated matter greatly if one wants to understand how images function as a form of testimony. While exhibitions are of course not the sole scene for the appearance of images, given the limits of the project within this book, I consider "the exhibition" as

the focal unit of my concern, hence opening the question of how an exhibition and its specific mise-en-scène enact "testimony."

35. This normative character of witnessing is the reason why it must be distinguished from other possible responses to testimony, such as mimicry, voyeurism, or spectatorship. Such practices depend on divorcing the testimonial referents from the transactional dynamics of lived engagements with traces of the past. As a result of this splitting, testimony is often heard or read as a phenomenon to be rendered meaningful within classification and analysis, or its force is perverted as it becomes a source of compulsive fascination. Rarely do such modes of apprehension call into question the epistemological and ethical frames through which one apprehends history. For further discussion of "just remembrance," see Simon, "Remembering Together: Interactive Social Media and the Formation of the Historical Present," in *Heritage and Social Media: Understanding Heritage in a Participatory Culture,* ed., Elisa Giaccardi (New York: Routledge, 2012), 89–106.
36. Kelly Oliver, *Witnessing: Beyond Recognition* (Minneapolis: University of Minnesota Press, 2001), 18.
37. Francisco Goya, *The Disasters of War* (London: Dover, 1967).
38. Sharon Sliwinski, "The Childhood of Human Rights: The Kodak on the Congo," *Journal of Visual Culture* 5, no. 3 (2006): 333–63.
39. Ernst Freidrich, *War Against War!* (Seattle: Real Comet Press, 1987).
40. Ariella Azoulay, *The Civil Contract of Photography* (Cambridge: MIT Press, 2008), 11.
41. Bal, "Pain of Images," in *Beautiful Suffering* (see ch. 1, n. 29). Further citations to this work are given in the text. For a further discussion of this issue see Barbie Zelizer, *About to Die: How News Images Move the Public* (Oxford: Oxford University Press, 2010).
42. Susan Sontag, *Regarding the Pain of Others* (New York: Picador, 2003), 62–63. Further citations to this work are given in the text.
43. Stephen Kinzer, "In Cincinnati, Art Bows to the Privacy of Death," *New York Times,* August 3, 2002, para. 3. http://www.nytimes.com/2002/08/03/arts/design/03MORG.html. Further citations to this work are given in the text.
44. Richmond Lattimore, trans., *The Iliad of Homer* (Chicago: University of Chicago Press, 1951). Further citations to this work are given in the text.

45. Butler, *Frames of War*.
46. Photos by Luc Delahaye/Magnum appended to "Fall of the Taliban," *Newsweek,* November 26, 2011, 21–29.
47. Apel, *Imagery of Lynching,* 2. Further citations to this work are given in the text.
48. Eleanor Watchtel, "Ghost Hunter" in *The Emergence of Memory: Conversations with W. G. Sebald,* ed. Lynne Sharon Schwartz (New York: Seven Stories Press, 2007), 37–62.
49. Reinhardt, "Picturing Violence: Aesthetics and the Anxiety of Critique" in *Beautiful Suffering,* 16. Further citations to this work are given in the text.
50. Alan Sekula, *Photography Against the Grain,* 57.
51. Roland Barthes, *Camera Lucida* (New York: Hill and Wang, 1981), 107.
52. Mark Simpson, "Archiving Hate: Lynching Postcards at the Limit of Social Circulation," *ESC English Studies in Canada* 30, no. 1. (2004): 17–38.
53. Simon, "Towards a Hopeful Practice of Worrying: The Problematics of Listening and the Educative Responsibilities of Canada's Truth and Reconciliation Commission," in *Reconciling Canada: Critical Perspectives on the Culture of Redress,* ed. Pauline Wakeman and Jennifer Henderson (Toronto: University of Toronto Press, 2013).
54. Reinhardt and Edwards "Traffic in Pain," from *Beautiful Suffering,* 8.
55. Martha Rosler, "The Look of War Photography" (lecture, Walker Art Center, Minneapolis, MN, November 16, 1981, quoted in Duganne, "Photography After the Fact," in *Beautiful Suffering,* 65.
56. Roger I. Simon, Mario DiPalantonio, and Mark Clamen, "Remembrance as Praxis and the Ethics of the Inter-Human," *Culture Machine* 4 (2002). http://www.culturemachine.net/ index.php/cm/article/viewArticle/272/257.
57. Edward Burtynsky, "Audio Commentary," *Manufactured Landscapes,* DVD, directed by Jennifer Baichwal (New York: Zeitgeist Films, 2007).
58. See Steven Galloway, *The Cellist of Sarajevo* (Toronto: Knopf Canada, 2008), 232–33.
59. Ken Gonzales Day, *Erased Lynching Series,* 2002–2010. http://

www.kengonzalesday.com/projects/erasedlynching/index.htm. Further citations to this work are given in the text.

60. Judith Butler makes a counterargument worth considering. She argues, "The face and name are not ours to know, and affirming this cognitive limit is a way of affirming the humanity that has escaped the visual control of the photograph." In a very direct sense, she supports the work of Ken Gonzalez-Day when she writes: "To expose the victim further would be to reiterate the crime, so the task would seem to be a full documentation of the acts of the torturer, as well as a full documentation of those who exposed, disseminated, and published the scandal—but all this without intensifying the 'exposure' of the victim, either through discursive or visual means." Butler, "Torture and the Ethics of Photography: Thinking with Sontag" in *Frames of War*, 95.
61. Butler, *Frames of War*. For Butler's discussion of "grievable life," see especially p. 14.
62. Azoulay, *Civil Contract* (see ch. 1, n. 40). Further citations to this work are given in the text.
63. Indicted by these exhibitions are the photographers, the white crowd, the systemic practice of lynching, the education system that has kept these images "hidden," the still-pervasive racism throughout America, etc.
64. Simpson, "Archiving Hate." Further citations to this work are given in the text.
65. See the notion of an image as dialectics at a standstill in W. Benjamin, *The Arcades Project* (Cambridge: Belknap Press of Harvard University Press, 1999) [N2, 3], 462.
66. John S. Willis, "Who Needs Multicultural Education? White Students, U.S. History, and the Construction of a Usable Past," *Anthropology and Education Quarterly* 27, no. 3 (1996): 365–89.
67. John L. Austin, *How to Do Things With Words* (Cambridge: Harvard University Press, 1975).
68. See Emmanuel Levinas, *Totality and Infinity,* trans. A. Lingis (Pittsburgh: Duquesne University Press, 1969); Idem., "Meaning and Sense," in *Collected Philosophical Papers,* trans. A. Lingis (Pittsburgh: Duquesne University Press, 1998).
69. Stanley Cavell, "Comments on Veena Das's Essay 'Language and Body: Transactions in the Construction of Pain," in *Social*

Suffering, ed. Arthur M. Kleinman, Veena Das, and Margaret M. Lock (Berkeley: University of California Press, 1997), 94. Further citations to this work are given in the text. See Cavell, "Knowing and Acknowledging," for further elaboration of these ideas.

70. Reinhardt, "Picturing Violence," in *Beautiful Suffering.* Further citations to this work are given in the text.
71. Sontag, *On Photography* (New York: Delta, 1978), 111, quoted in Reinhardt, "Picturing Violence," 31.
72. Cavell, "Knowing and Acknowledging," 263.
73. Cavell, "Between Acknowledgment and Avoidance" in *The Claim of Reason: Wittgenstein, Scepticism, Morality, and Tragedy* (Oxford: Oxford University Press, 1999), 428.
74. Ibid., 354.

CHAPTER 2. *WITHOUT SANCTUARY* EXHIBITIONS AT THE ANDY WARHOL MUSEUM AND CHICAGO HISTORICAL SOCIETY

1. Bal, "The Pain of Images," in *Beautiful Suffering* (see 224n29). For Bal's discussion of visual images, see p.102.
2. W. Benjamin, Convolute N 3, 1 in *The Arcades Project,* trans. Howard Eiland and Kevin McLaughlin (Cambridge: Belknap Press of Harvard University Press, 1999), 462–63 (see 227n65).
3. W. J. T. Mitchell, *Picture Theory* (Chicago: University of Chicago Press, 1994).
4. Georges Didi-Huberman, *Images in Spite of All: Four Photographs from Auschwitz,* ed. Shane B. Lillis (Chicago, University of Chicago Press, 2008), 155.
5. John Tagg, *The Disciplinary Frame: Photographic Truths and the Capture of Meaning* (Minneapolis, University of Minnesota Press, 2009).
6. Jacques Derrida, *Specters of Marx: The State of the Debt, the Work of Mourning, and the New International* (New York: Routledge, 2004), 16.
7. On display at the time of the *Without Sanctuary* exhibition was Happy *Warholidays, Andy Warhol's Holiday drawings.* As well, presented was the exhibition *Silver Clouds*—a room filled with helium balloons (silver clouds) that move with the air currents. The Andy

Warhol Museum is a seven-floor warehouse building displaying more than five hundred Andy Warhol works of art in all types of media. These include his Pop Art images, films, death and disaster series, and portraits.

8. James Allen, "Afterword," in *Without Sanctuary: Lynching Photography in America,* ed. James Allen (Santa Fe: Twin Palms Press, 1999).
9. Wall Panel, *Without Sanctuary: Lynching Photography in America,* Andy Warhol Museum, Pittsburgh, September 22, 2001-January 21, 2002. All further references to the Andy Warhol Museum are to this exhibition and are clearly identified in the body of the text.
10. When viewing the exhibition beginning with the earliest dated photograph, visitors encountered an image of the double lynching of two non–African Americans, J. L. Compton and Joseph Wilson, in Helena, Montana, in 1870.
11. Also displayed were two NAACP anti-lynching buttons, three NAACP anti-lynching pamphlets, and two NAACP broadsides, a version of a tabular display of statistics and alleged causes of lynchings in the years 1892–94 compiled by Ida B. Wells, and an NAACP poster announcing a protest in conjunction with murder of Emmett Till.
12. The collection is now owned by the National Center for Civil and Human Rights, Atlanta, Georgia. The opening for this new institution is scheduled for May 2014. http://www.cchrpartnership.org/index.html.
13. The Chicago Historical Society was undergoing extensive renovations at the time of their *Without Sanctuary* exhibit, and much of the museum space was closed off.
14. Maria Newman, "U.S. to Reopen Investigation of Emmett Till's Murder in 1955," *New York Times,* May 10, 2004. http://www.nytimes.com/2004/05/10/national/10CND-TILL.html, as quoted on Wall Panel at Chicago Historical Society.
15. See chapter 3 for comments from staff on this coincidence.
16. Wall Panel, *Without Sanctuary: Lynching Photography in America,* Chicago Historical Society, Chicago, June 4, 2005-December 4, 2005. All further references to the Chicago Historical Society are to this exhibition and are clearly identified in the body of the text.
17. The first of these amendments abolished American slavery, the second barred governments in the United States from preventing

a citizen from voting based on that citizen's race, color, or previous condition of servitude—i.e., slavery.

18. Inexplicably, while Jackson is identified in the book publication *Without Sanctuary: Lynching Photography in America,* on frequently accessed Web site presenting the Allen and Littlefield photographs (www.withoutsanctuary.org), the incorrect Andy Warhol Museum label is used along with the narrative explanation cited in the book (see photograph 17 on the Web site).
19. The text providing this framework was as follows: "Violence against African Americans was not new. Many whites considered Blacks barely human and racial ideologies helped support such views. During enslavement white slave holders inflicted a cruel spectrum of violence on African Americans. After emancipation the violence expanded, especially in the South to include outright murder. Endorsed by Whites such violence maintained a form of racial control in the absence of slavery."
20. Lois McMaster Bujold is an American science fiction author. The quote cited within the exhibit is from her novel *Diplomatic Immunity* (Riverdale, NY: Baen Books, 2002). The textual source of the quote was not provided in the Chicago Historical Society display.
21. Harold and Deluca have noted that "the power of Till's body is intensified not because it is a photo of a corpse but a photo of a face of a corpse, or what was a face. The kick in the gut offered by this photo is intensified by the dialogue between the photos of Till before he was murdered." Christine Harold and Kevin Michael Deluca, "Behold the Corpse: Violent Images and the Case of Emmett Till" *Rhetoric & Public Affairs* 8, no. 2 (2005): 274.
22. Harold and Deluca argue that encounters with Till's funeral image provoked "affect and action because it demonstrated that conventional boundaries—between self and others, North and South, life and death—were irrevocably blurred. . . . Till's head, swollen to three times its normal size, his individual features indistinguishable, missing an eye, an ear, and most of his teeth . . . all this [was set] in the frame of silk lined casket in a funeral home, a context in which if bodies are shown at all they are almost without exception displayed in a state of tranquility and peace—the body at rest, not at risk" ("Behold the Corpse," 281). The visual encounter with this image and the visceral reaction it demands, forced [and still forces]

"a reckoning, an active redistribution of knowledge that is different from what had sufficed before" ("Behold the Corpse," 281).

23. The *Independent* was an anti-lynching newspaper published at the turn of the nineteenth century and the early decades of the twentieth. It published reports on individual lynch murders as well as overall statistics on lynching in the United States.
24. From wall text at the Chicago Historical Society exhibit. See pp. 52–54 for full quotation.
25. Apel, *Imagery of Lynching*, 93 (see ch. 1, n.1).
26. Siegfried Kracauer, "La photographie," in *Le Voyage et la Danse: Figures de Ville et Vues de Films,* trans. S. Cornille (Saint-Denis: Presses Universitaires de Vincennes, 1996), 42–57, quoted in Didi-Huberman, *Images in Spite of All,* 173. Further citations to this work are given in the text.
27. Didi-Huberman discusses how reducing an image to a document amounts to a way of "being inattentive" to the image. See Didi-Huberman, *Images in Spite of All,* 34.
28. See pp. 52–54 for complete wall text statement.
29. Nancy, "Forbidden Representation" in *The Ground of the Image* (New York: Fordham University Press, 2005), 36.
30. Bennett, *Emphatic Vision,* 36.
31. See Gilles Deleuze, *Difference and Repetition,* trans. Paul Patton (New York: Columbia University Press, 1994).
32. Tagg, *Disciplinary Frame,* 68.

CHAPTER 3. THE CURATORIAL WORK OF EXHIBITING ARCHIVAL PHOTOGRAPHS OF LYNCHING IN AMERICA

1. Miguel Á. Hernández-Navarro, "The Curator's Demands: Toward an Ethics of Commitment." *Manifesta Journal* 12 (2010/2011): 7–8.
2. All interviews at Andy Warhol Museum were conducted by members of the research team (Lynn Teather and Claire-Estelle Daitch) in Pittsburgh from May 21–23, 2006. All interviews were conducted in confidentiality, and names of interviewees are withheld by mutual agreement. All further quotations from interviews at the Andy Warhol Museum are part of data from this set and are

identified clearly in the text. Therefore, separate notes will not be included for subsequent quotations from these interviews.

3. All interviews at Chicago Historical Society were conducted by members of the research team (Lynn Teather and Claire-Estelle Daitch) in Chicago on October 10, 2005. All interviews were conducted in confidentiality, and names of interviewees are withheld by mutual agreement. All further quotations from interviews at the Chicago Historical Society are part of data from this set and are identified clearly in the text. Therefore, separate notes will not be included for subsequent quotations from these interviews.
4. See pp. 52–54 for quotation from Theophus (Thee) Smith and for a discussion of "undeserved grace."
5. The exhibition *Keith Edmier and Farrah Fawcett* examined the connection between artist and muse through a series of collaborative sculptures and photographs by contemporary artist, Keith Edmier, and actress and artist, Farrah Fawcett.
6. *Clown Paintings: From the Collection of Diane Keaton and Others.* The exhibition included more than forty amateur clown paintings culled from the collections of actress Diane Keaton and gallery owner and collector Robert Berman.
7. Jessica Gogan, "The Warhol: Museum as Artist: Creative, Dialogic and Civic Practice," Case Study. *Animating Democracy* (Washington, DC., Americans for the Arts, n.d.): 4. http://www.AmericansForTheArts.org. Further citations to this work are given in the text.
8. Apel, *Imagery of Lynching,* op. cit.
9. Lynne Connor, "Hidden History: An Exploratory Case Study Looking at the Impact of the Andy Warhol Museum's *Without Sanctuary* Project," Case Study. *Animating Democracy* (Washington DC., Americans for the Arts, 2002). http://animatingdemocracy.org/sites/default/ files/documents/WOSanctuary_CaseStudy.pdf.
10. From description of the exhibition posted on the Chicago Historical Society Web site, http://www.chicagohistory.org/.
11. Harold and Deluca point out that while the black body in pain has served as a symbol of unmitigated white power, the corpse of Emmett Till became a visual trope illustrating the ugliness of racial violence and the aggregate power of the black community. They argue that this reconfiguration was, in part, an effect of the black community's embracing and foregrounding Till's abject body

rather than allowing it to be safely exiled from communal life. Harold and DeLuca, "Behold the Corpse," op. cit.

12. The August Wilson Center for African American Culture was in the process of building development at the time of the Andy Warhol Museum's *Without Sanctuary* exhibition.
13. While the numbers of African American visitors certainly increased during the run of the exhibition, as the head of visitor services emphasized, the museum "wanted everybody to come. . . . We wanted everyone to know about [the events depicted in the exhibition] because this [is] a history we don't normally talk about."
14. The artist educators responsible for the dialogues reported a variety of experiences. At times, the discussions took a turn likely to be disapproved of by some advisory committee members while seemingly remaining educationally significant. Thus, as artist educator 3 reported: "Although we didn't get to the institutional racism in some of those prominent white groups . . . what I thought was interesting that what came out was the biases that they had towards one another. You know . . . identifying the Jock biases versus the preps and all of those things in place. Even though they couldn't identify with the racism, they were able to identify with this bias, which I thought was really interesting. That was one of my observations with those groups and I saw a lot of it; some self-reflection with them wanting to connect with some sort of injustice and they identify with."
15. One of the artist educators reported: "At the opening we had an African drum group come and drum, it wasn't in the image space, it was in another one of the galleries, it was in the dialogue room. It was this huge, loud, wonderful drumming. It was this kind of honoring. This reverence is what was happening in this room."
16. *Possession Obsession* was an exhibition of objects from Andy Warhol's Personal Collection that ran from March 2, 2002 to May 19, 2002, at the Andy Warhol Museum. It was promoted as "a rare opportunity to reunite approximately 300 objects from Warhol's personal collection (sold at the legendary 1988 Sotheby's auction) in order to examine one of the least-studied aspects of his oeuvre: collecting." The exhibition focused on areas where "Warhol maintained a deep, abiding interest, such as 19th-century American furniture and folk art, cookie jars and other collectibles, Art Deco furniture and objects, Native American art and artifacts and fine

and costume jewelry" Indepth Arts News, "Possession Obsession: Objects from Andy Warhol's Personal Collection," *Absolute Arts.* http://www.absolutearts.com/artsnews/2002/03/04/29704.html, para. 1.

17. See the schematic layout of the Chicago Historical Society exhibit in chapter 2. The text editor is referring to a window in a standing wall near the Ku Klux Klan robe through which one could see elements of the later stages of the exhibition.

CHAPTER 4. PUBLIC PERFORMANCE IN THE SOCIAL SPACE OF MUSEUM COMMENT BOOKS

1. Sharon Macdonald, "Accessing Audiences: Visiting Visitor Books" *Museum and Society* 3, no. 3 (2005): 119.
2. Clearly, not all occasions of writing in comment books are the same. The contexts and formats can strongly affect what gets written. Performance is a phenomenon that is always highly contextual and not just in the sense of the material context of an exhibition per se. We know that this context includes the frameworks that produce comments as intelligible (to write outside these terms is to risk condemnation and dismissal if not sanction). Macdonald cites Tamar Katriel, who writes that in her work she found visitor books "a highly constraining frame of a tradition of self-selected, appreciative responses given out from guests to their hosts . . . very few comments I have seen were critical or indifferent in their response, and the few that were pointed out the need to improve one aspect of the display or another but never questioned the value or relevance of the enterprise as a whole." Tamar Katriel, *Performing the Past: A Study of Israeli Settlement Museums* (New Jersey: Lawrence Erlbaum Associates, 1997), 71 n. 5, quoted in Macdonald, "Assessing Audiences," 121. It would be worth considering why this was the case at the Israeli settler museums that Katriel discusses and, differently, how the visitor book at the *Without Sanctuary* exhibitions elicited very different performances than those structured as an appreciative comment from a guest to a host.
3. Susan Reid, "In the Name of the People. The Manege Affair Revisited," *Kritika: Explorations in Russian and Eurasian History* 6, no. 4 (2005): 682. Further citations to this work are given in the text.
4. See Pierre Bourdieu, *Distinction: A Social Critique of the Judgment*

of Taste, trans. Richard Nice (London: Routledge and Kegan Paul, 1984).

5. Paula Findlen, *Possessing Nature: Museums, Collecting, and Scientific Culture in Early Modern Italy* (Berkeley: University of California Press, 1994). Further citations to this work are given in the text.
6. Roger M. Buergel, Curator, *Documenta* 12. As quoted on, Debalie, "te gast/Documenta," May 12, 2007. http://www.debalie.nl/artikel.jsp?podiumid=overig&articleid=106675.
7. Macdonald, "Assessing Audiences," 122. Further citations to this work are given in the text.
8. In Lynne Connor's report on the Andy Warhol Museum exhibition cited in the previous chapter, she comments that she observed twice as many visitors reading the comment books than were writing in them.
9. Hannah Arendt, *The Human Condition* (Chicago: University of Chicago Press, 1998), 52–53.
10. Simpson, "Archiving Hate," 30.
11. Reid, "In the Name of the People," 682.
12. Sharon Macdonald notes, "Beyond [the] opportunity—or what some might even see as a kind of duty—to formulate a view, some visitors may experience writing as a need, as seems to be the case at the Anne Frank House in Amsterdam, where visitors queue up to write." Macdonald, "Accessing Audiences," 125. In our research visit to the *Without Sanctuary* exhibition at the Chicago Historical Society we observed visitors lining up to write comments.
13. There seemed to be an educational imperative to take in and acknowledge the fact of a murderous racism that was central to the history of the United States. For some who visited the Chicago Historical Society and Andy Warhol Museum, they experienced a revelation of a previously "hidden history." When this was the case, it may be presumed that visitors were being asked "to see" and testify to what others, primarily African Americans, have known for a long time (although it should be noted that in their comments many African Americans indicated they hadn't known much about what was shown—whether this refers to lynching in general or the specificity of the postcards is not clear).
14. Of course, the impulse to account for oneself through the writing of comments may be seen through a psychodynamic lens, as an attempted defense against the anxiety provoked by the images in the exhibition. On such terms, this anxiety stands as signal of a

danger to one's ego. This is a consequence of the images evoking an unmasterable affect that threatens a traumatic disintegration of the ego that would result in an unmanageable helplessness. Writing in a comment book and hence performing a response to the exhibition might thus be understood as a form of "signal anxiety," attempts to contain the primary anxiety that threatens to annihilate the ego. See Anna Freud, *The Ego and the Mechanisms of Defense* (London: Hogarth Press and Institute of Psycho-Analysis, 1937). This is particularly evident in many comments that express notions of what must be done in the face of evidence of the "inhumanity of man." This desire to redeem the violent brutality of the images will be discussed further in the chapter.

15. Apel, *Imagery of Lynching.*
16. See chapter 1 for a further discussion of "response-ability."
17. Butler, *Giving and Account of Oneself* (New York: Fordham University Press, 2005), 50.
18. See Arendt, "The Public Realm: The Common" in *The Human Condition,* 50–57.
19. All comments quoted in this chapter are either from the Andy Warhol Museum or the Chicago Historical Society. For all quotations from the comment books, the institution is clearly identified in the text. Therefore, separate notes will not be included for subsequent quotations from the comment books.
20. Within this set of comments, a distinction was made between an affective intensity that cannot be cognitively coded and expressed and the written comments that characterize an emotional state. Lexically specific characterizations of one's emotional state were coded separately from the expression of non-denotative graphic indicators of affective intensity (including exclamation points, underlining, large lettering, nonnormative use of page space in a comment book, nondeclarative pictures and doodles accompanying written comments).
21. This visual presentation of the comments and themes is based on a method used in an excellent article by Kevin Coffee, in which he presents thematic renderings of visitor comments following this same structure of offering the full comment followed by a listing of the thematic elements that appear within the comment. See Kevin Coffee, "Disturbing the Eternal Silence of the Gallery: A Site of Dialogue About Hunger in America," *Museum Management and*

Curatorship 26, no.1 (2011): 11–26. See especially pp. 20–24 for presentation of qualitative themes and sample comments.

22. Emotions or emotional states explicitly expressed in comments included: sadness, shame, embarrassment; fear, horror, abjection; shock, surprise; anger and hate; sympathy and compassion; confusion and the admission of the inability to find appropriate words; and gratefulness.
23. In addition, this category also tracked use of capital letters; prayers or verse; drawings; nonnormative use of space on the page; titled comments; and repeated words.
24. For an introduction to the notion of monstration, see Andre Gaudreault, "Narration and Monstration in the Cinema," *Journal of Film and Video* 39, no. 2 (1987): 29–36. See also Tom Gunning, "An Aesthetic of Astonishment: Early Film and the (In)credulous Spectator," in *Art and Text* 34 (1989): 114–33.
25. W. Benjamin, "Thesis on the Philosophy of History," 260.
26. Jonny Gammage, age thirty-one, was killed by police, Oct 12, 1995, at a traffic stop; five white policemen were involved.
27. Dana B. Polan, "'Above All Else to Make You See': Cinema and the Ideology of Spectacle," *boundary 2*, Vol. 11, no. 1/2 (1983): 135.
28. Mark Seltzer, "Wound Culture: Trauma in the Pathological Public Sphere," *October* 80 (1997): 3–26.
29. John Berger, "Photographs of Agony," in *About Looking* (Toronto: Random House Digital, 2011), 39–40.
30. Richard Sandell, *Museums, Prejudice, and the Reframing of Difference* (London: Routledge, 2007), 174. Further citations to this work are given in the text.
31. For further discussion of public-in-formation, see Craig Calhoun, "Imagining Solidarity: Cosmopolitanism, Constitutional Patriotism, and the Public Sphere," *Public Culture* 14, no. 1 (2002): 147–71.
32. Seltzer, "Wound Culture."
33. Arendt, *Human Condition*, 52.
34. James Allen, as reported in Caroline Abels, "Collector says exhibit provides 'visual vocabulary' of racism," *The Pittsburgh Post-Gazette*, September 22, 2001. http://old.post-gazette.com/ae/20010922allen0922fnp3.asp.
35. As noted earlier, displaying one's nonindifference may in some cases be rooted in narcissistic desire to put forward a "good performance"

that locates the self as "not racist," "not hateful." Quite differently, this nonindifference may also be a moment in which visitors are enacting the structure of feeling that accompanies participating in collective activity of remaking the world through professing and taking an active responsibility for the domain we live in.

36. Goldsby, *Spectacular Secret*, 214–82. Further citations to this work are given in the text.
37. Goldsby is here quoting from Roland Barthes, who in *Camera Lucida* observed that photographs may be thought of as absolute particulars—as ungeneralized encounters with the immediate and the "real"—noting that in its specificity and particularity a photograph demands that the viewer look at the thing to which it points. In this captured moment, the photograph seems indistinguishable from its referent, so that one seems to look at the person portrayed and not a photograph. Barthes, *Camera Lucida*, 4–5.
38. Perhaps the one exhibition that might be most associated with the substance of Goldsby's analysis was the first appearance of the picture postcards at the Roth Horowitz gallery in New York City.
39. Barbie Zelizer, *Remembering to Forget: Holocaust Memory Through the Camera's Eye* (Chicago, University of Chicago Press, 2000). See especially 100–10.
40. Anne Anlin Cheng, *The Melancholy of Race: Psychoanalysis, Assimilation, and Hidden Grief* (New York: Oxford University Press, 2001).
41. Frantz Fanon, *Black Skin, White Masks* (New York; Grove Press, 1967).
42. John Jackson Jr., *Racial Paranoia: The Unintended Consequences of Political Correctness: The New Reality of Race in America* (New York: Basic Civitas, 2008). Further citations to this work are given in the text.

CHAPTER 5: CURATORIAL JUDGMENT, THE PEDAGOGICAL FRAMING OF EXHIBITIONS, AND THE RELATION BETWEEN AFFECT AND THOUGHT

1. For example of such resonance, see Jacquie Soohen, "The case of the Jena 6: Black high school students charged with attempted murder for schoolyard fight after nooses are hung from a tree," *Democracy Now*, July 10, 2007. http://www.democracynow.org/

shows/2007/7/10. See also "Apparent B.C. hate crime leads to 3 arrests," *Canadian Broadcasting Company* (CBC), July 7, 2009, http://www.cbc.ca/canada/british-columbia/story/2009/07/07/bc-courtenay-hate-crime-reaction.html.

2. Reinhardt, Edwards, and Duganne, *Beautiful Suffering*.
3. Kevin Robins, *Into the Image: Culture and Politics in the Field of Vision* (London: Routledge, 1996), 77.
4. Cathy Caruth, *Unclaimed Experience: Trauma, Narrative, and History* (Baltimore: Johns Hopkins University Press, 1996).
5. Gerald Bruns. *Tragic Thoughts at the End of Philosophy: Language, Literature, and Ethical Theory* (Evanston: Northwestern University Press. 1999), 15.
6. Martha Langford. Comments made in discussion, Curating Difficult Knowledge Conference, Centre for Ethnographic Research and Exhibition in the Aftermath of Violence, Concordia University, Montreal, Quebec, April 16–18, 2009.
7. Wall panel from Chicago Historical Society exhibit. See pp. 52–54 for full text of wall panel.
8. Brian Massumi, "Introduction: Like a Thought," in *A Shock to Thought: Expression After Deleuze and Guattari*, ed. Brian Massumi (New York: Routledge, 2002), xiii–xxxix.
9. Geoffrey Batchen, Mick Gidley, Nancy K. Miller, and Jay Prosser, *Picturing Atrocity: Photography in Crisis* (London, Reaktion Books, 2012).
10. Sontag, *Regarding the Pain of Others*, 115.
11. Apel, "Lynching Photographs and the Politics of Public Shaming" in *Lynching Photographs*, 42–78.
12. Siegfried Kracauer, "The Head of the Medusa," in *Theory of Film* (Princeton: Princeton University Press, 1997), 305–306.
13. Derrida, "By Force of Mourning," *Critical Inquiry* 22, no.2 (1996): 179.
14. Bal, "The Pain of Images," 102.
15. Didi-Huberman, "Image Semblable ou Image Semblante," in *Images Malgré Tout* (Paris: Les Éditions de Minuit, 2003), 221. The original text reads, "*Mais l'horreur reflétée, reconduite, reconstruite comme image—non sans raison, Kracauer, comme le fera Godard, pense d'abord aux images d'archives—, peut être source de connaissance, à condition toutefois que l'on engage sa responsabilité dans le dispositif formel de l'image produite.*"

16. Didi-Huberman, *Images in Spite of All,* 178.
17. Deleuze, "What Is a Dispositif?" in *Michel Foucault, Philosopher,* trans. and ed. Timothy J. Armstrong (Brighton: Harvester Wheatsheaf, 1992), 159–68; Giorgio Agamben, *What is an Apparatus?* (Stanford: Stanford University Press, 2009).
18. Nancy, "Forbidden Representation," 36.
19. Cavell, "Knowing and Acknowledging," 238–66. See also Levinas, "Useless Suffering." As discussed in the previous chapter, the felt responsibility to express one's nonindifference was evident in the numerous and extensive visitor comments written at both exhibitions.
20. Bennett, *Emphatic Vision.* For Bennett's discussion of "the squirm," see especially p. 43.
21. Massumi, "The Autonomy of Affect" *Cultural Critique* 31 (1995): 104.
22. Justus Nieland, *Feeling Modern: The Eccentricities of Public Life* (Urbana: University of Illinois Press, 2008), 94.
23. Gilles Deleuze and Félix Guattari, *A Thousand Plateaus,* trans. Massumi (London and New York: Continuum, 2004).
24. Goldsby, *Spectacular Secret,* 13–14. Further citations to this work are given in the text. Goldsby's account is informed by citations from Samuel Burdett, "A Test of Lynch Law: An Exposé of Mob Violence and Courts of Hell" (Seattle: n.p., 1904), in D. A. P. Murray Pamphlet Collection (microfilm), United States Library of Congress.
25. Nancy, "Forbidden Representation," 38–39. Further citations to this work are given in the text.
26. This formulation is the inverse of what Nancy argues regarding "super-representation." He states that "super-representation . . . is a revelation that, in revealing, does not withdraw what is revealed but, on the contrary, exhibits it, imposes it, and fills every one of its fibers with presence and with the present." Nancy, "Forbidden Representation," 40.
27. It may reasonably be argued that in any form of super-representation that purports to provide full presence there is no face. The face that demands is not ready at hand, but one that is contains a hollowing.
28. Deleuze, *Difference and Repetition,* 139.
29. It is possible that the serial repetition of a large number of

photographs side by side may have mitigated the affective force of the visual event. However, it is also conceivable that this visual abundance of difficult images drove viewers to concentrate on specific photographs in the series. See Jennifer Bonnell and Roger I. Simon, "Difficult Exhibitions and Intimate Encounters," *Museum and Society* 5, no. 2 (2007): 65–85. http://www.le.ac.uk/ms/museumsociety.htm.

30. Michael Tymkiw, "Debunking the Myth of the *saubere Wehrmacht*," *Word and Image* 23, no. 4 (2007): 485–92. Tymkiw is quoting from Pierre Nora, "Between Memory and History: *les lieux de memoire*," *Representations* 26 (1989): 19.
31. Bernd Hüppauf, "Emptying the Gaze: Framing Violence through the Viewfinder" *New German Critique* 72 (1997): 6.
32. Reemtsma, quoted in Hüppauf, "Emptying the Gaze," 7. Here Hüppauf is quoting from Reemtsma, "*Ein Dokument der Verstorung. Zu einer Kritik der Ausstellung 'Vernichtungskrieg'*," *Merkur* 568 (1996): 643–46.
33. Jan Phillip Reemtsma, "Two Exhibitions—A Review," review of "*Verbrechen der Wehrmacht. Dimensionen des Vernichtungskrieges 1941–1944*" (*Crimes of the German Wehrmacht: Dimensions of a War of Annihilation, 1941–1944*), November 28, 2001-May 28, 2004. Hamburg, *Hamburger Institut für Sozialforschung*, n.d., 12. http://www.his-online.de/en/events/1095/. Further citations to this work are given in the text.
34. As will be discussed later in this chapter, various curators have chosen to reference the photographs under discussion on differing terms, most commonly as portraits or identity photographs. I will refer to the images as identity photographs unless referencing specific curators who preferred the term *portraits*.
35. Rachel Hughes offers an entirely different explanation: "The meticulous production of the prisoner portraits was an important element of administrative control. While the experience of being photographed undoubtedly intimidated prisoners, it is also imaginable that this repeated submission of individuals to 'identification,' the extensive photo archive produced and portrait photographs in circulation in the prison served to reinforce the total institution. The photographs were, for both prisoners and their masters, emblems of the regime's omnipotence and efficiency." Hughes, "The Abject Artefacts of Memory: Photographs from Cambodia's

Genocide" *Media, Culture and Society* 25, no. 1 (2003): 25. On the notion of "identification," Hughes is quoting from David Chandler, *Voices from S-21: Terror and History in Pol Pot's Secret Prison* (Chiang Mai: Silkworm Books, 1999), 14–40.

36. The museum hence was part of an attempt to produce a coherent narrative in which Cambodian memories of the last half of the twentieth century would fit with a narrative of "liberation and reconstruction at the hands of a benevolent and fraternal state" (Hughes, "Abject Artefacts," 26).
37. Photo Archive Group, *Tuol Sleng Museum of Genocide Project Summary*, (n.d.), cited in Hughes, "Abject Artefacts," 29.
38. The book *Killing Fields* was published by Twin Palms Press (the publisher of the book version of the *Without Sanctuary* photographs). It contained seventy-nine of the one hundred photographs, a short history of Tuol Sleng and the Khmer Rouge revolution, and a memoir by one the of the prison's seven survivors. Chris Riley and Douglas Niven, *The Killing Fields* (Santa Fe: Twin Palms Press, 1996).
39. Chris Riley is quoted by Lindsay French as saying, "We thought the images were powerful and spoke with a kind of directness about people's experiences under the Khmer Rouge. But so few people go to Phnom Penh and visit the Tuol Sleng Museum themselves. Our goal was to get the pictures out into the world, to enable more people to see them, and perhaps be inclined to learn something more about Cambodia." Lindsay French, "Exhibiting Terror" in *Truth Claims: Representation and Human Rights,* ed. Mark Phillip Bradley and Patrice Petro (New Brunswick: Rutgers University Press, 2002), 134.
40. Among the extensive number of sites where exhibitions of the Tuol Sleng prints have been presented are the Museum of Modern Art; the Photographic Resource Center in Boston; University of Arizona's Center for Creative Photography; the University of California at Riverside's California Museum of Photography; The Frederick Weisman Museum of Art, University of Minnesota; Ansel Adams Center for Photography in San Francisco, the Museum of Photographic Arts, San Diego, the Museum of Design in Zurich; the *Museet for Photokunst* in Odense (Denmark); the Australian Center for Photography in Sydney; the Canadian

Museum of Contemporary Photography in Ottawa; the *Rencontres Internationales de la Photographie* in Arles; and the *Parc de la Villette* in Paris.

41. The time frame of this exhibition is worthy of note. As Hughes explains, in July 1997 Cambodia's coalition government collapsed and a new government was formed. A few weeks after this, global news media screened a video showing Pol Pot being put on trial, denounced, and sentenced to life imprisonment by a remnant of his own Cambodian forces. This story along with photographs of Pol Pot also appeared on the front page of the *New York Times* on July 29, 1997. In the context of the speculation about the trial of Pol Pot under international law, as Hughes claims the S-21 photographs were seen less as tragic reminders of a peripheral past and instead as contemporary, crucial evidence that bore on a legal procedure.
42. Museum of Modern Art, "An exhibition of photographs of Khmer Rouge prisoners opens this month at the Museum of Modern Art," press release, May 1997, http://www.moma.org/docs/press_archives/7527/releases/MOMA_1997_0040_32.pdf?2010. For a review of the exhibition, see Guy Treblay, "Killing Fields of Vision," *The Village Voice,* June 3, 1997, 34.
43. Jeff Yang, lecture, cited in Trebay, "Killing Fields of Vision," 34.
44. Susan Kismaric, quoted in Trebay, "Killing Fields of Vision," 34. The next two citations from Kismaric also come from p. 34 of the Trebay article.
45. The problem with Kismaric's defense of the Museum of Modern Art exhibition is that it fails to address the implications of perpetrator photography's relation to art and the collecting and exhibiting policies of art institutions. This is extensively discussed in Thierry De Duve, "Art in the Face of Radical Evil" *October* 125 (2008): 3–23. See also the blog discussion "Collecting Atrocities" http://carefullyaimeddarts.wordpress.com/2009/03/26/collecting-atrocities/.
46. French, "Exhibiting Terror," 149.
47. Hughes argues that while is true that *Photographs from S-21* failed to recall the interconnectedness of Cambodia's modern history and that of the United States, it was not Museum of Modern Art's intention to provide visitors with a political history of Southeast

Asia within which to couch the S-21 photos. Rather, the curators' notion was to present the photographs as a relatively unmediated exhibition of vernacular works arguing that there were clear precedents for such a curatorial approach at their institution.

48. French assumes that what is disturbing about the photographs is their power to evoke our own suffering (or our own imagined death) and that this might be a first step toward understanding what is distinctive and particular about the Cambodian genocide.
49. See Paul Williams, "Witnessing Genocide: Vigilance and Remembrance at Tuol Sleng and Choeung Ek," *Holocaust and Genocide Studies* 18, no. 2 (2004): 234–55; Erik Palmer, "Richard Avedon, the Khmer Rouge, and the Ideological Power of Portraiture." Paper presented at the annual meeting of the International Communication Association, New York City. http://citation.allacademic.com/meta/p_mla_apa_research_citation/0/1/2/7/4/p12744_index.html.
50. Juan I-Jong, "An Interview with Christopher Riley and Douglas Niven," *Photographers International* 19 (April 1995): 98, as quoted in De Duve, "Art in the Face of Radical Evil," 11.
51. De Duve, "Art in the Face of Radical Evil," 20. Further citations to this work are given in the text. De Duve also provides an important articulation of the problematics of the aesthetics as discussed by Niven above.
52. Jenny Edkins, "Exposed Singularity" *Journal for Cultural Research* 9, no. 4 (2005): 259–386. Further citations to this work are given in the text.
53. Mark Kramer, e-mail message to author, January 2009. In early 2009, members of the research team contacted a number of institutions where the S-21 photographs had been exhibited with the goal of gaining further information about curatorial decision making and exhibition design. We initially asked six questions concerning image mounting, textual supplementation, signage, events that surrounded the exhibition, and curatorial decisions that were made within the institution. These questions were contextualized as being part of a book-length research project. Mark Kramer responded to our initial questions based on his coordination of an S-21 photograph exhibition at the University of Minnesota in 2001, and engaged with the author in further e-mail conversations about the exhibition. All subsequent references to Kramer are from

e-mails exchanged with the research team or the author in early 2009.

54. Edkins, "Exposed Singularity," 374.
55. Catherine Evans, quoted in Andrew Welsh-Huggins, "Exhibition puts a human face on genocide; 25 years on, exhibit's stark images define Pol Pot's brutal and blood-drenched reign of terror," *Toronto Star,* April 29, 2000. Further quotations from Evans are also from Welsh-Huggins's article.
56. Coreen Henry, "OSU Professor Discusses Cambodian Genocide." *The Lantern*, April 20, 2000.
57. Theodor Adorno, "Cultural Criticism and Society," in *Can One Live after Auschwitz?: A Philosophical Reader,* ed. Rolf Tiedemann (Stanford: Stanford University Press, 2003), 160.

CHAPTER 6. SOME CLOSING REMARKS ON CURATORIAL PRACTICE AND THE PURSUIT OF SOCIAL JUSTICE

1. Jack Jedwab, "History Knowledge and Trust In Sources." Association for Canadian Studies, http://www.acs-aec.ca/en/social-research/canadian-history-knowledge/, posted January 19, 2012. See Slide 19 for data.
2. See chapter 1, for my discussion of "difficult knowledge."
3. Hernández-Navarro, "The Curator's Demands."
4. Andrew Benjamin, *Present Hope: Philosophy, Architecture, Judaism* (New York: Routledge, 1997), 10.
5. Lauren Berlant, *Cruel Optimism* (Durham: Duke University Press, 2011). Further citations to this work are given in the text.
6. Michael Rothberg, *Multidirectional Memory: Remembering the Holocaust in an Age of Decolonization* (Stanford: Stanford University Press, 2009), 295.
7. Erica Lehrer, Cynthia Milton, and Monica Patterson, ed., *Curating Difficult Knowledge: Violent Pasts in Public Places* (New York: Palgrave Macmillan, 2011).
8. Rosalyn Deutsche, *Hiroshima after Iraq: Three Studies in Art and War* (New York, Columbia University Press, 2010), 5. Further citations to this work are given in the text.
9. Arendt, *The Human Condition*; Claude Lefort, *Democracy and*

Political Theory (Cambridge: MIT Press, 1989). For a discussion of the relationship between Arendt and Lefort, see Deutsche, *Hiroshima*.

10. Jens Andermann and Silke Arnold-de Simine, "Introduction: Memory, Community, and the New Museum" *Theory, Culture & Society* 29, no. 1 (2012): 3–13.
11. Alison Landsberg, *Prosthetic Memory: The Transformation of American Remembrance in the Age of Mass Culture* (New York: Columbia University Press, 2004).
12. Andermann and Arnold-de Simine, "Introduction."
13. Laura Levitt, "Intimate Engagements: A Holocaust Lesson," *Nashim: A Journal of Jewish Women's Studies & Gender Issues* 7 (2004): 190–205.
14. Paul Ricoeur, *Memory, History, Forgetting* (Chicago: University of Chicago Press, 2006), 89.
15. Andermann and Arnold-de Simine, "Introduction," 9.
16. Michael Morgan, *On Shame* (New York: Routledge, 2008), 21–22.
17. Berenice Fisher, "Guilt and Shame in the Women's Movement: The Radical Ideal of Action and Its Meaning for Feminist Intellectuals," *Feminist Studies* 10, no. 2 (1984): 185–212.
18. Morgan, *On Shame,* 29–30.
19. It should be noted that this sense of confusion was evident in the remarks written in the comment books at both the Chicago Historical Society and the Andy Warhol Museum.
20. See Kathleen Woodward, "Traumatic Shame: Toni Morrison, Televisual Culture, and the Cultural Politics of Emotion," *Cultural Critique* 46, (2000): 210–40; Sandra Bartky, "Shame and Gender: Contribution to a Phenomenology of Oppression," in *Femininity and Domination: Studies in the Phenomenology of Oppression* (New York and London: Routledge, 1990), 83–98.
21. Woodward, "Traumatic Shame," 227. Further citations to this work are given in the text.
22. Immanuel Kant, *The Critique of Pure Reason,* trans. J. M. D. Meiklejohn (Hazleton, PA: Pennsylvania State University Electronic Classics Series, 2010), 450.
23. Derrida, *Specters of Marx,* 54. Further citations to this work are given in the text.
24. Jocelyn Letoureau, "Remembering (from) Where You're Going: Memory as Legacy and Inheritance," in *A History for the Future:*

Rewriting Memory and Identity in Quebec, trans. Phyllis Aronoff and Howard Scott (Montreal and Kingston: McGill-Queen's University Press, 2004), 27.

25. Eric Santer, "Miracles Happen: Benjamin, Rosenzweig, Freud, and the Matter of the Neighbor," in *The Neighbor: Three Inquires in Political Theology,* ed. Slavoj Zizek, Eric L. Santner, and Kenneth Reinhard (Chicago: University of Chicago Press, 2006).
26. Edward S. Casey, "Public Memory in Place and Time," in *Framing Public Memory,* ed. Kendall R. Phillips (Tuscaloosa: University of Alabama Press, 2004), 17–44.

BIBLIOGRAPHY

Adorno, Theodor. "Cultural Criticism and Society." In *Can One Live after Auschwitz?: A Philosophical Reader*, edited by Rolf Tiedemann, 146–62. Stanford: Stanford University Press, 2003.

Agamben, Giorgio. *What Is an Apparatus?* Stanford: Stanford University Press, 2009.

Allen, James, ed. *Without Sanctuary: Lynching Photographs in America.* Santa Fe: Twin Palms Press, 1999.

Andermann, Jens, and Silke Arnold-de Simine. "Introduction: Memory, Community, and the New Museum." *Theory, Culture & Society* 29, no. 1 (2012): 3–13.

Apel, Dora. *Imagery of Lynching: Black Men, White Women, and the Mob.* New Brunswick: Rutgers University Press, 2004.

Arendt, Hannah. *The Human Condition.* Chicago: University of Chicago Press, 1998.

Austin, John L. *How to Do Things with Words.* Cambridge: Harvard University Press, 1975.

Azoulay, Ariella. *The Civil Contract of Photography.* Cambridge: MIT Press, 2008.

Bal, Mieke, "The Pain of Images." In *Beautiful Suffering,* edited by Reinhardt, Edwards, and Duganne, 93–115. Chicago: University of Chicago Press, 2006.

Barthes, Roland. *Camera Lucida.* New York: Hill and Wang, 1981.

Batchen, Geoffrey, Mick Gidley, Nancy K. Miller, and Jay Prosser. *Picturing Atrocity: Photography in Crisis*. London: Reaktion Books, 2012.

Benjamin, Andrew. *Present Hope: Philosophy, Architecture, Judaism*. New York: Routledge, 1997.

Benjamin, Walter. "Convolute N 3, 1." In *The Arcades Project,* translated by Howard Eiland and Kevin McLaughlin, 462–63. Cambridge: Belknap Press of Harvard University Press, 1999.

———. "Theses on the Philosophy of History." In *Illuminations: Essays and Reflections,* translated by Harry Zohn, 253–64. New York: Schocken Books, 1968.

Bennett, Jill. *Empathic Vision: Affect, Trauma, and Contemporary Art*. Stanford: Stanford University Press, 2005.

Berger, John. "Photographs of Agony." In *About Looking*. Toronto: Random House Digital, 2011.

Berlant, Lauren. *Cruel Optimism*. Durham: Duke University Press, 2011.

Britzman, Deborah. *Lost Subjects, Contested Objects: Toward a Psychoanalytic Inquiry of Learning*. Albany: State University of New York Press, 1998.

Bruns. Gerald. *Tragic Thoughts at the End of Philosophy: Language, Literature, and Ethical Theory*. Evanston: Northwestern University Press, 1999.

Burtynsky, Edward. "Audio Commentary." *Manufactured Landscapes*. DVD. Directed by Jennifer Baichwal. New York: Zeitgeist Films, 2007.

Butler, Judith. *Frames of War: When Is Life Grievable?* New York: Verso, 2009.

———. *Giving an Account of Oneself*. New York: Fordham University Press, 2005.

Carrigan, William D. *The Making of a Lynching Culture: Violence and Vigilantism in Central Texas, 1836–1916*. Urbana: University of Illinois Press, 2004.

Caruth, Cathy. *Unclaimed Experience: Trauma, Narrative, and History*. Baltimore: Johns Hopkins University Press, 1996.

Casey, Edward S. "Public Memory in Place and Time." In *Framing Public Memory,* edited by Kendall R. Phillips, 17–44. Tuscaloosa: University of Alabama Press, 2004.

Cavell, Stanley. "Between Acknowledgment and Avoidance." In *The*

Claim of Reason: Wittgenstein, Scepticism, Morality, and Tragedy. Oxford: Oxford University Press, 1999.

———. "Comments on Veena Das's Essay 'Language and Body: Transactions in the Construction of Pain." In *Social Suffering*, edited by Arthur M. Kleinman, Veena Das, and Margaret M. Lock, 93–98. Berkeley: University of California Press, 1997.

———. "Knowing and Acknowledging." In *Must We Mean What We Say?* 2nd ed., 238–66. Cambridge: Harvard University Press, 2002.

Cheng, Anne Anlin. *The Melancholy of Race: Psychoanalysis, Assimilation, and Hidden Grief.* New York: Oxford University Press, 2001.

Day, Ken Gonzales. *Erased Lynching Series*, 2002–2010. http://www.kengonzalesday.

De Duve, Thierry. "Art in the Face of Radical Evil." *October* 125 (2008): 3–23.

Deleuze, Gilles. "What is a Dispositif?" In *Michel Foucault, Philosopher*, translated and edited by Timothy J. Armstrong, 159–68. Brighton: Harvester Wheatsheaf, 1992.

———, and Félix Guattari. *A Thousand Plateaus.* Translated by Brian Massumi. London and New York: Continuum, 2004.

Derrida, Jacques. "By Force of Mourning." *Critical Inquiry* 22, no.2 (1996): 171–92.

———. *Specters of Marx: The State of the Debt, the Work of Mourning, and the New International.* New York: Routledge, 2004.

Deutsche, Rosalyn. *Hiroshima after Iraq: Three Studies in Art and War.* New York: Columbia University Press, 2010.

Didi-Huberman, Georges. *Images in Spite of All: Four Photographs from Auschwitz.* Translated by Shane B. Lillis. Chicago: University of Chicago Press, 2008.

———. *Images Malgré Tout.* Paris: Les Éditions de Minuit, 2003.

Edkins, Jenny. "Exposed Singularity." *Journal for Cultural Research* 9, no. 4 (2005): 259–386.

Fanon, Frantz. *Black Skin, White Masks.* New York: Grove Press, 1967.

Findlen, Paula. *Possessing Nature: Museums, Collecting, and Scientific Culture in Early Modern Italy.* Berkeley: University of California Press, 1994.

Fisher, Berenice. "Guilt and Shame in the Women's Movement: The Radical Ideal of Action and Its Meaning for Feminist Intellectuals." *Feminist Studies* 10, no. 2 (1984): 185–212.

Freidrich, Ernst. *War Against War!* Seattle: Real Comet Press, 1987.

French, Lindsay. "Exhibiting Terror." In *Truth Claims: Representation and Human Rights,* edited by Mark Phillip Bradley and Patrice Petro, 131–56. New Brunswick: Rutgers University Press, 2002.

Gibbs, Robert. "Messianic Epistemology: Thesis IV." In *Walter Benjamin and History,* edited by Andrew Benjamin, 197–214. New York: Continuum Press, 2005.

Goldsby, Jacqueline. *A Spectacular Secret: Lynching in American Life and Literature.* Chicago: University of Chicago Press, 2006.

Gordon, Avery. *Ghostly Matters: Haunting and the Sociological Imagination.* Minneapolis: University of Minnesota Press, 2008.

Goya, Francisco. *The Disasters of War.* London: Dover, 1967.

Harold, Christine, and Kevin Michael Deluca. "Behold the Corpse: Violent Images and the Case of Emmett Till." *Rhetoric & Public Affairs* 8, no. 2 (2005): 263–86.

Hernández-Navarro, Miguel Á. "The Curator's Demands: Toward an Ethics of Commitment." *Manifesta Journal* 12 (2010/2011): 5–12.

Hughes, Rachel. "The Abject Artefacts of Memory: Photographs from Cambodia's Genocide." *Media, Culture and Society* 25, no. 1 (2003): 23–44.

Hüppauf, Bernd. "Emptying the Gaze: Framing Violence through the Viewfinder." *New German Critique* 72 (1997): 3–44.

Jackson, John Jr. *Racial Paranoia: The Unintended Consequences of Political Correctness: The New Reality of Race in America.* New York: Basic Civitas, 2008.

Kant, Immanuel. *The Critique of Pure Reason.* Translated by J. M. D. Meiklejohn. Hazleton, PA: Pennsylvania State University Electronic Classics Series, 2010.

Kenaan, Hagi. "Facing Images." *Angelaki: Journal of the Theoretical Humanities* 16, no. 1 (2011): 143–59.

———. "What Makes an Image Singular Plural? Questions to Jean-Luc Nancy." *Journal of Visual Culture* 9, no.1 (2010): 63–76.

Kracauer, Siegfried. *Theory of Film.* Princeton: Princeton University Press, 1997.

Landsberg, Alison. *Prosthetic Memory: The Transformation of American Remembrance in the Age of Mass Culture.* New York: Columbia University Press, 2004.

Lattimore, Richmond, trans. *The Iliad of Homer.* Chicago: University of Chicago Press, 1951.

Lehrer, Erica, Cynthia Milton, and Monica Patterson, eds. *Curating Difficult Knowledge: Violent Pasts in Public Places.* New York: Palgrave Macmillan, 2011.

Letoureau, Jocelyn. "Remembering (from) Where You're Going: Memory as Legacy and Inheritance." In *A History for the Future: Rewriting Memory and Identity in Quebec*, translated by Phyllis Aronoff and Howard Scott, 3–29. Montreal and Kingston: McGill-Queen's University Press, 2004.

Levinas, Emmanuel. "Useless Suffering." In *Entre Nous: Thinking of the Other*, translated by Michael B. Smith and Barbara Harshay, 91–102. New York: Columbia University Press, 1998.

Levitt, Laura. "Intimate Engagements: A Holocaust Lesson." *Nashim: A Journal of Jewish Women's Studies & Gender Issues* 7 (2004): 190–205.

Macdonald, Sharon. "Accessing audiences: Visiting Visitor Books." *Museum and Society* 3, no. 3 (2005): 199–236.

Massumi, Brian. "Introduction: Like a Thought." In *A Shock to Thought: Expression After Deleuze and Guattari*, edited by Brian Massumi, xiii–xxxix. New York: Routledge, 2002.

———. "The Autonomy of Affect." *Cultural Critique* 31 (1995): 83–109.

Mitchell, W. J. T. *Picture Theory.* Chicago: University of Chicago Press, 1994.

Morgan, Michael. *On Shame.* New York: Routledge, 2008.

Nancy, Jean-Luc, *The Ground of the Image.* New York: Fordham University Press, 2005.

Nieland, Justus. *Feeling Modern: The Eccentricities of Public Life.* Urbana: University of Illinois Press, 2008.

Oliver, Kelly. *Witnessing: Beyond Recognition.* Minneapolis: University of Minnesota Press, 2001.

Pitt, Alice, and Deborah Britzman. "Speculations on Qualities of Difficult Knowledge in Teaching and Learning: An Experiment in Psychoanalytic Research." *International Journal of Qualitative Studies in Education* 16 (2003): 755–76.

Polan, Dana B. "'Above All Else to Make You See': Cinema and the Ideology of Spectacle," *boundary 2* 11, no. 1/2 (1983): 129–44.

Reemtsma, Jan Phillip. "Two Exhibitions—A Review." Review of "*Verbrechen der Wehrmacht. Dimensionen des Vernichtungskrieges*

1941–1944." (*Crimes of the German Wehrmacht: Dimensions of a War of Annihilation, 1941–1944*), November 28, 2001-May 28, 2004. Hamburg, *Hamburger Institut für Sozialforschung*, n.d., 12. http://www.his-online.de/en/events/1095/.

Reid, Susan. "In the Name of the People. The Manege Affair Revisited." *Kritika: Explorations in Russian and Eurasian History* 6, no. 4 (2005), 673–716.

Reinhardt, Mark. "Picturing Violence: Aesthetics and the Anxiety of Critique." In *Beautiful Suffering*, edited by Reinhardt, Edwards, and Duganne, 13-36. Chicago: University of Chicago Press, 2006.

Reinhardt, Mark and Holly Edwards. "Traffic in Pain." In *Beautiful Suffering, Photography and the Traffic in Pain*, edited by Reinhardt, Edwards, and Duganne, 7–12. Chicago: University of Chicago Press, 2006.

Reinhardt, Mark, Holly Edwards, and Erina Duganne, eds. *Beautiful Suffering: Photography and the Traffic in Pain*. Chicago: University of Chicago Press, 2006.

Ricoeur, Paul. *Memory, History, Forgetting*. Chicago: University of Chicago Press, 2006.

Robins, Kevin. *Into the Image: Culture and Politics in the Field of Vision*. London: Routledge, 1996.

Rothberg, Michael. *Multidirectional Memory: Remembering the Holocaust in an Age of Decolonization*. Stanford: Stanford University Press, 2009.

Said Edward, "The World, the Text, and the Critic." In *The World, The Text, and the Critic*, 31–53. Cambridge: Harvard University Press, 1984.

Sandell, Richard. *Museums, Prejudice and the Reframing of Difference*. London: Routledge, 2007.

Santer, Eric L. "Miracles Happen: Benjamin, Rosenzweig, Freud, and the Matter of the Neighbor." In *The Neighbor: Three Inquires in Political Theology*, edited by Slavoj Zizek, Eric L. Santner, and Kenneth Reinhard, 76–133. Chicago: University of Chicago Press, 2005.

Sekula, Alan. *Photography Against the Grain*. Halifax: Press of the Nova Scotia College of Art and Design, 1984.

Seltzer, Mark. "Wound Culture: Trauma in the Pathological Public Sphere." *October* 80 (1997): 3–26.

Simon, Roger I. "The Terrible Gift: Museums and the Possibility of

Hope Without Consolation." *Journal of Museum Management and Curatorship* 21, no. 3 (2006): 187–204.

———. "Towards a Hopeful Practice of Worrying: The Problematics of Listening and the Educative Responsibilities of Canada's Truth and Reconciliation Commission." In *Reconciling Canada: Critical Perspectives on the Culture of Redress,* edited by Pauline Wakeman and Jennifer Henderson, 129–42. Toronto: University of Toronto Press, 2013.

———, Mario Di Palantonio, and Mark Clamen. "Remembrance as Praxis and the Ethics of the Inter-Human." *Culture Machine* 4 (2002). http://www.culturemachine.net/ index.php/cm/article/viewArticle/272/257.

Simpson, Mark. "Archiving Hate: Lynching Postcards at the Limit of Social Circulation." *ESC English Studies in Canada* 30, no. 1. (2004): 17–38.

Sliwinski, Sharon. "The Childhood of Human Rights: The Kodak on the Congo." *Journal of Visual Culture* 5, no. 3 (2006): 333–63.

Sontag, Susan. *Regarding the Pain of Others.* New York: Picador, 2003.

Tagg, John. *The Disciplinary Frame: Photographic Truths and the Capture of Meaning.* Minneapolis: University of Minnesota Press, 2009.

Tymkiw, Michael. "Debunking the Myth of the *saubere Wehrmacht.*" *Word and Image* 23, no. 4 (2007): 485–92.

Watchtel, Eleanor. "Ghost Hunter." In *The Emergence of Memory: Conversations with W. G. Sebald,* edited by Lynne Sharon Schwartz, 37–62. New York: Seven Stories Press, 2007.

Willis, John S. "Who Needs Multicultural Education? White Students, U.S. History, and the Construction of a Usable Past." *Anthropology and Education Quarterly* 27, no. 3 (1996): 365–89.

Wodak, Ruth, and John E. Richardson. "On the Politics of Remembering (or Not)." *Critical Discourse Studies* 6, no. 4 (2009): 231–35.

Wood, Ann Louise, and Susan V. Donaldson. "Introduction: Lynching's Legacy in American Culture." *Mississippi Quarterly* 61, no. 1–2 (2008): 5–26.

Woodward, Kathleen. "Traumatic Shame: Toni Morrison, Televisual Culture, and the Cultural Politics of Emotion." *Cultural Critique* 46 (2000): 210–40.

Zelizer, Barbie. *Remembering to Forget: Holocaust Memory Through the Camera's Eye.* Chicago: University of Chicago Press, 2000.

INDEX